MEDIA TECHNOLOGIES AND THE DIGITAL HUMANITIES IN MEDIEVAL AND EARLY MODERN STUDIES

Edited by
Katharine D. Scherff and Lane J. Sobehrad

Routledge
Taylor & Francis Group
NEW YORK AND LONDON

Designed cover image: Digital image courtesy of the Getty's Open Content Program

First published 2023
by Routledge
605 Third Avenue, New York, NY 10158

and by Routledge
4 Park Square, Milton Park, Abingdon, Oxon, OX14 4RN

Routledge is an imprint of the Taylor & Francis Group, an informa business

Library of Congress Cataloging-in-Publication Data
Names: Scherff, Katharine, editor. | Sobehrad, Lane J., editor.
Title: Media technologies and the digital humanities in medieval and early modern studies / edited by Katharine D. Scherff and Lane J. Sobehrad.
Description: New York, NY : Routledge, 2023. | Includes bibliographical references.
Identifiers: LCCN 2022046263 (print) | LCCN 2022046264 (ebook) | ISBN 9781032265735 (hardback) | ISBN 9781032280493 (paperback) | ISBN 9781003295082 (ebook)
Subjects: LCSH: Middle Ages—Historiography. | Renaissance—Historiography. | Mass media—History. | History—Methodology. | Digital humanities.
Classification: LCC D116 .M358 2023 (print) | LCC D116 (ebook) | DDC 302.2309/02—dc23/eng/20221214
LC record available at https://lccn.loc.gov/2022046263
LC ebook record available at https://lccn.loc.gov/2022046264

ISBN: 9781032265735 (hbk)
ISBN: 9781032280493 (pbk)
ISBN: 9781003295082 (ebk)

DOI: 10.4324/9781003295082

Typeset in Bembo
by codeMantra

MEDIA TECHNOLOGIES AND THE DIGITAL HUMANITIES IN MEDIEVAL AND EARLY MODERN STUDIES

Through a multidisciplinary collection of case studies, this book explores the effects of the digital age on medieval and early modern studies.

Divided into five parts, the book examines how people, medieval and modern, engage with medieval media and technology through an exploration of the theory underpinning audience interactions with historical materials in the past and the real-world engagement of a twenty-first-century audience with medieval and early modern studies through the multimodal lens of a vast digital landscape. Each case study reveals the diversity of medieval media and technology and challenges readers to consider new types of literacy competencies as scholarly, rigorous methods of engaging in pre-modern investigations of materiality. Essays in the first section engage in the examination of medieval media, mediation, and technology from a theoretical framework, while the second section explores how digitization, smart technologies, digital mapping, and the internet have shaped medieval and early modern studies today.

The book will be of interest to students in undergraduate or graduate intermediate or advanced courses as well as scholars, in medieval studies, art history, architectural history, medieval history, literary history, and religious history.

Katharine D. Scherff is Postdoc Lecturer and teaches for the School of Art and the Medieval and Renaissance Studies Center at Texas Tech University.

Lane J. Sobehrad is Coordinator of Research and Innovation for Lubbock ISD.

CONTENTS

FIGURES

ACKNOWLEDGMENTS

We would like to most graciously thank our contributors for all their patience and excellent work. This volume would not be possible without their efforts. We would also like to acknowledge our anonymous referees, supportive readers, and editors at Routledge | Taylor & Francis Group. We would also like to thank our families for their immeasurable and enduring patience in all our projects.

CONTRIBUTORS

Brittany Forniotis is a doctoral candidate at Duke University in the Department of Art, Art History, and Visual Studies. Her research encompasses medieval and early modern architectural theory and practice in the Mediterranean, with a focus on cultural and intellectual exchange and connections to the history of science and medicine. Her dissertation project examines the architectural history of premodern hospitals in the Mediterranean as a specifically transcultural phenomenon.

Dr. Eric R. Hupe is an Assistant Professor of Art History at Lafayette College where he teaches courses on Italian Renaissance and Baroque art. His research investigates the relationship between optical science, theology, and art in Renaissance Italy. In his courses, Eric prioritizes close looking as he attempts to immerse his students in the art they study by using VR technology. Dr. Hupe is the director of VRART, a digital initiative that creates VR/XR content for teaching art history. Caitlyn Carr is a junior undergraduate student at Lafayette College majoring in Art and English. Caitlyn is an appointed EXCEL Scholar working with Professor Hupe. She is a co-contributor of the VRART initiative.

Nancy Haijing Jiang received her PhD from Northwestern University, USA with a dissertation that explores how Latin and vernacular religious writers in fourteenth- to fifteenth-century Europe drew from their economic contexts and experiences to construct innovative narratives about sin and salvation. Nancy has taught in English literature departments at Northwestern University and the University of Warwick, UK. Her current project investigates the intersections between women's credit practices and female religious writings in pre-modern England.

Margaret Mansfield is a doctoral candidate at University of California, Santa Barbara, and Kress Foundation Fellow in the History of Art at Leiden University. Her dissertation, "Image Reincarnation in Early Modern Dutch Illustrated Travelogues," examines the production and dissemination of accounts of the Indian subcontinent, specifically of the ten avatars of Vishnu mythology to an Early Modern European readership. This research analyzes the recycling or recontextualization of images as molded by the social networks of the authors, engravers, publishers, and financers of the publications. Margaret is also involved with a collaborative project funded by the NEH concerning Bernard Picart's, Cérémonies et coutumes religieuses de tous les peuples du monde.

Katharine D. Scherff received her PhD in 2019 from Texas Tech University in Interdisciplinary Studies in Fine Arts with an emphasis in Medieval and Early Modern material culture. As a scholar of media theory, Medieval European Art History, and visual culture, Katharine's interests center on art of the fourteenth and fifteenth centuries with an emphasis in materiality, liturgical ritual, and contemporary media technology. An interest in interdisciplinary discourse and critical theory shapes her research in religious materiality, perception, and viewership. In addition, Katharine enjoys scholarly and pedagogical research in queer and gender theory. Her previously published work, *Saint Quiteria: Virgin and Martyr: An Analysis of Her Cult Veneration and Iconography in France and The Iberian Peninsula* (2012) is the most complete monograph on the Iberian martyr Saint Quiteria. Current projects include the manuscript – *The Virtual Liturgy and Ritual Artifacts in Medieval and Early Modern Studies*, a manuscript soon to be published by Routledge, and an article for *Peregrinations: Journal of Medieval Art and Architecture*, "Walking with Helena: An Examination of a Gendered Model for Women and Medieval Pilgrimage in Northern Spain" (2023). Katharine has presented papers and organized sessions at international and regional conferences. Katharine is currently a post-doc lecturer at Texas Tech University and teaches for the School of Art and the Medieval and Renaissance Studies Center.

Sr. Albert Marie Surmanski, OP is a member of the Dominican Sisters of Mary, Mother of the Eucharist. She is a Full Professor of Theology at the University of St. Thomas in Houston where she also teaches at St. Mary's Seminary. Her main area of research is medieval sacramental theology with a focus on Albert the Great and Aquinas. She has published a translation of Albert the Great's work *On the Body of the Lord*, in the CUA press series, *The Fathers of the Church Medieval Continuation*, as well as a forthcoming translation of Aquinas's Commentary on the Psalms for the Aquinas Institute. She has published articles in various journals including *Logos*, *Antiphon*, *Nova et Vetera*, and *Franciscan Studies.*

Anne Betty Weinshenker, PhD, Professor Emerita of Art History at Montclair State University, is a specialist in eighteenth-century western European art. Her study of French sculpture during that period led to the publication of several articles and her monograph, *A God or a Bench: Sculpture as a Problematic Art during the Ancien Régime* (2008). More recently, she has been investigating the transnational cycle of paintings and prints known as the Tombeaux des princes, on which she published articles in *The Papers of the Bibliographical Society of America* (2016) and the anthology *Adapting the Eighteenth Century* (2020); another is currently in press.

Susan Sobehrad has served students in public education for 30 years at all levels. She has a Master's degree in science education and is a nationally certified project-based learning trainer. Her post-graduate research focuses on creativity in digital spaces. Susan Sobehrad is a nationally certified PBL trainer and has served as an instructional coach and facilitator at multiple project-based campuses utilizing 30 years of teaching experience.

Beatrice Bottomley is a doctoral candidate at the Warburg Institute, supported by a studentship from the London Arts and Humanities Partnership (LAHP). Beatrice's research examines the interplay among text, image, and material culture in the production and transmission of knowledge in the premodern and early modern Islamic world and Europe.

Arianna Dalla Costa is a doctoral candidate in Intellectual History at the Warburg Institute, University of London. Her project is funded by the Gerda Henkel Foundation. Her current project looks at the Latin geomantic tradition of the twelfth to fourteenth centuries and includes the critical edition of the Liber arenalis scientiae, which was translated from Arabic into Latin by Plato of Tivoli in 1135. Her research interests include the transmission of scientific doctrines from the Islamic to the Christian world, the edition of medieval texts, the relationship between word and image, and the use of diagrams to convey information in medieval science.

Lane J. Sobehrad, PhD, is the coordinator of Research and Innovation for Lubbock ISD where he has successfully applied for over $20,000,000 in funding to develop and implement innovative educational programming. His medieval research focuses on undergraduate history education with an emphasis on project-based learning strategies, which can be found most recently in *Medieval History in the Modern Classroom* (2022).

INTRODUCTION

Media Technologies and the Digital Humanities

Katharine D. Scherff and Lane J. Sobehrad

Do not to seek the old in the new, but find something new in the old.[1]

The digital age has shaped our ways of viewing ourselves, society, and culture. Since 2000, regular use of the internet among Americans has risen from around 50% to over 90%. For people under sixty-five, regular internet usage is nearly universal.[2] For education and industries, access to the internet is no longer a convenience, it is a necessity. It has also reframed and revealed new perspectives on how medievalists engage with historical phenomena in the classroom, during the research process, and in promulgating new findings through presentations, publications, and other research products.

Pervasive use of digital tools does not necessarily correlate with effective use of those tools. PowerPoint slides continue to be a common feature in the college lecture hall, only skimming the surface of the enormous diversity of media available in digital spaces for teaching and learning. Presenting medieval studies in this way does not reflect the type of work done by medieval studies in 2022 and presents a false image of the field to students and the general public. In the most basic sense, the digital age has dramatically shifted the accessibility of medieval media and the modality through which people use it. Hours upon hours previously spent in archival reading rooms have been replaced with screen time as major archival locations, such as the Bibliotheque Nationale, British Library, and Vatican Library, have endeavored upon major digitization initiatives – Gallica, Digitised Manuscripts, and DigVatLib, respectively. These efforts have made tens of thousands of manuscripts available to researchers around the world in extremely high-quality images. Similarly, the production of academic papers, books, and volumes is now developed primarily, if not exclusively, through virtual communication over digital space – where would medieval publishing houses be without access to Adobe pdfs? The myriad of societal effects due to the COVID-19 pandemic has highlighted the importance of digital access, digital literacies, and the impacts of media on cultural studies. That is, in understanding medieval and early modern media at a deeper epistemological level, scholars may better understand historical contexts and

DOI: 10.4324/9781003295082-1

their populations, thereby facilitating new perspectives. Furthermore, a deeper, more varied understanding of past media will help us understand contemporary and future media and their role in academia.

This multidisciplinary project explores the effects of the digital age on medieval and early modern studies. We aim to examine how people, medieval and modern, engage with medieval media and technology through an exploration of the theory that underpinned audience interactions with historical materials in the past and the real-world engagement of a twenty-first-century audience with medieval and early modern studies through the multimodal lens of a vast digital landscape. Each contribution reveals the diversity of premodern media and media technologies thereby challenging the misconception of a divided world that places at odds pre-electric and electric chronologies – that is, old vs. new media – and asks readers to consider new types of literacy competencies as scholarly, rigorous methods of engaging in premodern investigations of materiality.

This volume is a representation of scholars participating in emerging discourses that will, in some small way, guide the future of medieval and early modern studies. The audiences engaging with this work are likely those who directly and indirectly participate in these academic fields, with a secondary goal to maintain general accessibility to readers who seek to learn more about these eras beyond what they are fed by entertainment and popular media. We argue that the variety of approaches presented here strengthen and diversify those interests. Medieval and early modern studies are reorienting their focus to a richer and more diverse framework that engages with other methodologies beyond traditional self-imposed boundaries of period, geography, and discipline. More specifically, it is our hope that the synthesis of these modalities of analysis will further subvert colonialism and imperialist constructs that medieval and early modern studies have been so beholden to these many decades.

As it explores a burgeoning methodological framework, this volume participates in new discussions through the exemplars detailed below. The increasing prevalence of new media and digital methodologies over the last few decades in medieval and early modern scholarship underpins the relationship between what is old and what is new, blurring the boundaries between them. The authors in this volume have placed their work at this intersection between media studies and the digital humanities. Beatrice Bottomley and Arianna Dalla Costa, for example, discuss how medieval readers accessed and used texts but, critically, show how the use of external tools transforms text-based information through a "mechanization of thought and reality" with cipher disks. Brittany Forniotis argues that early modern maps are not always maps, wherein geospatial positioning takes a backseat to architectural imagery that reflects the socio-cultural context of the cartographer and their audience. That is, the ink on a page cannot provide its full meaning merely through literal comprehension, as Sister Albert Marie Surmanski contends in her discussion of the many uses of tongues in Psalms. Audiences must have access points through which media can be explored, manipulated, and interpreted.

The digital humanities is a relatively new field in academia, which, upon the advent of its inauguration as a permanent office in the National Endowment for the Humanities in 2008, has been an expansive force in new media literacies.[3] The efforts of its federal program officers and grantees have also proved both attractive and effective, as federal funding for the Office of Digital Humanities has more than doubled from $2,000,000 in 2008 to nearly $5,000,000 in 2019.[4] This scholarly intersection of computing and digital technologies has generally been associated with new media and, in many instances, is described with this characteristic as a lens through which to examine past humanities and histories by way of new media. In a 2009 essay in *Cinema Journal*, Tara McPhereson demonstrated how the divisions between the digital humanities and new media have been historically hyperbolic.[5]

Where the digital humanities utilize media technologies as a means of methodological analysis, for media studies it is these very methodologies of communication that are the object of analysis. For example, a digital humanities scholar might use a software-based mapping program to perform a historical investigation. A media scholar might look at the software-based mapping program as an object of inquiry in and of itself. Concomitantly, both strategies are a lens through which to peer into the past. As much as the two fields are their own kind, they are also enmeshed where their use, practices, meanings, and functions are self-referential. That is, our relationship to media is shaped by our perceptions of media.

We cannot, however, disregard that historically media studies and the digital humanities have been assumed to be two divergent disciplines, isolating them into relatively separate infrastructures and differing histories. Jentery Sayers connotes that this is largely due to the disciplines' contrary theories and histories.[6] As we concur with these assertions, it is our intention that essays not only complement each other but also that the two disciplines are intrinsically linked. Understanding media means comprehending the technologies employed. Media studies is the academic investigation of mass media – its content, perception, and the way in which it shapes culture and history. Like all historiographies, the objective of media history is to realize the historical trajectory and processes of those histories. First, the constructs of media are largely sorted into contemporary and traditional media. Since the advent of modernity in the nineteenth century, the invention, evolution, and effects of media had largely gone unstudied until the latter half of the twentieth century. Historically, *traditional forms of media* consisted of radio, television, and print media, whereas *contemporary media* consists of social media, digital text, video games, and others of the same kind.

Early media studies in Germany formed much of the foundations of the discourse surrounding traditional forms of media. Media ensembles, social historical study, and the interactions and connectivity of differing media were principally examined by German scholars and were largely restricted to that of visual media like newspapers.[7] German theorists in the Frankfurt School (f. 1918) largely saw media as a propagandic tool for the dictatorial and authoritative systems seen to manipulate the masses.[8] However, it is the digital age which transformed the field as we begin to see the emphasis of the communicative and interdisciplinary nature of media. This shift emphasized the dynamics and influences of media as they shape and are shaped by their environments. As media and media environments became more complex, the scholarship surrounding revealed the intricate and dynamic complexities of communication spheres. Traditional forms of media were largely the center of Marshall McLuhan's focus. A Canadian media theorist, he was particularly interested in the effects of mass media, thought, and human nature. Predominantly, he was occupied with the golden age of television of the 1960s. Predicting the fourth era of media, he postulated in his 1964 collaborative work *The Global Village*, a new era – the electronic age – a "global village" which pervasively maintained the Marxist construct that all would have equal access to information and technology.[9] Along a similar trajectory, the German cultural critic Walter Benjamin's essay "The Work of Art in the Age of Mechanical Reproduction" (1935) has also, to some extent, been pointed to as an early contributor to media studies.[10]

Humanities scholars have, of course, participated in the development of products in the new electronic age, taking advantage of the mathematical power of computers and the ability of the internet to offer dynamically accessible and updateable work products. These efforts eventually came to be called the Digital Humanities, which *Digital Humanities Quarterly*, explains as, "a diverse and still emerging field that encompasses the practice of humanities research in and through information technology, and the exploration of how the humanities may evolve through their engagement with technology, media, and computational methods."[11] Initial efforts can be dated to at least 1946, when Father Roberto Busa began a career-long project indexing every word in the works of Thomas Aquinas. This concordance, the *Index Thomisticus,* was joined by Thomas Watson and IBM in 1949. Busa's work is important not only for its seminal role in the field of the digital humanities, but because it is illustrative of the exponentially increasing ability of new technology to make research more efficient and its products more accessible. This project highlights the rapid advancement in computationally based research as the over 10,000,000 words in his project transitioned from a warehouse of punched cards to 1,800 magnetic tapes in the 1950s to a single CD-ROM in 2004, and finally an ethereal existence online beginning in 2005.[12] Busa's project illustrates how media can be both *physically* condensed, but *virtually* expanded. Curiously, McLuhan and Busa, both at the forefront of the emergence of their respective fields, were medievalists.[13]

Early periodization of media studies and the digital humanities immediately encounters historiography's debate over modernity. Building on his teacher, Harold Innis, McLuhan divided and defined three eras of communication which assumed *three eras of literacy* – the oral – where early humankind first acquired speech to the developed early literacies; writing/print – from on the invention of writing to the electronic forms of writing; and electric/electronic – that is, the communication era of the electric flow of communication. The way scholars demarcate media is dependent on the historical milieu. The internet, for example, while certainly requiring access to electricity to function, is not what was used in McLuhan's definition of electronic media, which focused on audio/visual technologies. The internet includes these technologies but contains as much digital writing as it does audio/visual material. Likewise, the Middle Age saw a gradual shift in the importance of writing/print over its millennium, but oral traditions remained a critically important form of communication in every culture. Where television was the dominant media in the 1960s, by the early 1970s, media studies broadened, expanding as a methodology used in a wide range of fields, including film studies.[14] Universities in Europe and Australia established coursework within this relatively new area of study.[15] In turn, the radical feminist response to the traditional hostile treatment of women in media ushered in the rise of feminist media theory. Thus, television, film, advertisements, and concepts of domestic and economic determinism deconstructed the person/political relationship which greatly informed research through to the 1980s.[16]

In 1985, Friedrich Kittler described media in terms of discourse networks that were at the foremost of cultural techniques. These "network of technologies and institutions that allow a given culture to select store and process relevant data" pointed to the cultural implementations and development of literacies.[17] A pillar within media studies, his work was largely derived from poststructuralists including Jacques Derrida, Jacques Lacan, and Michel Foucault. Noticeably like McLuhan's aphorism "the medium is the message," Kittler's systems of notations assert that the way in which information is physically recorded and later disseminated could delineate pertinent meaning.[18] In *Discourse Networks 1800/1900,* however, he framed network technologies within the confines of titled centuries prescribing a logic of technological determinism.[19] The problem rests, then, with placing media technologies in a position of complete power over society and driving society forward.

Comparatively, though the digital humanities could perform large computations related to word frequency and usage in the mid-twentieth century, it could not use its new mechanical tools to support much of the progressive changes in its associated fields as noted above. Busa was restricted by the technology of his time, and it is why he and his contemporaries focused their electronically based research on linear, logical tasks.[20] Commonplace features used today, such as search queries or file organization, were not yet possible. At that time, computers could not recognize special characters or lower-case letters. Scholars wanting to use technology to evaluate medieval text instead relied on additional notations to indicate non-standard characters, necessitating additional literacy competency in addition to the paleogeography and codicology needed to interpret text in the first place. It was not until *The Dictionary of Old English,* established in 1981, that medievalists began to use computers to tackle more complex problems across medieval media.[21] While the *Index Thomisticus* restricted itself to texts on parchment or paper, *The DOE* incorporated Old English text wherever it was found to build its dictionary and text body, including stone monuments, jewelry, and art. Yet other problems remained, such as special characters, which could not be solved until the creation of flexible text formats like Unicode in the early 1990s.[22]

The internet's place in the digital humanities contributed less to brute computing strength needed for projects like Busa's, but completely transformed the way in which people accessed medieval content. Paul Halsall's Internet Medieval History Sourcebook began in 1996 hosted by Fordham University, and it made primary source texts much more accessible to everyone. We contend it is one of the most important public-facing medieval studies projects to ever be undertaken.[23] While the work that went into it did not offer ground-breaking insight on a particular topic, it arguably has done more to promote medieval studies to the general public that just about any other medieval studies product. For institutions with substantial manuscript holdings, the 1990s saw the beginning of digitization projects, like the British Library's Turning the Pages, which began in 1997, and allowed anyone with internet access the ability to view its rare books and manuscripts in a realistic, online setting. Critically, researchers were no longer restricted to what they might gain in a short trip to the archives, the archives had made themselves a globally accessible, immediately available communication resource.

It is evident through the fast-paced evolution of both electronic media and computationally based tools that this progress has made research using electronic media more accessible and efficient favoring the new. The distinction between old and new media has been rather controversial. Media theorists, historically, have not considered an application of modern media constructs to the medieval and early modern periods, an era before digital and automatic compilation, storage, and dissemination of information. To emphasize this difference, in 2003 Wolfgang Ernst made the rather decisive assertion that the Middle Ages were definitively *amedial*, isolated premodern media. Championing the expulsion of non-automatic materials, Ernst argued to reserve the term for only modern technologies. That would, therefore, negate the classification and analysis of all media before modernity. This resounding assertion that, "there are no medieval media," only fortified the problems with periodization and disciplinary boundaries, reinforcing contention and division between the pre-modernists and modernists.[24] Accordingly, Ernst suggests that media and mediation are always tethered to modern material support, a rather disparaging and limiting view of medieval and early modern literacies.[25] McLuhan and Innis asserted that there are many modes of media, proposing that meaning can be channeled through varying modes, whether visual or verbal.[26] Elleström discusses the variants of media in four modes: *material, sensorial, spatiotemporal,* and *semiotic.* He defines *material modality* as a "latent corporeal interface of the medium."[27] Media is, then, indexical and, therefore, not reducible to its physical properties; however, neither is it dependent on material. Therefore, old and new media, in actuality, are far less divisive. Busa's project illustrates this, as his team moved their work products from punch cards to magnetic tapes to book form to, finally, a website. His initial production of punch cards required the user to wait a long period of time, understand complicated annotations, had to be accessed in person, required a large amount of physical space to store the research products and, critically, could not be readily reproduced. The update to a CD made information quicker to access, easier to read through a computer, could be accessed anywhere, required very little space, and was quickly reproducible. However, you still needed to have a physical copy of the CD to access the information. The website, by contrast, can be accessed in seconds, requires no space, has no need to be reproduced, and can be accessed anywhere in the world. The cultural background of these changes to the format of the *Index Thonisticus* reflects the nature of communication in their respective time periods. Research was an act of patience; it can now act with immediacy. Busa waited for the evening news, we can log-on to Twitter *right now.* As Ilana Gershon suggests,

> [e]ach new medium is instantly enmeshed in a web of media ideologies – old media determine how new media will be perceived. At the same time, every new medium alters how the already existing media are understood to shape communication.[28]

Media archaeologists including Siegfried Zielinksi and Jussi Parikka challenge the notion of the historical framework surrounding the geology of media, progression, and technological determinism.[29] In the 1999 publication *Remediation: Understanding New Media,* Jay David Bolter and Richard Gruisin positioned concepts of remediation as a more nuanced understanding of media, where new media does not merely emulate but situates media within a cultural condition in which notions of old and new, at times, are less distinguished.[30] This belief suggests that media is an ever adaptive and reciprocal force that shapes and reshapes itself. Media is far less defined than the hierarchies proposed by earlier theorists, instead its importance is highly subjective and contextual.[31] The works by Martin Foys, Lars Elleström, and the most recent 2022 volume from Thora Brylowe and Stephen Yeager illustrate the transcendence of the media concept demonstrating the trend of a wider acceptance of media and mediation beyond the constraints of historical periodization.[32] To reinforce the methodology of media archaeology, the way to understand the present and the future is through the revelations of the past.

Using this perspective, let us "remediate" Beowulf through Keven Kiernan's development of *Electronic Beowulf,* initiated in 1993. It started as a digitization of Cotton Vitellius A.xv. In 1993, digitization was still in its infancy, but the re-production of medieval manuscripts in a higher quality format than microfilm, and a much cheaper alternative to facsimiles, was still a major step forward. As it evolved into its iteration, *Electronic Beowulf 4.0* made use of digital tools to update traditional structures found in critical editions of texts.

For example, it not only offers the text in parallel columns so the reader can compare the transcription to translation, but also allows the reader to place manuscript images alongside them in a tripartite format. It provides footnotes, a glossary, and commentary, but the reader has no need to flip to the back of the book, as these resources are available dynamically, in-line with the text selection.[33] The reader also has the choice to compare manuscripts complete with paleographic resources and commentary. *Electronic Beowulf* is well-situated as an example where new media has adapted itself from old media to reflect cultural changes and the current needs of the people utilizing its communicative properties. Books can become more than text on a page in a digital space, but only if the author has the wherewithal to recognize and use the tools at hand.

Framing the Book

As many of the methodological treatises on the differing media types have predominantly focused on new media, we often conjure ideas of modern media like social media or the internet. In a broad sense, media is a means of communication which does not differentiate between old and new. Media has agency and meaning as conveyors of information. Elleström defines medium as a "'middle'...a channel for the mediation of information."[34] When McLuhan asserted, "the medium is the message," he maintained that the nature of the object is more important than its content. In this instance, the message – all messages – are media.[35] Media is without borders, and it is diverse with many shared characteristics. Media is an extension of the body, the brain, consciousness, and the physical to be self-outward; it is "the extension of man."[36] Therefore, the media and digital studies use the middle and examine the middle to better understand the past, present, and future. For McLuhan, the fact that we are watching television far outweighs its content. The aesthetics of the television set, the act of congregation, its geography within homes, businesses, and restaurants construct a peer group – a fellowship with a single consciousness.[37] Media technologies then, create complex social networks which greatly influence cultural and social perception and reception.

Katharine D Scherff defines media and media technologies that generate and modulate the individual and collective structure of sacredness among assemblages of humans and non-humans. She works within the framework that media is largely based on perception and reception, expounding upon the concepts of mediation and screens. Interpreting the sacred extends beyond sacred spaces, as Sister Albert Marie Surmanski focuses her work on humanity's original media, the tongue, and Thomas Aquinas' struggle to interpret its various interpretive uses in Psalms. The tongue acts as both a medium and a mediator to communicate divine knowledge through the senses and sensory experiences. The spiritual meaning generated in these sacred spaces had many applications for medieval people, as Nancy Haijing Jiang explores the productive influence of fiscal accounting culture on the literature of vernacular penitential instruction. Here she explores technological networks through collaborative process that tied sinners to each other in chains of relational accountability. While many have observed that confession is primarily an expression of interior subjectivity, this pedagogical overlap between accounting and penance demonstrates that confession can also be an important communal practice that fostered layers of new relational responsibilities between confessors, penitents, and their fellow neighbors.

Media generates meaning in a variety of modalities, spiritual, fiscal, or otherwise. Brittany Forniotis discusses maps that are not maps, but indicators of cultural predilections of architectural features reinforcing the societal norms of their creators. These chorographies were less useful for practical directions to a particular location but are visual tools that provide insight into how early modern people viewed the world around them. However, chorographies require their audiences to have a level of cultural understanding in order to generate meaning from visual images. Beatrice Bottomley and Arianna Dalla Costa, on the other hand, explain how paper "machines" can be used to acquire meaning through the use of a text where it would otherwise remain hidden or difficult to understand. Ramon Llull's *ars combinatoria*, for example, provides a symbolic alphabet to be used in conjunction with the reading of a text, allowing the reader a physical tool that offers a scaffold for readers to identify absolute (i.e. divine) principles and moral guidance. Modern tools offer additional pathways to meaning, as Anne Betty Weinshenker discusses modern viewership and research of the Anglo-Irish impresario, Owen McSwiny's cycle of some twenty large-size allegorical paintings commemorating English nobles. She argues that her investigation and, by association, other arts historians' investigations can be made more robust by accessing the art both digitally and in-person. Digital investigation allows the researcher to interact more personally with the art, observing fine details otherwise easily overlooked but of iconographic significance.

Eric Hupe and Caitlyn Carr's essay expands upon this concept of digital viewership through their development of art history as an academic discipline where classroom teaching remains dependent on technologies that reproduce images. They explore how as image technology advances, so too must the methods art historians use for teaching and conducting research. This article explores new approaches for teaching Renaissance art history that harnesses the full potential of immersive technology. Rather than relying on two-dimensional images to recreate the experience of an architectural space on a flat screen, VR technology allows students to experience these sites with their instructors in digital spaces. Similarly, but less immersive, Margaret Mansfield discusses an interactive in-class simulation where students gain both a broad and individualized understanding of the seventeenth-century Dutch art market viewed through the corrective lens that digital technology provides them. Students are able to concurrently develop the knowledge and understanding of early modern Netherlands along with real-world tools used by historians and art historians. Practical application is key to the continued development of medieval and early modern studies. Lane Sobehrad and Susan Sobehrad discuss how even a basic understanding of multimodality and new literacies may offer medievalists strategies for incorporating complex medieval and early modern topics in an undergraduate setting. As is often the case with academic research in the humanities, it is not always clear how the work of medievalists is either useful to learners or offers any practical insight into modern life. The educator must act as a mediator to ensure that the learner has the necessary tools to access information and meaning in their classroom environment.

These curated chapters reflect the sentiments suggested at the start to not, "seek the old in the new, but find something new in the old."[38] Applying the paradigms and methodologies of media studies to our research and pedagogical practices offers a chance to glean a better understanding of premodern art, sacred practices, and literacies. Historians and art historians have continually reimagined their disciplines through the discovery of new evidence, the development of new approaches to evaluating extant evidence, and by using new tools that alter the ways in which people engage with the past. This volume emphasizes the latter by reframing our understandings of media technologies, in and outside of the digital period, in effort to demonstrate that the ways historical phenomena are accessed are just as important as the information contained therein.

Notes

1 Siegfried Zielinski, *Deep Time of the Media: Toward an Archaeology of Hearing and Seeing by Technical Means*, trans. Gloria Custance (Cambridge, MA: MIT Press, 2006), 3.
2 Pew Research Center, "Internet/Broadband Fact Sheet," https://www.pewresearch.org/internet/fact-sheet/internet-broadband/, accessed February 21, 2022.
3 Tara McPherson, "Introduction: Media Studies and the Digital Humanities," *Cinema Journal* 48, no. 2 (2009): 119–23, 119.
4 Additional budget and funding information may be found at, National Endowment for the Humanities, "Budget/Performance," *National Endowment for the Humanities*, https://www.neh.gov/about/budget-performance, accessed April 29, 2022.
5 Tara McPherson, "Introduction: Media Studies and the Digital Humanities," *Cinema Journal* 48, no. 2 (2009): 119–23.
6 Jentery Sayers (ed.), *The Routledge Companion to Media Studies and Digital Humanities* (New York: Routledge, 2020), 1.
7 Inge Marszolek and Yvonne Robel, "The Communicative Construction of Collectivities: An Interdisciplinary Approach to Media History," *Historical Social Research/Historische Sozialforschung* 41, no. 1 (155) (2016): 328–57, 333.
8 Marszolek and Robel, "The Communicative Construction of Collectivities," 333. Also see Bernd Sösemann, *Propaganda. Medien und Offentlichkeit in der NS-Diktatur*, vol. 1 and 2 (Stuttgart: Steiner, 2011).
9 See Marshall McLuhan and Bruce Powers, *The Global Village: Transformations in World Life and Media in the 21st Century* (Oxford: Oxford University Press, 1989).
10 See Walter Benjamin, "The Work of Art in the Age of Mechanical Reproduction," in Hannah Arendt (ed), Translated by Harry Zohn, *Illuminations* (London: Pimlico, 1999), 217–253.
11 Digital Humanities Quarterly, "About DHQ," *dhq*, http://www.digitalhumanities.org/dhq/about/about.html, accessed January 15, 2021.
12 See Eduardo Bernot and Enrique Alarcon, eds., *Corpus Thomisticum: Index Thomisticum* (Ravenna: Società CAEL, 2005), https://www.corpusthomisticum.org/it/index.age.
13 Marshall McLuhan studied Western Civilization at St Louis University. He had a particular affinity for classical, medieval, and Renaissance thought (Philip Marchand, *Marshall McLuhan: The Medium and the Messenger: A Biography* (Cambridge: MIT Press, 1998), 54–5.
14 A student of McLuhan, Walter J. Ong, analyzed the human consciousness in its transitions from these transitions from an oral to literate culture. See Walter J. Ong, *Orality and Literacy: The Technologizing of the Word* (New York: Routledge, 1982).
15 John Hartley, *Communication, Cultural and Media Studies: The Key Concepts*. 3rd edition. (London: Routledge, 2002), ix–x.
16 Sue Thorham, et al. (eds.), *Media Studies A Reader*. 3rd edition (New York: New York University Press, 2009), 345.
17 Friedrich A. Kittler, *Discourse Networks, 1800/1900*, trans. Michael Metteer and Chris Cullens (Stanford, CA: Stanford University Press, 1990), 369.
18 Marshall McLuhan, *Understanding Media: The Extensions of Man* (Cambridge, MA: The MIT Press, 1994), 7.
19 Kirk Ambrose, *The Art Bulletin* 93, no. 1 (2011): 110–13, 110.
20 Susan Hockey, "The History of Humanities Computing," in *A Companion to Digital Humanities*, eds. Susan Schreibman, Ray Siemens, and John Unsworth (Oxford: Blackwell, 2004), http://www.digitalhumanities.org/companion/, accessed December 12, 2020.
21 Robert Getz and Stephen Pelle, eds., *The Dictionary of Old English* (Toronto: University of Toronto, 2020), https://www.doe.utoronto.ca/pages/index.html, accessed December 15, 2020; Angus Cameron, Ashley Crandell Amos, Sharon Butler, and Antonette diPaolo Healey, *The Dictionary of Old English Corpus in Electronic Form* (Toronto: University of Toronto Press, 1981).
22 The Unicode Consortium, *The Unicode Standard: Worldwide Character Encoding, Version 1.0*, 2 vol. (Reading: Addison-Wesley Publishing, 1990–2).
23 See Paul Halsall, "The Internet History Sourcebooks Project," https://sourcebooks.fordham.edu/index.asp.
24 "Verkürzt gesagt, eskalieren mittelalterliche Kulturtechniken erst postum zu Medien." Ernst, "'Medien,'" 347. Wolfgang Ernst, "'Medien' im Mittelalter? – Kulturtechnische Retrospektive,"

in *Goetz Mediävis-tik im 21. Jahrhundert: Stand und Perspektiven der interdisziplinaren Mittelalterforschung*, eds. Hans-Werner Goetz and Jorg Janut (Munich: Fink, 2003), 347–57. Paper from the proceedings of the congress *Goetz Mediävis-tik im 21. Jahrhundert*, as cited in Erik Born, "Media Archaeology, Cultural Techniques, and the Middles Ages: An Approach to the Study of Media before the Media," *Seminar* 52, no. 2 (May 2016), 110.

25 Erik Born, "Media Archaeology, Cultural Techniques, and the Middles Ages: An Approach to the Study of Media before the Media," *Seminar* 52, no. 2 (May 2016), 110.

26 Lars Elleström, "Media, Modality and Modes," in *Media Borders, Multimodality and Intermediality*, ed. Lars Elleström (New York: Palgrave Macmillan, 2010), 14. I will revisit the four modalities of media in Chapter 3.

27 Lars Elleström, "Media," 17.

28 Ilana Gershon, "Media Ideologies: An Introduction," *Journal of Linguistic Anthropology* 20, no. 2 (2010): 283–93, 287.

29 See Jussi Parikka, *What Is Media Archaeology* (London: Polity Press, 2012) and Siegfried Zielinksi, *Deep Time of the Media: Toward an Archaeology of Hearing and Seeing by Technical Means* (Cambridge, MA: MIT University Press, 2006). Media archaeology has emerged from many directions including Michel Foucault's archaeology of knowledge and Walter Benjamin's critical writings on the impact of reproduction.

30 See: Jay David Bolter and Richard Grusin, *Remediation: Understanding New Media* (Cambridge, MA: The MIT Press, 1999). Jussi Parikka discusses their interrelation design in *What Is Media Archaeology* (London: Polity Press, 2012), 3. Manuel Menke and Christian Schwarzenegger elaborate on this idea in "On the Relativity of Old and New Media: A Lifeworld Perspective," *Convergence: The international Journal of Research into New Media Technologies* 25, no. 4 (2009): 657–72, 660.

31 Bolter and Grusin, *Remediation*, 105. Also see: Jay David Bolter, Blair MacIntyre, Maribeth Gandy, and Petra Schweitzer, "New Media and the Permanent Crisis of Aura," *The International Journal of Research into New Media Technologies* 12, no. 1 (2006): 21–39.

32 Lars Elleström, "Media, Modality and Modes," in *Media Borders, Multimodality and Intermediality*, ed. Lars Elleström (New York: Palgrave Macmillan, 2010), Martin Foys "The Remanence of Medieval Media," in *The Routledge Research Companion to Digital Medieval Literature*, eds. Jennifer E. Boyle and Helen J. Burgess (New York: Routledge, 2018), 9–30; Foys, *Virtually Anglo-Saxon: Old Media, New Media, and Early Medieval Studies in the Late Age of Print* (Gainesville: University Press of Florida, 2007); and Thora Brylowe and Stephen (eds.), *Old Media and the Medieval Concept* (Montreal: Concordia University Press, 2021).

33 Kevin Kiernan, ed. *Electronic Beowulf 4.0* (British Library, 2015), https://ebeowulf.uky.edu/ebeo4.0/start.html, accessed January 5, 2021.

34 Lars Elleström, "The Modalities of Media: A Model for Understanding Intermedial Relations," in *Media Borders, Multimodality and Intermediality*, ed. L. Elleström (London: Palgrave Macmillan, 2010), 13.

35 Marshall McLuhan, *Understanding Media: The Extensions of Man* (Cambridge, MA: The MIT Press, 1994), 7.

36 Marshall McLuhan, *Understanding Media: The Extensions of Man* (Cambridge, MA: The MIT Press, 1994), 1.

37 See McLuhan, *Understanding Media* (Cambridge, MA: The MIT Press, 1994).

38 Siegfried Zielinski, *Deep Time of the Media: Toward an Archaeology of Hearing and Seeing by Technical Means*, trans. Gloria Custance (Cambridge, MA: MIT Press, 2006), 3.

PART I

Text or Tool? - Beyond the Narrative

1

FROM AUDITS TO CONFESSIONALS

The Influence of Accounting Technology on Medieval Penitential Pedagogy

Nancy Haijing Jiang

For better or worse, technology has always shaped the ways in which people practiced religion in the West. One *New York Times* article on an iTunes application called 'Confession: A Roman Catholic App' captures this convergence in all its intricate, and sometimes humorous, complexity. Still in use today, the app prepares penitents before in-person confession by providing them with a detailed questionnaire of sins so that they can better articulate their vices to the confessor. The user can even pre-select their sins on the app, storing them manually to erase later once confession is complete. Met with a mixture of enthusiasm, bemusement, and suspicion, the app caused quite a stir for some members of the Catholic community – from those who heralded it as the long-awaited tool for reviving lay interest in confession to the disgruntled cynics, like Rev. Father Federico Lombardi, who tersely responded to a reporter's request for comment that 'one cannot speak in any way of "confession by iPhone."'[1]

While it appears that something like a 'confession app' can only exist in our techno-centric modern age, the medieval penitential system likewise intersected with contemporary technological advancements, sometimes in surprisingly similar ways to our current era. One remarkable parallel with the confession app can be found in the famous Vernon Manuscript (c.1390–410): a miscellany of Middle English religious writing containing several works of penitential instruction.[2] In the middle of the manuscript, there is an intricate grid-shaped diagram to help readers prepare for confession that closely resembles a late medieval accounting technology.[3] The diagram, known as the 'Vernon Paternoster Table,' lays out the seven petitions of the Lord's Prayer, the seven gifts of the Holy Spirit, the Seven Deadly Sins, and their corresponding virtues in an intricate checkered formation similar to a reckoning board used in medieval auditing procedures.[4] These boards were often placed in the center of an auditing space, encircled by various members of a manor, household, or religious institution as they calculated their estates' revenues and debts by moving counters, or 'jetons,' along its squares.[5] As on an actual reckoning board, the Vernon Table is also interspersed with significant roundels that resemble jetons, as if encouraging penitents to prepare for confession by calculating, quite literally, the particular virtues that will balance

DOI: 10.4324/9781003295082-3

out their vices. Furthermore, just like a reckoning board, this diagram would have been publicly presented. The manuscript's unusually large size (weighing 48.75 lbs. and measuring 544 × 393 mm) meant that it was likely on display in an abbey, and the Vernon Table, with its central placement and large, elaborate design, potentially the page displayed.[6] Just as members of an abbey would have gathered around a reckoning board during an audit to ensure that their abbey was not in financial debt, so too could they have gathered around the Vernon Table in group prayer, reading out loud the vices and virtues to ensure collective penitential vigilance against spiritual debt, reminding each other to cancel their sins in confession.[7]

The table designer, like the creator of the confession app, appropriated contemporary technology to teach confessional preparation. Only in this case, rather than just creating a device for *individual* devotion, the designer also fashioned a tool to promote shared moral and confessional responsibility. This pedagogical move, I argue, is not unique. Indeed, my chapter examines numerous other instances in late medieval texts of penitential instruction that showcase instructors using accounting technologies to engage penitents in confession and, in that process, encourage an ethic of collective spiritual and moral accountability (Figures 1.1 and 1.2).

Some scholars have already observed that medieval accounting technologies and concepts greatly influenced the penitential system, although most, like Rev. Lombardi, viewed this influence with deep suspicion. This period, as a number of scholars have pointed out, saw an exponential growth in 'counting piety': a method of praying taught by numerous devotional handbooks that calculated the specific number of prayers required for a certain amount of heavenly rewards.[8] Purgatorial doctrine, too, took on greater arithmetical complexity as penitents learned to keep, in Jacque Le Goff's words, 'double-entry accounts with respect to earthly time and time in purgatory,' tallying up their penitential ventures, such as prayers, pilgrimages, and alms-giving, as 'spiritual guarantees' against purgatorial fire.[9] Even as lay penitents learned to calculate sins and penances in their personal salvation, an increasing number of churches and confraternities also started to use bookkeeping tools to track the alms from those penitents, tallying up the goods gained from penitential almsgiving to sum up their institutional growth.[10] Reading their use of accounting technology as inextricably linked to a proto-capitalistic agenda, scholars saw the overlap between accounting and penitential practice as a sign of 'a piety trapped in a commercial mentality,' a profit-centric force that transformed true devotion into selfish, accumulative gain.[11]

My chapter challenges this scholarly consensus in two significant ways. First, by examining medieval technologies of accounting (tally sticks, account books, and reckoning boards) in their historical contexts, I highlight how they were used not simply to tabulate profits and expenditures but also – and sometimes more often – to maintain the fabric of social relations and collective ethical accountability. Even as they were made to service the expanding market economy of late medieval England, these technologies also reflected and actually helped to cultivate, the religious and ethical imperatives still governing English society and commerce.[12] Second, I illuminate how writers of penitential instruction harnessed accounting technologies not to generate a self-centered, profit-motivated spirituality but to cultivate a more robust system of shared moral responsibility. From penitential manuals, like Robert Mannyng's *Handlyng Synne* (c.1330), to sermon treatises, these texts appropriated the technological developments in accounting to teach confession as a tool for spiritual accountability – one that fostered networks of interpersonal and interconnecting penitential accounts and reinforced the important role that all penitents have to secure their salvation collectively. Foucault famously defined confession as a 'technology of the self,' highlighting how its systematic structure and guided self-reflective questions led penitents to articulate their inner being and develop their own individual subjectivity.[13] Yet by engaging with

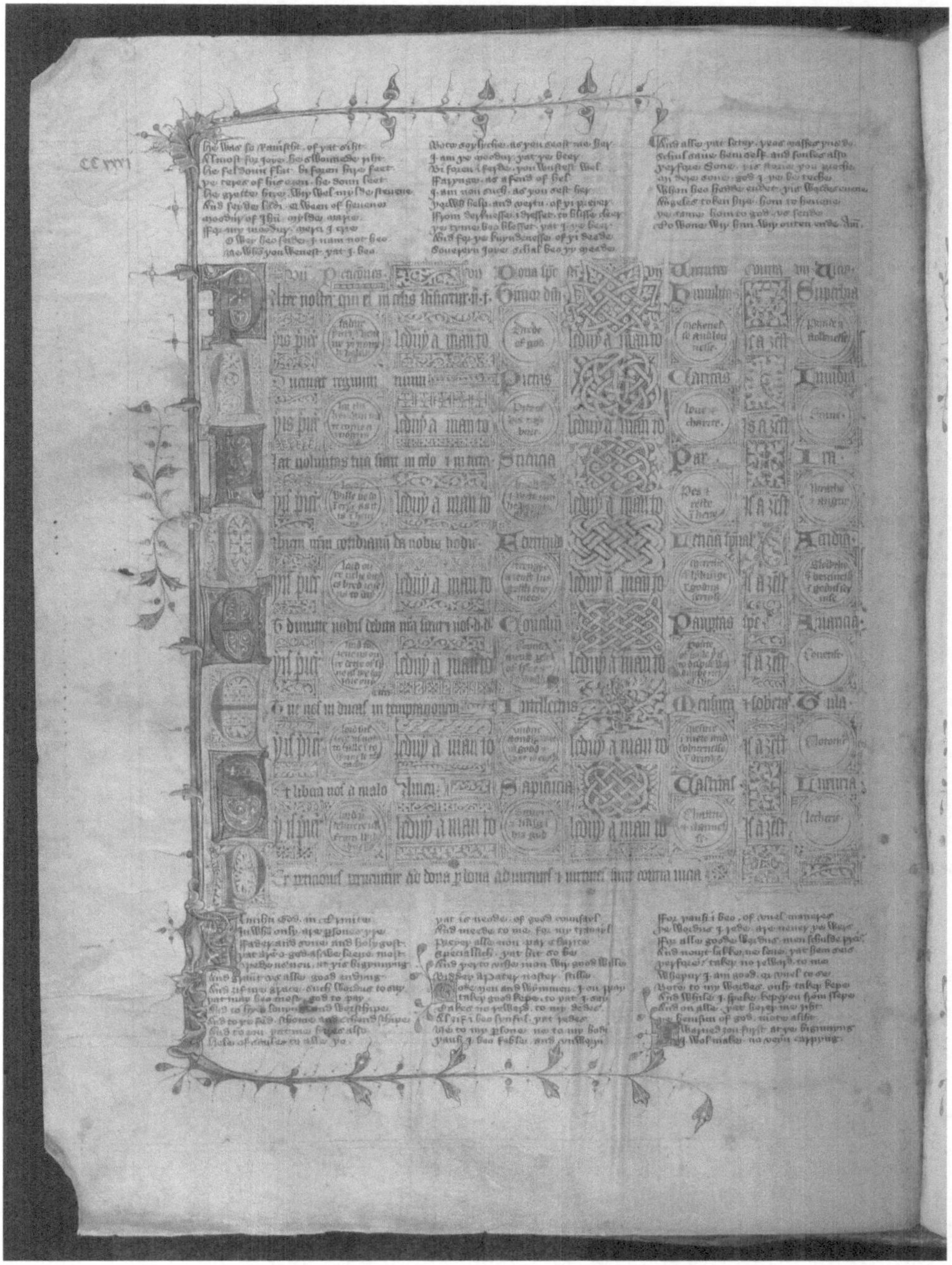

FIGURE 1.1 f. 231v of the Vernon Manuscript, Bodleian Library, MS Eng. poet. a. 1.

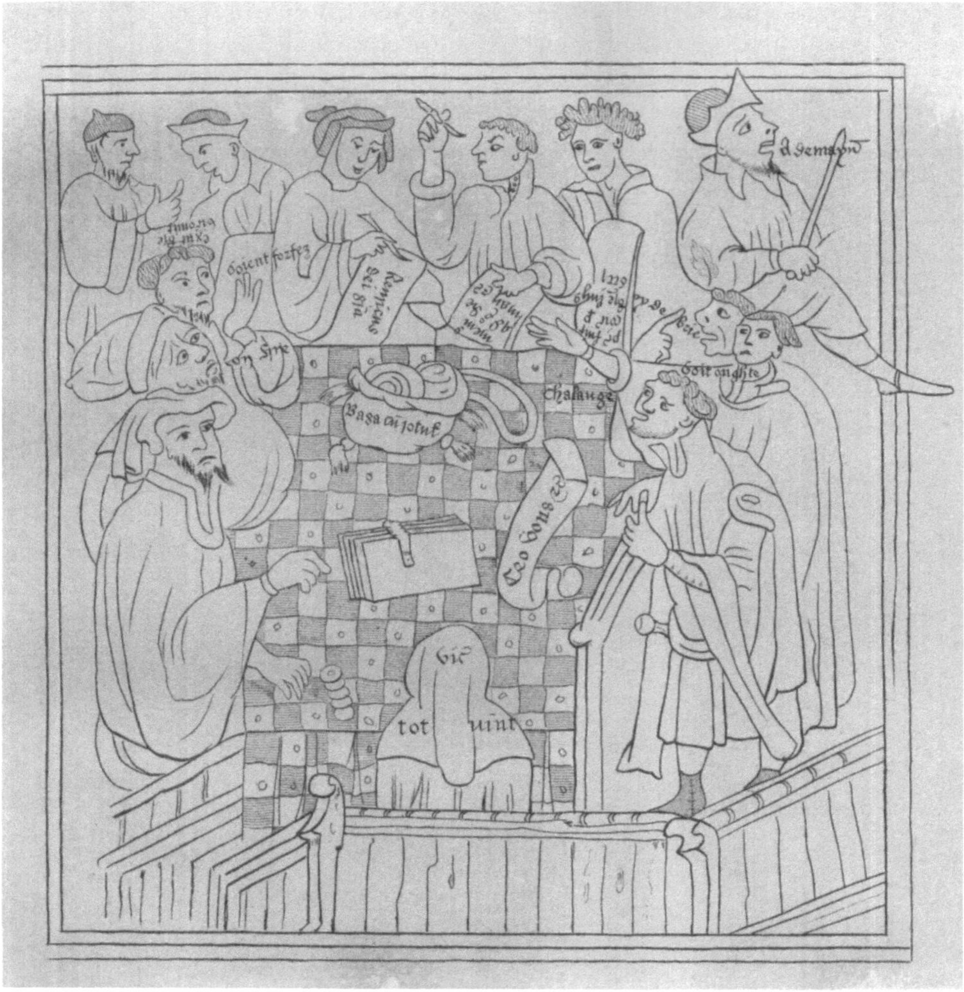

FIGURE 1.2 A scene showing the Dublin Court of the Exchequer wherein accountants and sheriff encircle a large reckoning board.[63]

contemporary technologies of accounting, the writers explored in this chapter demonstrate that confession could also be an important communal apparatus that fostered layers of new relational responsibilities between penitents and their local communities.

Accounting Technologies in Late Medieval England

Late medieval England's expanding commercial culture required greater accounting dexterity and new technologies to meet this demand. By the fourteenth century, accounting ledgers had become essential equipment not only for the merchant trader but also for any successfully managed manor, guild, religious institution, or rich household.[14] Tallies (long sticks of wood with carved notches to record transactions) became a regular part of manorial estate management and day-to-day credit arrangements.[15] Reckoning boards and jetons, too, were increasingly used in urban spaces to facilitate exchanges and calculate expenditure.[16] These technologies paved the way for greater accounting literacy not only among industrious traders or paid clerks but also, at some level, among nearly all strata of medieval society. The *Account Books of Beaulieu Abbey*, for example, consist of approximately fifty interlocking accounts to be rendered, as Rosemary O'Neill posits, 'by the most humble of manorial workers, including milkmaids and swineherds' in order to ensure abbey stability.[17]

While it is tempting to read this increase in accounting literacy among medieval subjects as a direct precursor of modern capitalist thinking, accountancy in this period was actually far from being the system of capital accumulation we think of today.[18] Most medieval manor accounts show no strong indication that they were used for determining profit but rather, as Jonathon Sabapathy highlights, manorial accounting was more often than not an exercise to ensure manorial officers practiced correct stewardship.[19] Focusing on late medieval Italy, James Aho argues that merchants developed accounting not initially for calculating profit but for demonstrating their debt and resource management skills before their community in order to bolster their trading reputations.[20] For example, Leon Battista Alberti (a prominent member of the renowned Florentine banking family) argued that it was his 'ethical duty to write everything down…so that [he] should seem more diligent.'[21] My discussion of accounting technologies aims to understand these tools in light of this conception of medieval accountancy: a system concerned not just with profit-making but also with ethical obligation. In doing so, I suggest that even as medieval subjects used technologies of accounting to tabulate resources and profits, they also harnessed them to generate collaborative relationships of shared responsibility and dependency, in particular, in the handling of financial debt.

As a number of scholars have shown, debt was ubiquitous in the late medieval period.[22] People frequently bought and sold on credit in markets, shops, and among friends, rarely paying with money up front because of perennial bullion shortage across medieval Europe.[23] From the urban trader to the manorial lord, to the rural villager, everyone was literally indebted to everyone else all the time in a long 'chain of debt,' as Martha Howell explains, that linked people across villages, cities, and even continents.[24] In an economic climate with long chains of interconnected loans, debt was therefore not just a personal issue but often a shared burden.[25] One debtor's ill-managed obligations would have undermined the financial standing of all others who were serially connected to him in the chain of debt, causing a disastrous domino effect of debt collapses. What is more, given the spiritual associations with debt in this period, the implications of this collective debt were more than simply economic.[26] A common late medieval theological manual applied the Seventh Commandment against stealing to all those who 'nell not pay here dette that thei oweth [will not pay the debt that they owe],' hence constituting outstanding debts as a deadly sin.[27] Ill-managed debt, then, did not just negatively impact the economic standing of an entire community but also jeopardized everyone's salvation. Consequently, keeping diligent accounts in order to manage resources and repay debts on time was more than a savvy economic skill but was considered, as Aho argues, 'a cardinal virtue' and 'an expression of a late medieval project in moral improvement.'[28] Put another way, accounting in this period became the virtuous antidote to the vice of debt – a virtue that must be cultivated collectively because of how intricately each person's debts were enmeshed with another.

Accounting technologies were crucial instruments for fostering this virtue of collaborative accountability, increasingly becoming tools not only for record keeping but also for mediation that kept people in economic arrangements accountable. For example, tally sticks, which had for centuries been used as recording devices, were now passed between debtors and creditors as tools of interpersonal accountability.[29] In late medieval England, debtors would record their loans on a tally by carving notches down the middle of the stick. After splitting the tally in two, they would hand one part to the creditor as a pledge of repayment while keeping the other as a record of transaction. With the tally, creditors could hold their debtors accountable with a visible receipt of their promise while debtors could ensure that their creditors did not overcharge them when collecting debt. A case found in the 1368 entry of the *Plea and Memoranda Rolls* of London demonstrates how the exchange of tallies between Thomas Andrew, Sir John de Cobham, and three other Londoners to whom Andrew owed about £35 kept all of them accountable in a multi-layered credit relationship. Instead of paying the three Londoners in cash, Andrew presented a tally that recorded £54 10s 5d owed to him by Sir John de Cobham, promising to repay everything once Cobham fulfilled his side of the obligation. Evidently satisfied, the creditors dropped their charges.[30] In this case, the tally was used as a negotiable financial instrument while serving as a trustworthy token of promise that mediated between many debtors and creditors. Such accounting devices maintained the long chains of debt through systems of accountability while reinforcing the interdependency and trust so crucial for economic relationships of obligation.

Late medieval manorial accounting also adopted (and adapted) tallies as instruments of interpersonal accountability for the yearly audit to mitigate manorial debt. In the fourteenth-century manor, tallies mediated the accounting procedures conducted between bailiffs, reeves, clerks, and manorial officers. During the fiscal year, their transactions would be noted on split tally sticks so that numerous parties had records of their exchange.[31] These transactions could range from collecting rent and sales to paying workers, with tallies acting simultaneously as receipts, records of transaction, and even pledges of payment should anyone lack the cash to pay upfront. At the end of the fiscal year, bailiffs would collect these tallies to determine an accurate account of the manor's expenditures and loans, ensuring that the manor's debts would be repaid on time. This introduction of tallies into manorial accounting procedures decentralized its administrative hierarchy by distributing the work of accounting across the manor, as reflected in the late medieval manorial auditing process.[32] Before the fourteenth century, accounts were created and finalized by a small circle of men chosen by the lord of the manor who oversaw the work of all manorial members.[33] By the fourteenth century, the bailiff would create a version of accounts using the tallies from numerous manorial workers. Then he would take these accounts to an audit, orally presenting them before the lord who could question and renegotiate these records until they arrive at a collectively agreed account, at which point an accounting clerk would help finalize it in writing.[34] In other words, the introduction of tallies into manorial management meant that accounting was no longer the job of only a small group of higher-ups.[35] Instead, it became a cooperative exchange that involved all echelons of manorial members, fostering a collective ethic of interpersonal accountability within the manor estate.

Accounting ledgers, while not typically passed between people as tallies, also became tools of interpersonal mediation in their own right, especially among the merchant classes. In particular, one method of mercantile bookkeeping called 'bookkeeping barter' generated mutual accountability among fellow traders by facilitating concessions of credit between continuous trading relationships.[36] This method consisted of each party recording what the other owed in a ledger and, periodically, bringing the account books to mutually strike out their debts and pay only the imbalances in cash. In doing so, merchants also created a system for reciprocal account book invigilation, sharing their texts for interpersonal scrutiny so that no errors will be made in the process of striking out debts. During a period of scant bullion, bookkeeping barter was common among buyers and sellers of every caliber, especially among merchants who relied heavily on credit transactions. The back-and-forth running accounts found in London wool merchant Gilbert Maghfeld's account book (c.1390–5), especially between him and John Kempston, a cloth merchant based in Hadleigh, are some of the clearest instances of this system in operation.[37] Bookkeeping barter not only ensured that both parties could effectively manage their debts even if cash was wanting; it cultivated bonds of reciprocal trust and alliance so crucial for maintaining the numerous credit arrangements on which merchants built their trade.[38]

Of course, the increasing reliance and accessibility of these accounting technologies also created new dangers. As Dorothea Oschinsky notes, untrustworthy or careless bailiffs, reeves, and manorial officers frequently failed to produce clear tallies or records, making the process of accurately assessing a manor's profits and debts nightmarish for accounting clerks and leaving ample room for theft and fraud.[39] Mercantile ledgers were equally suspectable to such instances of human oversight and abuse as indicated by a selection of medieval court cases where merchants were tried for fraudulent account books.[40] Yet the period's anxiety about erroneous accounts did not curb its enthusiasm for accounting technologies nor the hope that these tools could cultivate a virtue of collective accountability. Indeed, in the face of individual debt-management failure or accounting fraud, the task of ensuring accounting technologies was properly employed became an even more collaborative enterprise. What occurred after the accounting failures of Edward de Courtenay's steward in 1384 and the prioress of Harrold Priory in 1442 highlights this fact especially clearly.

In the summer of 1442, when the prioress of Harrold Priory in Lincolnshire failed to make correct tallies and landed her priory in debt, William Alnwick, the bishop of Lincolnshire, urged that she always 'make tayles or som remembraunce writene be twix yow and the sellers [make tallies or some written reminders between you and the sellers]' and commissioned her entire community to invigilate her endeavors.[41] He even threatened to suspend the prioress unless she showed her 'fulle and plenare accompte [plain account]' to all her chapter sisters every year so that 'hit may be knawen to thaym what plyte your place yerely standes yn [they may know the yearly conditions of your abbey].'[42] The prioress's account books and tallies, then, become not just instruments of interpersonal accountability but also of collective interest that required the efforts of an entire community to operate well. Likewise, when Courtenay's steward was charged with disallowed expenses because he did not keep his accounts properly, Courtenay ordered that the entire household should help survey the steward's accounting to avoid such errors in the future.[43] Yet more than just asking the community to shoulder the steward's accounting burden, Courtney also took responsibility for the steward's accounting failures, resolving the steward's financial grievances by helping to repay his debts.[44] Perhaps to maintain the appearance of a well-managed household, Courtenay saw it as his responsibility to help clear his steward's accounts.[45] Like the prioress' tallies and account books, then, the steward's accounting technologies were tools that both cultivated and required collective accountability. Failure to use these tools effectively, and the economic burdens that arose from such errors, implicated numerous people who were all tasked with the responsibility of ensuring that accounting instruments were properly used.

Far from being instruments of capital accumulation as have been previously assumed, medieval accounting technologies must be understood as tools adapted and honed by medieval subjects deeply concerned with integrating their ethical and even spiritual imperatives with their expanding economic contexts. In doing so, we gather that these tools helped to cultivate relationships of collaborative accountability crucial for maintaining the long chains of debt that marked the economic landscape of late medieval England. As we turn from the world of commerce to one of penance, it becomes clear that this ethic of collective accountability conversed with and filtered into numerous aspects of the medieval lived experience, including the penitential system.

Accounting for Sin in the Confessional Audit

Long before these developments in accounting technology and strategy took place, medieval theologians and writers frequently discussed Christ's second coming in terms of a future 'reckoning' before God's throne. Building on the already pervasive language of accounting in the Bible – in particular, images of a 'Book of Life,' opened by God on Judgement Day, which records the saved and damned – writers presented God's court of justice as a terrifying and all-encompassing audit with a divine 'Auditor' who will render each individual answerable for their thoughts, words, and deeds.[46] The clearest example of this can be found in Thomas Wimbledon's sermon *Redde Rationem* (c.1388), wherein Christ is described as a 'householdere [head of the household]' and each Christian as a steward who, at Judgement Day – must 'ȝelde rekenynge of [his] baile [yield an account of his stewardship].'[47] In penitential traditions, descriptions of a Final Reckoning often overlapped with the popular medieval trope of the 'book of conscience': the human heart or mind as an inner text.[48] Combined with the prospect of a divine audit, the 'book of conscience' became a sort of personalized 'account book' of deeds to be scrutinized by God at that Final Reckoning where he will render a final and unchangeable verdict based on every deed marked in this personalized spiritual ledger.[49]

The exemplum of King Coenred's knight found in Bede's *Ecclesiastical History* (5.13) (c.651–731) – a tale that is frequently reiterated in late medieval sermons and handbooks on penance – encapsulates the terror of this divine audit metaphor.[50] The narrative opens with the king calling his knight to repent and turn from his sins. The knight refuses and soon falls into a grave illness. Hearing that his knight was in such an affliction, King Coenred rushes to his bedside, again pleading with him to repent. Yet the knight still refuses, having already succumbed to despair because of a dream he had before the king's arrival. In the dream, the knight was presented with two books: one small volume held by angels that was filled with his good deeds and the other an enormous codex of his sins carried by an army of evil spirits. After the knight examined these texts, upon which was written his every thought, word, and deed, the evil spirits claimed the knight's soul for Satan. In the wake of this terrifying personal reckoning that awaits him at God's throne, the knight dies despairing at his unchanging, and unchangeable, fate. The knight's deathbed tableau, therefore, captures the necessity of repentance and the dangers of lax penitential vigilance, all held together by an extended metaphor of a divine audit wherein every person's account book of conscience will be read from cover to cover with no room for intercession or mediation if spiritual debts are left unsettled.

As the Middle Ages progressed, however, writers of penitential instruction transplanted these images of accounting from Judgement Day into their discussions about confession to imagine a provisional audit *before* God's Final Reckoning. Furthermore, by conversing directly with some of the accounting technologies burgeoning in the late medieval period, these writers presented a confessional auditing space where the settlement of debts, mediation, and collaboration was entirely possible, much like a secular accounting audit. One such example can be found in the fourteenth-century vernacular penitential manual, *The Book of Vices and Virtues* (c.1370): a handbook, translated from a popular French penitential *Somme le Roi* (c.1279), written to teach lay penitents to confess their sins.[51] The writer of the *Book* included a number of interesting textual additions to his French source that indicate his interest in and knowledge of medieval accounting procedures and technologies.[52] In the section on 'Confession,' for instance, the writer reminds his reader that a penitent should:

> ȝelde acountes & answer of to God and to his bailiff, þat is his schrifte-fadre, and schulle þenke also on hemself, as he þat is a-iorned to yelde acounte of his receiȝtes and of his dispences to-fore his lord [...] For þeiȝ þei failen at here acountes, God wole not faile at his whan he comeþ.
>
> *(174.4–13)*

> [yield accounts and answer to God and to his bailiff, that is his confessor, and should also think of himself as one who is appointed to yield an account of his receipts and dispenses before his lord. For though they might fail at their accounts, God will not fail at his when he comes]

Here, the writer is not merely invoking a familiar metaphor of Judgement Day but defines the penitent's entire confessional experience through the lens of fiscal accounting strategy. Unlike the knight's heavenly account book, here the penitent has control over his or her 'acountes' as if they are tangible records that can be altered and exchanged to shape the course of a person's history – as 'receiȝtes' that he or she can use 'to receive' salvation.[53] While the divine 'Auditor' still looms ominously, the overall message of this passage is one of action rather than fear. Here, penitents have the privilege of readying their accounts in a confessional audit, using them to ensure salvation before entering God's divine audit where the terms are far less revocable.

Moreover, in this preliminary auditing space, accounting ceases to be a strictly individualistic endeavor. In figuring the 'shrifte-fadre' as God's 'bailiff,' the writer of the *Book* implies that confession is not just the penitent's personal enterprise but also a collaboration shared with the confessor: a bailiff who acts as an intercessor between the penitent and God. Indeed, readers can infer that the confessor, being a 'bailiff,' must also present an account of his own 'receiȝtes' and 'dispences' before his lord one day and that these 'acountes' will be entirely contingent on how well his penitents render theirs. What is more, the presence of 'receiȝtes' suggests that this process of collaboration could encompass a far broader scope of persons than just the penitent and confessor. Just as tallies in medieval accounting acted as receipts that manorial workers collected from their transactions with other people, the 'receiȝtes' in the *Book* also intimate that the penitent's confessional accounts are partially constructed from what he or she has given to and 'received' from others in day-to-day interactions. In other words, these confessional 'acountes' connect the penitent not only to his or her confessor but also to others in the immediate community, invoking a larger network of interconnected penitential accounts all circumscribing the confessional audit. Far from being unique to the *Book* author, this interest in cultivating communal confessional accountancy by invoking contemporary accounting technologies was shared by numerous late medieval penitential instructors – from sermon writers to later adaptors of Bede's exemplum.

The emergence of the confessional as a collaborative audit began with a new penitential system, as it developed in the twelfth century, that greatly transformed the confessor–penitent relationship. During the time of Bede's *Ecclesiastical History* (c.651–731), penances issued by confessors were particularly harsh, including, but not exclusive to, penalties such as ten winters of fasting for fornicating with an animal, or one year's fasting for breaking into a neighbor's property.[54] Because of these extremities, lay penitents would typically not confess until their deathbed or would only confess after committing especially grave sins for which they desperately needed to atone.[55] Yet after the Fourth Lateran Council (1215) mandated annual confession for every Christian, they also stressed that confessors must now inquire after the circumstances of the sinner and sin, adapting and administering penances that were feasible for each penitent so that he or she would willingly return to confession year after year.[56] Emphasizing a level of priest-lay cooperation as part of this new confessional practice, the *Omnis utriusque sexus* figures the confessor as a healing doctor administering yearly remedies of reconciliation:

> Sacerdos autem sit discretus et cautus, ut more periti medici superinfundat vinum et oleum vulneribus sauciati [The priest shall be discerning and prudent, so that like a skilled doctor he may pour wine and oil over the wounds of the injured one].[57]

That is, with a cooperative and compassionate confessor, penitents were now able to repeatedly alter their records of sin before Judgement Day: an opportunity that Coenred's knight was never truly offered.

The penitential manuals and sermons published after Lateran IV's pedagogical programs, implemented in part to engage all penitents in this model of confession, taught the laity about this newly defined dynamic with the confessor, often by appropriating the collaborative accounting relationships found within the medieval manor. Like the *Book* writer, one early fifteenth-century Ash Wednesday Sermon teaches sinners to prepare for a confession like an accounting audit:

> Although it sometimes happens that some people who have fallen into sin are negligent of their salvation and do not know the words to express their confession, the confessor should nevertheless support them humbly, comfort them, and help them. *Just as a clerk helps the bailiff to make his account*, so must the priest ask his penitent about the Ten Commandment and the seven deadly sins with their branches and circumstances in order and inform him in any of these as best he can [emphasis mine].[58]

Presenting a nuanced variant to the *Book*, the Ash Wednesday preacher positions the confessor in a definitively ancillary position to the penitent by reversing the hierarchal order we expect from such a relationship: the penitent is now the bailiff while the confessor is a helpful clerk. Far removed from the exacting the harsh pre-Lateran IV figure, then, this sermon writer presents the confessor as a helper and fellow accountant alongside his penitent-bailiff-ready accounts, ready to mitigate any accounting failures a penitent might have. Indeed, since some literate penitents were even encouraged to take written accounts into the confession to help them remember their sins,[59] one can easily speculate how confessors might have probed, negotiated, and helped construct these records with their penitent to assign the correct penances, just like clerks would pour over account books and tallies with bailiffs to ensure against arrears for the yearly audit. The Ash Wednesday preacher's rendition of the confessor and penitent as clerk and bailiff, then, could be more than just a metaphorical parallel but also a pragmatic overlap – one that captures the collaborative dynamic of the new confessor–penitent relationship and emphasizes the overlap of interpersonal accountability between the audit and confessional.

Even as post-Lateran IV confession stressed confessor–penitent collaboration, it also emphasized a collective ethic of confessional vigilance that stretches beyond just the penitent and his or her confessor. In the late medieval period, there was a growing sense that a sinner's penitential accounts are deeply enmeshed with those in his or her community: neighbors, servants, and family members. The *Prick of Conscience* (c.1330–50), a popular Middle English penitential poem, reminds readers that at the Last Judgement, all people must render an account of those for whom they are socially and spiritually responsible: 'Fadur and modur at that day/shul acounte … of here children [Father and mother on that day shall account for their children]' 'lordes eke of her meynye [lords also for their household],' 'maysteres of here disciples [masters for their disciples]' (5.1773–9), and every person for the neighbors they failed to help.[60] In this view, it is not merely the individual's imperative to use confession to erase his or her debts before Judgement Day but also the community's to ensure his or her confessional participation –a community that will equally suffer should the penitent's spiritual debts be left unsettled.

Nowhere are the interconnected natures of these penitential accounts more prevalent than in Robert Mannyng's retelling of Bede's exemplum in *Handlyng Synne* (c.1330): a Middle English verse penitential handbook.[61] By engaging with the late medieval account book as a technology that promotes and requires interpersonal accountability – especially when individual accounting failure occurs – Mannyng transforms the knight's spiritual ledger into a shared responsibility. Whereas Bede's knight is the only one answerable for the sins in his account book, the spiritual debts of Mannyng's knight are erasable by the collective penitential vigilance of those connected to the knight, those who are responsible for and implicated by the knight's actions. That is, Mannyng's retelling of Bede's exemplum teaches that the 'account book of conscience,' just like a fiscal account book, must be maintained by collective accountability in order to ensure a clear account before God's Final Reckoning.

In *Handlyng Synne*, Mannyng draws the knight's relationship with the king into sharper focus, reframing the knight's own debts of sin as a burden that the king also shares.[62] Elaborating upon his source, Mannyng emphasizes how the king benefits materially from the knight's worldly machinations:

> no man myght trowe him weyl,
> where þat he myght make a wanlace
> and any þyng to þe kyng purchace

he ne lette for no false oth
þat he ne made ofte dysheresun
And holy cherche traueyled with tresun
For wrong ne lefte he nyȝt ne day,
But onely he serued þe kyng to pay.

(4375–83)

[No man could trust him securely. Wherever he could make a dishonest deal and acquire anything for the king, he would not refrain because of any false oath. In the process, he often disinherited people and betrayed holy Church, for he did not forsake wrongdoing either by night or by day but served only to please the king.]

In this passage, Mannyng notes that the knight's actions stem not just from selfish ambition but also his desire to please ('to pay') his king: an act of subordination to his earthly king that is ultimately an act of 'tresun' against his heavenly one. Mannyng's emphasis on the connection between the knight's corruption and the king's pleasure constructs a close relationship of interdependence. In other words, Mannyng rewrites the king as one who has far greater stakes in the knight's repentance and penitential restitution than the figure in Bede's exemplum. Therefore, the king's insistence on the knight's confession is more than the pious undertaking of a devout ruler but the desperate urgency of someone who is implicated in the knight's corruption and whose own penitential accounts are deeply enmeshed with that of his loyal servant.

In fact, Mannyng makes this fact overtly clear when he adds a new moral to Bede's exemplum that reminds rulers who benefit from corrupt subordinates that their own spiritual lives will be equally jeopardized:

And þys ys a custummable þyng
Now, wyþ euery lordyng,
Þat, ȝyf his stuwarde hym oght wynne,
Be hyt wyþ ryght, or wyþ synne,
Hym wyl he holde most pryue
Of alle þo þat wyþ hym be.
But as he takeþ þerof þe frame
He shal haue parte of synne and shame.

(4413–20)

[And this is now the custom with every lord: if his steward wins him any profit, whether rightfully or sinfully, he will trust him the most among all his followers. But just as he takes a share in the profit, he shall have a share in the sin and shame.]

By placing this new moral directly before the knight's deathbed tableau, Mannyng shifts the perspective of that scene from one of the individuals to shared culpability. The king, because he 'takeþ þerof þe frame' of the knight's deceits, must 'haue parte of synne and shame' in the knight's reckoning process. The relative lack of specificity in the last two lines implies that this lesson applies not only to kings or 'lordyngs' who disregard the spiritual depravity of their knights and 'stuwards' but also to anyone who gained materially from the sins of another. Indeed, Mannyng's new moral implies that one sinner's unsettled spiritual debts will negatively impact the penitential accounts books of every other person who benefited from his actions, no matter what their station. Furthermore, the placement of this moral immediately after the king's attempt to persuade the knight toward confession suggests that one way to insure against such a disastrous domino effect of one unbalanced account after another is to practice interpersonal confessional vigilance. That is, like Edward de Courtenay who scrupulously monitored the accounts of his steward to curtail further negative impact on himself, penitents should likewise the conditions of sin within their household or those with whom they shared profits, urging them to confession when necessary – just like the king in this story.

The sense of collective accountability that circumscribe the knight's deathbed vision is further accentuated by the presentation of his account book of conscience. During this dream sequence, the summation of the knight's account book is not a private examination but a public performance as the knight is asked to orally read his books, 'al y hyt redde wyþ opon mouthe [I read it all with open mouth]' (4442), sounding out his accounts before angels and demons just as bailiffs would read aloud their tallies and accounts before their lords and stewards in a formal, oral review. The knight's account book of conscience is imagined, then, not as a private, inner 'Book of the Heart' but a publicly shared document, one to which the demons, angels, and even the king are privy. Put another way, the knight's account book – like that of the prioress and Courtenay's steward – is an object of collective interest and, especially for the king, an important shared responsibility.

The ultimately unbalanced condition of the knight's account book in Mannyng's retelling has, therefore, a somewhat different message from the warning provided in Bede's original narrative. First, the knight's final tragic ending in Mannyng's version is caused not by the number of sins in his book but rather by his failure to confess and clear his record of sin earlier: 'ȝyf y shulde haue any grace/y shulde haue asked whan y had space [if I should have any grace, I would have asked for forgiveness when I had time]' (4499–52). Here, the knight's unsettled accounts are a lesson against wasting opportune 'space' to ask for the remission of his sins, rather than simply a warning about the perils of wrongdoing. Yet in a narrative where the king had partial responsibility over the knight's repentance and restitution, the knight's failed confession and unbalanced account book inevitably leave another 'space' of conjecture within the narrative: a reverberating rebuke at the king's ultimately failed responsibilities and, thereby, compromised spiritual accounts. Put another way, this space opens an invitation to all of Mannyng's readers not simply to deal with their own account books of conscience in confession but also to be mindful of the accounts of all those whom they 'takeþ þerof þe frame.' By exploiting contemporary accounting technologies, Mannyng's version of Bede's exemplum also meditates on the inherently interpersonal and communal aspects of the confessional process, teaching this practice as a collaborative endeavor that requires multiple persons to ensure that a sinner's account book of conscience is not in the red.

Examining how advancements in accounting instruments intersected with and bolstered penitential instruction helps us see the productive overlaps between the world of commerce and confession that are frequently obscured when we equate the medieval marketplace to a capitalist prototype. Indeed, this intersection between accounting and penance testifies to the creative ways in which medieval subjects used the technologies and strategies from that expanding marketplace to teach each other the various responsibilities they owe to their fellow humans. The accounting technologies at the heart of this chapter, then, did not, as Rev. Lombardi may have feared, induce mechanical reductions of sincere penitential piety, nor did they replace true spirituality with a profit-driven inferior model. Rather, they actually facilitated a crucial exchange between the medieval church and marketplace that encouraged participants in both spaces to interrogate and expand the responsibilities and possibilities of an actively confessing Christian community.

Notes

1 Laura Goodstein, "App Can't Replace Confession, Vactican Says," *The New York Times*, February 10, 2011, <https://www.nytimes.com/2011/02/10/technology/10vatican.html> accessed November 24, 2020.

2 For discussions on the Vernon Manuscript's dating, composition, and origins, see *Studies in the Vernon Manuscript*, ed. Derek Pearsall (Cambridge: D.S. Brewer, 1990), and *The Making of the Vernon Manuscript*, ed. Wendy Scase (Turnhout: Brepols, 2013).

3 While a number of scholars have written on the Vernon Paternoster Table, the overlap between its design and medieval accounting technology has gone unnoticed. For a recent discussion on the Vernon Table, see Kathyrn Vulic, 'The Vernon Paternoster Diagram, Medieval Graphic Design, and the *Parson's Tale*,' in *Chaucer: Visual Approaches*, eds. Susanna Fein and David Raybin (University Park: Pennsylvania State University Press, 2016), 59–88.

4 For general information on medieval auditing procedures, see Dorothea Oschinsky's introduction to her translation of *Walter of Henley and Other Treatises on Estate Management and Accounting* (Oxford: Oxford Clarendon Press, 1971). For a discussion on reckoning boards see William T. Baxter, 'Early Accounting: The Tally and the Checker-Board,' in *Accounting History: Some British Contributions*, eds. R.H. Parker and B.S. Yamey (Oxford: Clarendon Press, 1994), 197–235.

5 On the use of jetons, see Michael Mitchiner, *Jetons, Medalets, and Tokens* (Hawkins: London, 1998).

6 Ralph P. Robinson, 'The Vernon Manuscript as a "Coucher Book,"' in *Studies on the Vernon Manuscript*, ed. Derek Pearsall (Cambridge: D.S. Brewer, 1990), 15–28.

7 For discussions on medieval estates management in abbeys, see Ulla Sander Olsen, 'Work and Work Ethics in the Nunnery of Syon Abbey in the Fifteenth Century,' in *The Medieval Mystical Tradition in England: Exeter Symposium V*, ed. Marion Glasscoe (Woodbridge: D.S. Brewer, 1992), 134.

8 Thomas Lentes, 'Counting Piety in the Late Middle Ages,' in *Ordering Medieval Society: Perspectives on Intellectual and Practical Modes of Shaping Social Relations*, ed. Bernard Jussen (Cambridge: Cambridge University Press, 1998), 55–91.

9 Jacque Le Goff, *The Birth of Purgatory* (Chicago: Chicago University Press, 1986), 229.

10 Ibid., 62–3.

11 Lentes, 'Counting Piety,' 67. For a more in depth reading of the potential inferiority of counting piety, see Rachel Fulton Brown, 'Praying by Numbers,' *Studies in Medieval and Renaissance History*, 3, no. 4 (1990): 185–250, and Martha Rust, 'The Arma Christi and the Ethics of Reckoning,' in *Medieval and Early Modern Culture*, eds. Lisa Cooper and Andrea Denny-Brown (Abingdon: Ashgate, 2014), 143–69.

12 Recent scholars of medieval economic history have convincingly highlighted the numerous ways in which commercial culture in the late Middle Ages was not actually antithetical to a religious framework but accepted and even thrived within it. See James Davis, *Medieval Market Morality: Law and Ethics in the English Marketplace 1200–1500* (Cambridge: Cambridge University Press, 2012), and Martha Howell, *Commerce Before Capitalism* (Cambridge: Cambridge University Press, 2010).

13 Michel Foucault, *History of Sexuality* (New York: Random House, 1978); *Technologies of the Self* (Amherst: University of Massachusetts Press, 1988). On scholars who have dealt with these questions in medieval literature, see Mary Flowers Braswell, *The Medieval Sinner: Characterisation and Confession in the Literature of the Middle Ages* (Rutherford: Fairleigh Dickinson University Press, 1983); Jerry Root, *Space to Speak: The Confessional Subject in Medieval Literature* (New York: Peter Lang, 1997); Karma Lochrie, *Covert Operations: The Medieval Uses of Secrecy* (Philadelphia: University of Pennsylvania Press, 1999); Katherine Little, *Confession and Resistance: Defining the Self in Late Medieval England* (Notre Dame: University of Notre Dame Press, 2006).

14 For general discussion of medieval European account books see Raymond De Roover, 'The Development of Accounting Prior to Luca Pacioli According to the Account-Books of Medieval Merchants,' in *Studies in the History of Accounting*, ed. Ananias C. Littleton (London: Sweet & Maxwell, 1956), 114–74.
15 For discussion of tallies in medieval England, see William T. Baxter, 'Early Accounting: The Tally and the Checker-Board,' in *Accounting History: Some British Contributions*, eds. Robert H. Parker and Basil S. Yamey (Oxford: Clarendon Press, 1994), 197–235.
16 Francis P. Barnard, *The Casting-Counter and the Counting Board* (Oxford: Clarendon Press, 1916).
17 Rosemary O'Neill, 'Counting Sheep in the C-Text of *Piers Plowman*,' *The Yearbook of Langland Studies*, 29 (2015): 89–116, at 96.
18 Marxist theorists such as Max Weber and Werner Sombart helped to perpetuate the narrative that medieval accounting directly heralded modern capitalist rationality. For Weber and Sombart's influence on accounting historiography see Bruce G. Carruthers and Wendy Nelson Espeland, 'Accounting for Rationality: Double-entry Bookkeeping and the Theory of Economic Rationality,' *American Journal of Sociology*, 97 (1991): 31–69.
19 Jonathon Sabathany, *Officers and Accountability in Medieval England, 1170–1300* (Oxford: Oxford University Press, 2014), 82.
20 James Aho, *Confession and Bookkeeping: The Religious, Moral, and Rhetorical Roots of Modern Accounting* (Albany: State University of New York, 2005), xiii. For more recent discussion on accountancy and justification, see Larita Killian, 'Accounting as Personal Apology,' *Accounting and the Public Interest*, 14 (2014): 34–47.
21 Cited in Aho, *Confession*, 36.
22 On the proliferation of debt and credit in medieval England see *Credit and Debt in Medieval England c. 1180–1350*, eds. Phillipp R. Schofield and Nicholas Mayhew (Oxford: Oxbow Books, 2002). For a general discussion on the role of debt throughout history, see David Graeber, *Debt: The First 5000 years* (New York: Melville House, 2011).
23 For discussion of money and credit in bullion shortage, see Pamela Nightingale, 'Money and Credit in the Economy of Late Medieval England,' in *Medieval Money Matters*, ed. Diana Woods (Oxford: Oxford University Press, 2004), 53.
24 Howell, *Commerce*, 27.
25 An excellent example of the collective responsibility of debt can be found in *Warden's Accounts and Court Minute Books of the Goldsmith's Mistery of London 1334–1446*, ed. Lisa Jefferson (Woodbridge: Boydell Press, 2009), 127. According to an entry made in 1370, debt had become so expansive in this guild that wardens had to 'take distress' of any such debtor, to 'constrain them to settle the payment,' lest more complaints are brought forth.
26 *Middle English Dictionary*, 'dette' n. 1.a. whatever someone owes; 3.a. moral or religious obligation; and 4.a. sin.
27 *Memoriale Credencium: A Late Middle English Manuel of Theology edited from MS Bodley Tanner 201*, ed. J.H.L. Kengen (Nijmegen: Department of English, 1980), 40.
28 Aho, *Confession*, 37.
29 Hilary Jenkinson, 'Medieval Tallies, Public and Private,' *Archaeologia* (1923–4): 289–351.
30 *Calendar of Plea and Memoranda Rolls Preserved among the Archives of the Corporation of the City of London at Guildhall, A.D. 1323–1482*, ed. Arthur H. Thomas, vol. 3 (Cambridge: Cambridge University Press, 1921–62), 89–90. For a discussion of this case in relation to the culture of debt in London, see Bertolet, *Chaucer, Gower, Hoccleve and the Commercial Practices of Late Fourteenth-Century London* (Farnham: Ashgate, 2013), 93–4.
31 For the use of tallies in medieval manorial accounting, see Osckinsky, *Walter of Henley*, 222–4.
32 Paul D. A. Harvey suggests that the presence of tallies introduced a 'phase two' of manorial auditing in fourteenth-century England compared the previous "phase one" accounting which was managed more centrally. See Harvey, *Manorial Records of Cuxham, Oxfordshire, circa 1200–1359* (London: Royal Commission on Historical Manuscripts, 1976), 33–4.
33 Sabathany, *Officers and Accountability*, 72.
34 Ibid., 73.
35 Harvey, *Manorial Records*, 34.
36 Margery James, 'A London Merchant of the Fourteenth Century,' *The Economic History Review*, 8, no. 3 (1956): 364–75, at 369.
37 Ibid., 369.

38 By the early modern period, this practice extended well beyond the mercantile sphere. For example, Craig Muldrew details the case of Adam Eyre, a seventeenth-century yeoman, whose debts were subtracted from the rent that his creditor owed him, writing in his journal that they met 'to cast up our reconings.' See Muldrew, 'Interpreting the Market: The Ethics of Credit and Community Relations in Early Modern England,' *Social History*, 18, no. 2 (1993): 163–83, at 173.

39 Oschinsky, *Walter of Henley*, 220–1. Chaucer's Reeve in the *General Prologue* is a prime example of corruption present in the manorial accounting process. Not only does the Reeve understand all the potential tricks other members of the manor could perform he also abuses his position for personal gain since (I.601–2).

40 Andrew Galloway, 'The Account Book and the Treasure: Gilbert Maghfeld's Textual Economy and the Poetics of Mercantile Accounting in Ricardian Literature,' *Studies in the Age of Chaucer*, 33 (2011): 65–124, at 80.

41 *Visitations of Religious Houses in the Diocese of Lincoln*, ed. A. Hamilton Thompson (Lincoln: Lincoln Record Society, 1929), 131.

42 Ibid., 131.

43 Devon, RO CR 491. Cited in *Household Accounts from Medieval England*, ed. C.M. Woolgar (Oxford: Oxford University Press, 1992–3), 48.

44 Ibid., 48.

45 For a discussion of the serially connected nature of household reputations in late medieval England, especially in relation to mercantile families, see Bertolet, *Chaucer, Gower, Hoccleve*, 81–104. For discussion of household reputation and mercantile credit see Craig Muldrew, *The Economy of Obligation: The Culture of Credit and Social Relations in Early Modern England* (New York: St. Martin's Press, 1998).

46 Scriptural references to the Book of Life which God will open on Judgement Day can be found in Revelation 20: 12–15, and Daniel 7:10.

47 Thomas Wimbledon, *Wimbledon's Sermon: Redde Rationem Villicationis Tue*, ed. Ione Kemp Knight (Pittsburgh: Duquesne University Press, 1967), 123.

48 For more discussions on the book of conscience see Mary Carruthers, *The Book of Memory: A Study of Memory in Medieval Culture* (Cambridge: Cambridge University Press, 2008), and Eric Jager, *Book of the Heart* (Chicago: University of Chicago Press, 2000).

49 While the name 'Final Reckoning' is not as frequently used to describe Christ's Second coming as terms such as 'Judgement Day' or 'Day of Doom,' I choose to use this term because it better captures the sense of divine judgment as a settling of accounts—an image crucial to this entire chapter.

50 Bede, *Historia Ecclesiastica Gentis Anglorum*, ed. Charles Plummer (Oxford: Clarendon Press, 1896), 366–8.

51 Boasting of nine extant volumes, *The Book of Vices and Virtues* is one of most popular penitential manuals in Middle English. For general information on this text and its French source, see W. Nelson Francis, 'Introduction,' in *The Book of Vices and Virtues*, ed. W. Nelson Francis, EETS, o.s. 69 (London: Oxford University Press, 1942), i–lxxxi.

52 There are many other Middle English translations of the *Somme le Roi*. The parallel text to the *Book* is Dan Michel's *Ayenbite of Inwit* (c.1340). Caxton's *Royal Book* (c.1489) is the other, much later, prose translation of the *Somme*. *Speculum Vitae* (c.1350–70) is an extended verse translation of the French text and *The Mirror of Lewd Men and Women* (c.1425) is a prose translation of *Speculum Vitae*. While this passage is found in the *Somme*, neither *Speculum Vitae* nor the *Mirror* contain it. Furthermore, while the French writer does use the language of accounting, he does not specify that the confessor is a 'bailiff,' calling him 'priest' instead.

53 *Middle English Dictionary*, 'receite' 1: 'the amount of money received by a person' (i.e. income); 2 (a): 'the receiving of something,' and 'ledger detailing monies received.'

54 For further discussion on pre-Lateran IV penances, see Thomas Tentler, *Sin and Confession on the Eve of the Reformation* (Princeton: Princeton University Press, 1977), 3–16.

55 The irregularity of confession during this period, especially among laypeople, also stemmed from a pervasive condemnation of iterative penance. The Third Council of Toledo (589), for example, stipulated that confession of sin and reconciliation to the church should only occur once in a lifetime and condemned the custom of granting repeated penances. For general information on this matter, see Bernhard Boschmann, *Penance and the Anointing of the Sick*, ed. and trans. Francis Courtney (New York: Herder and Herder, 1964), 104.

56 For general discussion of the transformation of penance after Lateran IV, see Tentler, *Sin and Confession*, 57.

57 Latin text and English translation of the *Omnis utriusque sexus* can be found in the *Decrees of Ecumenical Councils*, ed. Norman Tanner (London: Sheed & Ward, 1990), 245.

58 *Preaching in the Age of Chaucer: Selected Sermons in Translation*, ed. Siegfried Wenzel (Washington: Catholic University of America Press, 2008), 91.

59 An example of priests requiring this written confession for literate congregants can be found in the early fourteenth-century *Manipulus curatorum* written by Guido de Monte Rocherii. This text is cited in Tentler, *Sin and Confession*, 89.

60 'Men shul not oonly to acountes go / for hemselfe bot als for mo that is tos say of uche neyghebore / that fel to hem to doon socoure [People shall not only make an accounting for themselves, but also for others, that is, for every neighbor to whom they should have given aid]' (5.1764–7), in *Prick of Conscience*, ed. James Morey (Kalamazoo: Medieval Institute Publications, 2012).

61 All references are taken from *Robert of Brunne's 'Handlyng Synne'*, ed. Frederick J. Furnivall. EETS. o.s. 119, 123 (London: Kegan Paul, Trench, Trübner, 1901).

62 My account of this retellings of Bede's exemplum bears some resemblance to Rosemary O'Neill's discussion of accounting imagery in sermon exempla tradition within her unpublished PhD thesis 'Accounting for Salvation in Middle English Literature,' PhD Diss (University of Pennsylvania, 2009). O'Neill and I agree on how later retellings of the Bede exemplum incorporate contemporary accounting procedures to emphasize that the penitent could have changed the contents of his own book of conscience and to, thereby, alter the outcome at God's final audit (see O'Neill, Diss, 40). What O'Neill does not address in her account of these later exempla retellings is their emphasis on king's responsibility over the accounts of the knight, a crucial departure from Bede's exemplum that has previously gone unnoticed by other scholars.

63 The image is a tracing of the original sketch found in the *Red Book of the Irish Exchequer* by James Frederick Ferguson. See Frederick in 'A Calendar of the Contents of the Red Book of the Irish Exchequer,' *Proceedings and Transactions of the Kilkenny and South-East of Ireland Archaeological Society, 3*, no. 1 (1854): 34–52, at 46–7. The image, while depicting a scene in Dublin, closely resembles the English Exchequer. The accounting and auditing processes of the English Exchequer filtered into manorial and household accounting processes by the early fourteenth century. For the connections between English Exchequer accounting and manorial accounting, see Oschinsky, *Walter of Henley*, 213–15.

Bibliography

Manuscript

Oxford, Bodleian Library MS Eng. poet. a. 1.

Primary Sources

Bede, Historia Ecclesiastica Gentis Anglorum, ed. Charles Plummer. Oxford: Clarendon Press, 1896.

Calendar of Plea and Memoranda Rolls Preserved among the Archives of the Corporation of the City of London at Guildhall, A.D. 1323–1482, ed. A.H. Thomas. vol 3. Cambridge: Cambridge University Press, 1921–62.

Decrees of Ecumenical Councils, ed. Norman Tanner. London: Sheed & Ward, 1990.

Ferguson, James Frederick. 'A Calendar of the Contents of the Red Book of the Irish Exchequer.' *Proceedings and Transactions of the Kilkenny and South-East of Ireland Archaeological Society* 3 1 (1854): 34–52.

Household Accounts from Medieval England, ed. C.M. Woolgar. Oxford: Oxford University Press, 1992–3.

Mannyng, Robert. Robert of Brunne's 'Handlyng Synne', ed. Frederick J. Furnivall. EETS. o.s. 119, 123. London: Kegan Paul, Trench, Trübner, 1901.

Memoriale Credencium: A Late Middle English Manuel of Theology edited from MS Bodley Tanner 201, ed. J.H.L. Kengen. Nijmegen: Department of English, 1980.

Prick of Conscience, ed. James Morey. Kalamazoo: Medieval Institute Publications, 2012.
The Book of Vices and Virtues, ed. W. Nelson Francis, EETS, o.s. 69. London: Oxford University Press, 1942.
Visitations of Religious Houses in the Diocese of Lincoln, ed. A. Hamilton Thompson. Lincoln: Lincoln Record Society, 1929.
Walter of Henley. *Walter of Henley and Other Treatises on Estate Management and Accounting*, ed. Dorothea Oschinsky. Oxford: Oxford Clarendon Press, 1971.
Warden's Accounts and Court Minute Books of the Goldsmith's Mistery of London 1334–1446, ed. Lisa Jefferson. Woodbridge: Boydell Press, 2009.
Wenzel, Siegfried, ed. *Preaching in the Age of Chaucer: Selected Sermons in Translation*. Washington: Catholic University of America Press, 2008.
Wimbledon, Thomas. *Wimbledon's Sermon: Redde Rationem Villicationis Tue*, ed. Ione Kemp Knight. Pittsburgh: Duquesne University Press, 1967.

Secondary Sources

Aho, James. *Confession and Bookkeeping: The Religious, Moral, and Rhetorical Roots of Modern Accounting*. Albany: State University of New York, 2005.
Barnard, Francis Pierrepont. *The Casting-Counter and the Counting Board*. Oxford: Clarendon Press, 1916.
Baxter, William T. 'Early Accounting: The Tally and the Checker-Board.' In *Accounting History: Some British Contributions*, eds. Robert H. Parker and Basil S. Yamey. Oxford: Clarendon Press, 1994. Pp. 197–235.
Bertolet, Craig E. *Chaucer, Gower, Hoccleve and the Commercial Practices of Late Fourteenth-Century London*. Farnham: Ashgate, 2013.
Boschmann, Bernhard. *Penance and the Anointing of the Sick*, ed. and trans. Francis Courtney. New York: Herder and Herder, 1964.
Braswell, Mary Flowers. *The Medieval Sinner: Characterisation and Confession in the Literature of the Middle Ages*. Rutherford: Fairleigh Dickinson University Press, 1983.
Brown, Rachel Fulton. 'Praying by Numbers.' *Studies in Medieval and Renaissance History* 3, no. 4 (1990): 185–250.
Carruthers, Bruce G., and Wendy Nelson Espeland. 'Accounting for Rationality: Double-entry Bookkeeping and the Theory of Economic Rationality.' *American Journal of Sociology* 97 (1991): 31–69.
Carruthers, Mary. *The Book of Memory: A Study of Memory in Medieval Culture*. Cambridge: Cambridge University Press, 2008.
Davis, James. *Medieval Market Morality: Law and Ethics in the English Marketplace 1200–1500*. Cambridge: Cambridge University Press, 2012.
De Roover, Raymond. 'The Development of Accounting Prior to Luca Pacioli According to the Account-Books of Medieval Merchants.' In *Studies in the History of Accounting*, ed. A. Charles Littleton. London: Sweet & Maxwell, 1956. Pp. 114–74.
Foucault, Michel. *History of Sexuality*. Vol. 1. An Introduction. New York: Random House, 1978.
———. *Technologies of the Self*. Amherst: University of Massachusetts Press, 1988.
Galloway, Andrew. 'The Account Book and the Treasure: Gilbert Maghfeld's Textual Economy and the Poetics of Mercantile Accounting in Ricardian Literature.' *Studies in the Age of Chaucer* 33 (2011): 65–124.
Goodstein, Laura. 'App Can't Replace Confession, Vactican Says.' *The New York Times*, February 10, 2011.
Graeber, David. *Debt: The First 5000 Years*. New York: Melville House, 2011.
Harvey, Paul D. A. *Manorial Records of Cuxham, Oxfordshire, circa 1200–1359*. London: Royal Commission on Historical Manuscripts, 1976.

Howell, Martha. *Commerce Before Capitalism*. Cambridge: Cambridge University Press, 2010.

Jager, Eric. *Book of the Heart*. Chicago: University of Chicago Press, 2000.

James, Margery. 'A London Merchant of the Fourteenth Century.' *The Economic History Review* 8, no. 3 (1956): 364–75.

Jenkinson, Hilary. 'Medieval Tallies, Public and Private.' *Archaeologia* (1923–4): 289–351.

Killian, Larita. 'Accounting as Personal Apology.' *Accounting and the Public Interest* 14 (2014): 34–47.

Le Goff, Jacque. *The Birth of Purgatory*. Chicago: Chicago University Press, 1986.

Lentes, Thomas. 'Counting Piety in the Late Middle Ages.' In *Ordering Medieval Society: Perspectives on Intellectual and Practical Modes of Shaping Social Relations*, ed. Bernard Jussen. Cambridge: Cambridge University Press, 1998. Pp. 55–91.

Little, Katherine. *Confession and Resistance: Defining the Self in Late Medieval England*. Notre Dame: University of Notre Dame Press, 2006.

Lochrie, Karma. *Covert Operations: The Medieval Uses of Secrecy*. Philadelphia: University of Pennsylvania Press, 1999.

Mitchiner, Michael. *Jetons, Medalets, and Tokens*. Hawkins: London, 1998.

Muldrew, Craig. 'Interpreting the Market: The Ethics of Credit and Community Relations in Early Modern England.' *Social History* 18, no. 2 (1993): 163–83.

———. *The Economy of Obligation: The Culture of Credit and Social Relations in Early Modern England*. New York: St. Martin's Press, 1998.

Nightingale, Pamela. 'Money and Credit in the Economy of Late Medieval England.' In *Medieval Money Matters*, ed. Diana Woods. Oxford: Oxford University Press, 2004.

Olsen, Ulla Sander. 'Work and Work Ethics in the Nunnery of Syon Abbey in the Fifteenth Century.' In *The Medieval Mystical Tradition in England: Exeter Symposium V*, ed. Marion Glasscoe. Woodbridge: D.S. Brewer, 1992.

O'Neill, Rosemary. 'Accounting for Salvation in Middle English Literature.' PhD diss., University of Pennsylvania, 2009.

———. 'Counting Sheep in the C-Text of Piers Plowman.' *The Yearbook of Langland Studies* 29 (2015): 89–116.

Pearsall, Derek, ed. *Studies in the Vernon Manuscript*. Cambridge: D.S. Brewer, 1990.

Robinson, Ralph P. 'The Vernon Manuscript as a "Coucher Book."' In *Studies on the Vernon Manuscript*, ed. Derek Pearsall. Cambridge: D.S. Brewer, 1990. pp. 15–28.

Root, Jerry. *Space to Speak: The Confessional Subject in Medieval Literature*. New York: Peter Lang, 1997.

Rust, Martha. 'The Arma Christi and the Ethics of Reckoning.' In *Medieval and Early Modern Culture*, eds. Lisa Cooper and Andrea Denny-Brown. Abingdon: Ashgate, 2014. Pp. 143–69.

Sabathany, Jonathon. *Officers and Accountability in Medieval England, 1170–1300*. Oxford: Oxford University Press, 2014.

Scase, Wendy, ed. *The Making of the Vernon Manuscript*. Turnhout: Brepols, 2013.

Schofield, Phillipp R., and Nicholas Mayhew, eds. *Credit and Debt in Medieval England c. 1180–1350*. Oxford: Oxbow Books, 2002.

Tentler, Thomas. *Sin and Confession on the Eve of the Reformation*. Princeton: Princeton University Press, 1977.

Vulic, Kathyrn. 'The Vernon Paternoster Diagram, Medieval Graphic design, and the Parson's Tale.' In *Chaucer: Visual Approaches*, eds. Susanna Fein and David Raybin. University Park: Pennsylvania State University Press, 2016. Pp. 59–88.

2

AS NIMBLE AS THE PEN OF A SCRIBE

The Mediating Tongue in Aquinas's *Commentary on the Psalms*

Albert Marie Surmanski

Since the *Book of Psalms* is a collection of songs, it is not surprising that the tongue features prominently in it. These poems are not only songs to be sung, but they are songs that exhort the singer to sing, and songs that reflect on the action of singing.[1] The treatment of the tongue in the *Book of Psalms* is diverse and symbolic. The tongue is a weapon used to revile enemies, flattering and deceitful, a means of sin, and an almost untamable source of temptation. Yet, it is also the instrument for the encouragement of others and the praise of God. The tongue as the seat of the sense of taste becomes a metaphorical image for experience of the divine goodness. Tied to the intelligence and sociability of human language, the flexibility of the human tongue expresses the contradictions and possibilities of the human condition.

In his *Commentary on the Psalms,* Thomas Aquinas takes up the biblical portrait of the tongue and examines it in the scholastic language of the 1200s. His analysis is shaped by his own vocation as a preacher and teacher, someone deeply concerned with communication. Although the tongue itself is a part of the human body and not a distinct object as many media are, Aquinas consistently discusses the tongue as mediating meaning between heart and body, between one person and another, and even between God and humanity. In his discussion, Aquinas reveals several elements of his own anthropology, especially his own virtue ethics with its emphasis on the habituation of interior responses through repeated action. Aquinas's explication of Psalm tongue imagery also illumines his understanding of the human person as oriented toward communion with others, God's influence on humanity as the first cause, and elements of his Christology. This investigation will first briefly consider the background and sources of Aquinas's *Commentary on the Psalms.* Then it will examine the tongue as a mediator of meaning, focusing on several aspects of Aquinas's analysis, especially his concern for the moral qualities of speech. It will conclude with a consideration of Aquinas's understanding of the mediation of divine revelation through the Scriptures, and his rare use of the tongue as an image of Christ himself.

DOI: 10.4324/9781003295082-4

Background

A short overview of the characteristics of Aquinas's *Commentary on the Psalms* illustrates its scope and importance. Aquinas composed his *Commentary on the Psalms* at the end of his life, between 1272 and 1273 CE. He stopped actively producing academic work in 1273, the year before his death. This means that his *Commentary on the Psalms* is one of his latest works. He broke off this text about the same time that he interrupted the third part of his masterwork, the *Summa Theologiae*.[2] This means that the *Commentary on the Psalms* reflects the same mature theology found in Aquinas's *Summa*.

Although from the same period of his life as his *Summa*, Aquinas's *Commentary on the Psalms* lacks the craftsmanship of the other work.[3] The *Commentary on the Psalms* was a series of lectures given to the Dominican school at Naples. It has come down to us as a *reportatio*, that is, notes taken down by a student, in this case an uncorrected student transcription.[4] As a result, the text is unpolished and rough in places. The *Commentary on the Psalms* is limited in scope as well as style; it does not cover the entire Biblical books of 150 Psalms, ending at Psalm 54. This means that themes are only traced through the first third of the *Book of Psalms*. In terms of structure, Aquinas suggests that the work can be broken into thematic groups of ten Psalms. The major structural form of the *Commentary on the Psalms*, however, is given by the individual Psalms. Within each Psalm, Aquinas first gives a *divisio*, describing the overall structure of each Psalm, and then continues with a verse-by-verse explanation of the text.

The Biblical *Book of Psalms* is an ancient collection of hymns, written in Hebrew (although a few Psalms may have had pre-Biblical Egyptian or Canaanite versions) and cherished by both Jewish and Christian traditions. Some Psalms are understood to date from as early as 1000 BCE, while others may be from hundreds of years later. Exegetes suggest that several earlier compilations or songbooks were compiled into the current form of the book several hundred years before Christ.[5] The ancient origins of this book mean that its imagery may be only imperfectly understood by those who encountered it centuries later; its revered origins mean that many authors have nevertheless attempted such interpretation.

According to Marcia Colish, Psalms was the "most beloved" Biblical book of both patristic and medieval exegetes.[6] In commenting on it, Aquinas takes his place within a long tradition of Psalm commentary. He wrote within the "analytic, detached, critical...doctrinal and systematic" style of scholastic commentary that emerged in the twelfth century to provide texts appropriate for the cathedral schools and university debates.[7] Aquinas draws heavily upon Peter Lombard, one of the most important twelfth-century commentators. Aquinas also cites the *Glossa Ordinaria* and several earlier writers on the Psalms: Origen (200s CE), Augustine (400s), and Cassiodorus (500s). Although he does not cite him, Aquinas shows influence from the Psalm commentary of the Dominican Hugh of St. Cher who wrote just before Aquinas.[8] In addition, Aquinas draws on the ideas and spiritual insights of a host of works (not necessarily Psalm commentaries) from other authors, including, but not limited to Aristotle (300s BCE), Jerome (400s CE), John Chrysostom (400s), Pseudo-Dionysius (500s), Boethius (500s), Gregory the Great (500s), and Anselm (1100s). Although the medieval Jewish community did curate a version of Scripture that is now known as the Masoretic Text, Aquinas would have worked exclusively from Latin and (occasionally) Greek texts.[9] He had a limited contact with Hebrew words and interpretations through the work of Jerome.

One important methodological tool that Aquinas received from the tradition is the division of Biblical interpretation into four main senses, which are the literal/historical sense and the three spiritual senses, which are the allegorical, moral, and anagogical. This four-fold division structures Aquinas's commentary on each Psalm and therefore is necessary for understanding his exegesis of texts involving the tongue. In his exegesis, he follows a pattern in which he begins with the literal sense of each passage and then moves into whichever spiritual senses he finds applicable.

The four-fold division is ancient, having roots at least as far back as the writings of Origen.[10] According to this understanding, God shaped both the text and events recorded in the Bible so as to have several layers of meaning. The literal or historical sense is the basic meaning of the text. Some other medieval authors, such as Albert the Great Aquinas's teacher, identified the literal sense of the text with the intention of the human author in distinction from the spiritual senses that are present in the text through the intention of the Holy Spirit.[11] Aquinas prefers to describe the literal sense in more ontological terms as the words, events, and ideas to which the Biblical text refers. This sense includes the interpretation of the meaning of any literary devices or figures of speech. For example, a text that declares, "God is a rock" would have the literal/historical meaning of a metaphorical statement about God's strength and stability, not a claim that God is a large chunk of granite.[12] Since Aquinas writes as a believing Christian who understands the scriptures to be the inspired Word of God, the literal meaning of a Psalm may be as varied as King David writing about his sorrow after his betrayal by his son to a direct prophecy about Christ.[13]

According to Aquinas's Aristotelian epistemology, just as spiritual and intellectual understanding are founded upon the human sense knowledge of sight, touch, tastes, etc., so the three spiritual senses are, in turn, founded upon the literal sense.[14] For Aquinas, in the spiritual senses of Scripture, the words and events described by the literal sense take on a deeper meaning so as to point to other realities.[15] In the allegorical sense, they foreshadow Christ and the Church. In the moral, they give examples of how or how not to act. In the anagogical they point to eternal life. Working within the tradition of this four-fold exegesis, Aquinas often finds spiritual readings in the text of the Psalms – particularly moral meanings. His first concern, however, is the literal/historical meaning upon which he believes the others to be based.[16] It is important to be aware that the spiritual senses are secondary levels which build upon but do not displace the literal meaning. Thus, when Aquinas says that the tongue is Christ, he is not claiming that the text directly teaches about Christ; it (literally) teaches about the Psalmist singing, and in turn, that singing (allegorically) represents something about Christ as Mediator. Thus, in surveying Aquinas's understanding of the tongue in the Psalms, one often moves from a literal reading, to a moral, to an allegorical.

The Sword and Arrow: Tongue as Mediating Harm

A first tongue-related theme in Aquinas's *Commentary on the Psalms* is the tongue as a weapon. Aquinas uses this theme to transform many texts which do not make mention of human speech into metaphors for the linguistic attack. In the Vulgate text of the Psalms, 17 of the first 54 Psalms include the word *lingua*, which literally means tongue or language.[17] Aquinas considers the tongue in each of these Psalms but also introduces a discussion of the tongue in his Prologue and in his commentary on an additional 12 Psalms.[18] This means that he discusses some aspect of the tongue in around 55% of the Psalms covered in his commentary. While instances in which Aquinas mentions the tongue are divided approximately evenly between those which are positive and those which are negative, the metaphor of weapons is one of the ways in which he transforms several of the Psalms which do not mention the tongue into places to teach about this provocative bodily member.

When Aquinas speaks about the dangers of the tongue, he cites two particular texts to aid his interpretation. These are Psalm 56 (57):5 which reads, "Their tongue was a sharp sword," (Douay-Rheims), and Jeremiah 9:8, which reads, "Their tongue is a piercing arrow, it has spoken deceit."[19] Both of these quotes are from sections of the Bible outside the scope of Aquinas's own commentary, but Aquinas introduces them to clarify other texts. These two texts, with their metaphorical characterizations of the tongue as different types of weapons, express the ability of human speech to harm through straightforward or deceitful means. The tongue as a sword is the direct attack of someone who either plots or insults or defames openly.[20] As a piercing arrow, the tongue is used to hurt subtly, or from a distance, to flatter, hide plots, detract, deceive, or defraud.[21]

Aquinas appears to have found this paired set of texts in his Dominican brother Hugh of St. Cher. Hugh uses them to explain tongue imagery in his *Psalterium cum Postilla* but not as frequently as Aquinas.[22] Neither Augustine nor Peter Lombard (two of Aquinas's favorite sources) employs them to interpret the first 54 Psalms.[23] In commenting on Psalm 36, Lombard does connect open violence to the sword and hidden violence to the arrow, but he does not take the further step to use Aquinas's texts to make the connection to open and hidden *verbal* violence.[24]

Aquinas employs these chosen texts in two ways. First, as discussed, he uses them to transform Psalms about battle into texts about speech. In doing so, he begins with a secondary literal sense which reads the weapons as metaphors and then offers a connected moral sense. Aquinas certainly knows that, in the primary literal sense, the Psalms are about real battle, with perhaps, attached moral lessons about warfare. As objects of warfare, mediators of bodily harm, the sword and arrow would not play significant parts in the lives of Aquinas's Dominican students. These young preachers were being trained to wield language, not weapons. By interpreting the sword and arrow as violent speech, Aquinas widens the applicability of the texts. He uses the more exciting images – the sword and the arrow – to reveal danger hidden in the apparently tamer object – the tongue. Aquinas dramatizes the power of the human tongue. By paralleling it to the objects of sword and arrow, he cast the tongue itself as an object – not merely a body part, but a weapon his students must learn to wield.

The second way Aquinas uses these texts is to classify the types of harm the tongue inflicts. The texts refer to public or stealthy defamation and opposition – two different types of verbal attacks. Here, Aquinas the teacher supplies pastoral tools to help others to grow in virtue and avoid sin. The concern about growth fits well with Aquinas's virtue ethics. In Aquinas's anthropology, the human person has both a physical body and a spiritual soul, which is both the animating "form" of the body and also the intellectual immortal mind.[25] Aquinas follows Aristotle in insisting on the importance of sensation as the beginning of knowledge.[26] The human person perceives things with the physical senses, which send impressions to be coordinated by the "common sense" – a function of the brain.[27] Sense images provide the material for intellectual understanding. In this process, the intellect "illuminates" sense images to grasp the identity of things and to judge and reason about causes and meaning. The emotions are physically based responses which parallel this process by responding to sense impressions and imagination and ultimately engage the reasoning intellect and will.[28]

While the movement of knowledge runs from sense to mind, the ordering of virtue proceeds in the opposite direction. The practice of virtue (strengths often formed by repeated actions) habituates different faculties of the human person (practical reason, will, and emotions) to respond according to reason enlightened by faith.[29] These virtues integrate the person's various powers, enabling self-mastery, as well as harmonious societal relationships.[30] In Christian life, faith and love enlighten and "form" the moral virtues so that they are exercised not only in a way that allows the person to achieve natural human goods such as health, and good family relationships, but also to do this out of love of God and influenced by revelation and religious duty.[31] Since reason plays an important role in virtue, the understanding of both motivation and of which actions to choose to form one's responses is a valuable tool for moral growth.

Aquinas's exegesis of the sword as tongue reveals his interest in habituation toward virtue. He advises his students,

> The sword is used to speak of striking verbally...This sword is in its sheath as long as it is in the heart, but then sometimes it is brought out and so it is drawn. Therefore, first we should take care not to have this sword. If it is there, then, second, we should not draw it. If it remains long in the sheath, first it will rust, then it will be consumed and hatred and the will to injure will cool.[32]

Aquinas describes a chosen pattern of action intended to form patterns of emotional response. He advises the student to keep the sword of angry words sheathed, so that the anger can gradually weaken, just as a sheathed sword will eventually rust. In this way, he gives counsel for developing the virtue of meekness, which moderates and orders anger as part of the cardinal virtue of temperance.[33] The tongue is presented as an object over which the human person exercises agency, choosing to be silent rather than vent his anger. In doing so, the restrained tongue mediates his choice to his emotions. Keeping the tongue "in its sheath" communicates the willed choice of the person to his emotional interior.

Aquinas continues to show attentiveness to the complexities of the human condition and stages of growth in moral behavior when he analyzes the level of culpability in various sins of the tongue. Aquinas says, "Sometimes someone hurts another [verbally] ... unexpectedly through his weakness, and this is clear when he is immediately sorry. But when he hurts another out of malice then he rejoices in what he has done."[34] In another place Aquinas notes, "If someone says something inordinate from a slip of the tongue, it is borne easily."[35] Here, Aquinas draws on the philosophy of Aristotle who distinguishes between the virtuous man (who chooses and executes the good), the vicious man (who chooses and executes what is evil), and the man considered to be merely morally "incontinent" that is, of goodwill but weak moral control (he tries to choose what is good, but fails at moments, due to passion).[36]

Aquinas is teaching his students how to understand the mediation of the tongue. Not all offensive words come from the same root. Therefore, not all should wound to the same degree. When offended, the one who has received sharp words needs to continue to observe the offender. The offensive words themselves do not carry the full communication. If the offender has spoken out of thoughtlessness or sudden anger, his tongue (by an apology) or his face (by sorrow or sheepishness) will reveal that he does bear deep-seated ill-will toward the offended person. Conversely, if the offender gloats or seems pleased with the hurt he has caused by his words, his malice is revealed to be deeply entrenched and thus more dangerous. The tongue and face continue to mediate meaning after the initial vocalization, revealing to the bystander the depth and source of offensive words.

This observation by Aquinas has (unsurprising) implications for the current-day use of social media. In the conversation that Aquinas describes the tongue and the face are the media through which communication occurs, even after the initial speech. Aquinas does not specify exactly what makes the person who speaks out of thoughtlessness recant. It might be his own tongue – actually hearing his own vehemence spoken aloud makes him realize that he has crossed a boundary that should not have been crossed. It might be that seeing the face of the hearer prompts the speaker's sheepish or apologetic reaction. Then, further words, or perhaps the very facial expression of the speaker, communicate his sorrow for his inordinate speech. In the encounter, it is the close contact between the two persons which opens the way to reconciliation. These subtle cues are not all present in a current-day encounter using a telephone. Fewer of them are present in texting or many other forms of social media. An exception, to an extent, might be video messaging. Aquinas's teaching reminds us that the "flattened" communication in which the face and voice of the speaker are not presented to an attentive hearer may exacerbate conflicts which could be more easily smoothed over in the direct presence of the other.

Aquinas's observations about the different levels of harm and different motivations for harm are also meant to be advice to his students about their own speech. Recognizing the sources of harsh words can serve as a first step to correcting the vices which cause them. Am I weak, easily overcome by anger or annoyance? Or am I motivated by some deeper malicious jealousy? Once the student has identified from where his words are coming, he is equipped to study their deeper roots. Recognizing the root of verbal offense – weakness, as opposed to festering malice or envy – would make it easier to plan how to mitigate their sinful tendencies.

It may be also that Aquinas does not want his students to be burdened by unreasonable guilt when they hear a denunciation of evil words. Scripture has strong things to say about the destructive potential of the tongue. A quick outburst from lack of self-control may be wrong, but it would be a different sort of wrong than planned, malicious harm. This weighing would have been important for either penitents or confessors in the sacrament of confession, where people disclose their sins in order to reject them and change their lives with the help of God. Aquinas draws on Scripture to support the recognition that entirely innocent speech is very difficult. He quotes the Epistle of James, "If any man offend not in word, the same is a perfect man."[37] Inordinate speech is so easy that avoiding it is a mark of perfection that he does not seem to expect his students to have yet fully attained. This is comforting and human.

The Tongue as a Mediator to Self and Others

When Aquinas recognizes that to avoid all verbal sin shows a high level of virtue, he acknowledges the tongue as a mediator of the heart. In discussing the movement from interior to exterior, he gives a classic progression of action, saying that evil is, "first in the heart…second in the mouth…third in works."[38] Because of the unity of mind and body, what is thought in the mind is almost always expressed by the tongue. Aquinas says, "The tongue is the organ in which the interior thoughts of the heart are immediately expressed. So whatever is in the heart is quickly expressed by the tongue and one should diligently guard it."[39] Following the Psalmist, Aquinas advises that one guard his tongue. He adds that, "a man should place a guard over his heart," the seat of emotion and desire.[40] The heart and tongue are two links in the chain of communication, so powerful and difficult to regulate.

The tongue first mediates the person to herself. If what is in the mouth was first in the heart, then the tongue can reveal to a person her inner attitudes and thoughts, crystallizing them toward action. When the Psalmist says, "my tongue shall meditate upon your justice," Aquinas notes that the tongue can be said to meditate because the tongue can refer to the interior speech by which we clarify our thoughts to ourselves, or because we speak outwardly from the "prior meditation" of the heart.[41] What someone vocalizes reveals her interior, first of all to herself. Words that roll off the tongue may reveal hidden frustration, anger, or jealousy. Or the tongue may reveal by joy which amplifies itself through speech. In commenting on Psalm 15 (16) Aquinas says that, "joy rushes forth exteriorly into vocal praise."[42] The praise deepens and affirms the intentions of the heart, bringing interior thoughts and feelings to a new birth of a deeper reality.

In this movement of mediation, the tongue also mediates to others. The overflow from heart to word is a movement that serves to connect one person to those around her. Aquinas agrees with Aristotle that the human person is naturally social – able to achieve happiness (and survival) only through association with others.[43] Therefore, this mediation to others is an essential part of being human. Aquinas's examination of the mediation of harmful intentions was considered above. There are also many places where Aquinas discusses the tongue as mediating positive news or emotions. One such instance is found where Aquinas gives an allegorical interpretation of Psalm 18. Here, the "heavens" which "declare the glory of God" to all "tongues and languages" become the Apostles, preaching the truth of Christ to the whole world.[44] Aquinas interprets "tongue" to mean either dialect or style of speech, referring more directly to the product rather than the organ of production. He notes that the Apostles varied their style of speech to suit hearers, casting them as effective teachers.[45]

In other cases, Aquinas understands the tongue to communicate an emotional state rather than news. He says that the tongue will, "meditate your [God's] justice" because the one who ponders the goodness of God will speak outwardly from the "prior meditation" of the heart, continuing on to "bless the Lord" for others to also hear and be moved to praise.[46] Such an outburst might include information, such as a recounting of God's mighty works, or it might simply consist in joyful cries. In commenting on Psalm 5 (6), he says that, "a man cannot rejoice well about anything alone, but when he has friends, they participate in his good, and so he says, 'But let all be glad who hope in you. They shall rejoice forever.'"[47] Spoken words of rejoicing increase joy and unite friends more closely together.

Words spoken by the tongue also mediate between the person and God. In Psalm 50, the Psalmist promises, "Deliver me from blood, O God, God of my salvation and my tongue will extol your justice."[48] In this text, the singer uses his tongue to beg help from God, showing trust by speaking these words in time of trial. Aquinas interprets this verse as expressing the Psalmist's trust that God alone can save him, thereby confessing faith in God's unity, power, and goodness, while also praying to God for aid.[49] Surely God knows the heart, but speaking binds the speaker and God closer together. In his *Summa,* Aquinas teaches that God, as the first cause, often chooses to work through secondary causes.[50] Although God knows what people need before they pray, he chooses to use their prayers as channels through which to grant his gifts, both spiritual and physical.[51] In this case, the Psalmist's tongue can be seen as forming the mediatorial words through which God will grant the needed help.

The Psalmist promises the Lord that he will praise him when he is rescued. Aquinas holds that God does not need human praise for his own satisfaction, but chooses to share his goodness and joy with humanity.[52] When people praise God in prayer, their prayer serves to excite and deepen devotion, enabling them to rejoice in the goodness of God as well as to proclaim God to others.[53] It seems that the singer tastes God's goodness through his joy in speaking the praise of God.

Tongue as Mediating Taste

In Psalm 33 (34), Aquinas delves into the sweet effect of prayer when he comments on the verse, "Taste and see that the Lord is sweet."[54] The singer first exhorts the listener to "magnify the Lord with me" and then describes tasting the sweetness of the Lord.[55] The Psalmist explores the tongue as a sense organ, rather than an instrument of speech, although the two overlap. It is almost as though the communicative power of the tongue reverses so that the words themselves become sweet morsels to be savored. Instead of sending information outward, the tongue brings the experience of God's goodness inwards. The praise of God opens the one who prays to the experience of the goodness of God.

In analyzing this verse, Aquinas notes that taste refers to the "experience of the divine goodness" as something present within the soul of the one praying.[56] This presence takes place through "security of affection," a mystical experience in which the presence of the Lord draws and delights the heart through love.[57] In this way, the presence of God is known through his effect on the will and perhaps on the emotions as well.[58] Aquinas describes this as taste because physical taste involves contact just as this mystical awareness of God involves a certain contact with God through love.[59] The communicative level which Aquinas recognizes in taste was accepted by the natural philosophy of his own day. While medieval people, following Aristotle, considered a sight to be the leading sense for understanding, taste and smell held a particular prominence within the science of medicine. Within this science, they were recognized as crucial for discerning the natures of various remedies.[60] Anyone who has ever taken an exploratory sip of sour milk or hot chocolate knows that taste can give information as either a warning or an invitation. So, just as taste receives knowledge about the desirable nature of the tasted through contact, Aquinas teaches that the contact of the joyful heart with the divine goodness yields intellectual certainty, serving as a sort of confirming revelation of God.

Tongue as Mediating the Divine

Not only used by the human person to pray to God or praise him, but the tongue is also used by God as a medium of divine inspiration. Aquinas does not give a full theory of Biblical inspiration in his *Commentary on the Psalms*, but his discussion of the tongue outlines the human and divine elements he understands to belong to the inspiration of Scripture. Both of these can be seen in his exegesis of Psalm 44 (45):2. The Psalmist says, "My heart has uttered a good word; I speak my works to the king; my tongue is the pen of a scribe who writes swiftly."[61] Aquinas interprets the good word of the heart as the human element of the Psalm because,

> Utterance flows from overabundance or completeness; so this signifies that he speaks out of an abundance of devotion and wisdom ... the writing of the Psalm is attributed to the heart, out of whose great devotion it was composed... he pronounces the praises of Christ from the heart.[62]

Aquinas recognizes both wisdom and devotion in the heart of the speaker. The wisdom is about Christ, who had not yet come into the world when the Psalms were written, so it involves a revelation from God, but it rests in the mind of the speaker, moving him to experience the joy which sings in the words of this Psalm. It is significant that Aquinas recognizes that the Psalms express real human experience. God gives understanding and experience to the Psalmist which blend with and illuminates his natural understanding and experience. This is not a description of a sort of verbal inspiration in which God would dictate words to the human author or directly move the writer's tongue or pen.[63]

Yet, Aquinas does hold firmly that the Psalm is divinely inspired. In his Prologue to his *Commentary,* Aquinas says, "my tongue is like the pen of a scribe" to emphasize that the speech of the Lord (i.e. the Holy Spirit) is *the* source of the book of the Psalms.[64] Within Psalm 44 (45), he interprets the "tongue" in this line as signifying the author himself who is moved by the scribe, the Holy Spirit. Then Aquinas shifts his reading mode, placing these words in the mouth of the Psalmist: "It should not be understood that I made this by myself, but by the help of the Holy Spirit, who used my tongue as a scribe uses a pen." The tongue is no longer the Psalmist as a person, having been reduced to only his divinely connected tongue. Aquinas comments, "And so the principle author of this Psalm is the Holy Spirit."[65] This might at first seem to contradict the claim that God inspires by giving wisdom and devotion to the author rather than by moving his tongue directly. To grasp Aquinas's understanding, both elements must be held together. The human author knows and experiences divine meaning within himself, but is also guided by the Holy Spirit in the very act of his external expression. God works as a first cause through the genuinely real causality of the human author. Aquinas's exegesis gives a picture of the Holy Spirit putting wisdom into the heart of the Psalmist, who grasps it and feels its impact on his life, literally and spiritually formulating words and ideas. Then he writes, expressing himself, while guided by the Spirit of God so as to write what is pleasing to God. In giving this interpretation, Aquinas understands himself to be giving a literal interpretation of the processes of the inspired song described in the Psalm.

Having established the literal sense, Aquinas then offers a moral reading. In this interpretation, he reads the tongue and the pen as saying something about the applicability of the Scriptures. Aquinas says that the fact that the Psalm was first uttered by the tongue teaches that it is useful for those who lived at the time it was first sung. That it was written down expresses it is also useful for those who will come in the future.[66] This seems to correspond to the proverb "*verba fugit, littera manet*" (words are fleeting; text remains). Aquinas recognizes an immediacy in the mediation of the tongue. Before the ability to capture sound recordings, the tongue carried the sound from person to person only. Therefore, the tongue indicates a certain human presence and contemporariness, in contrast to the pen, which records for the future.

Beyond strict Biblical inspiration, Aquinas allows the work of the "tongue of God" to take place whenever people are inspired to understand the wisdom of God. He says,

> In Sacred Scripture, operations which are the operation of a [first] principle are metaphorically signified through instruments or members, and by the tongue the action of God is signified. The action of a tongue is that through it the wisdom of the heart is passed on to others. God… speaks when he pours his wisdom into rational minds.[67]

Aquinas reads the metaphor of the speech of God to express the various ways in which God inspires a human person with his wisdom. He next speaks about the way in which God's wisdom is imprinted in the creation and thus able to be "read" by the person who looks at creation. It seems, then, that the "tongue" of God, inspiring the human person, acts in any way that God may best help the human mind grasp the world. This includes everything from God strengthening and supporting human natural investigation into the structure of reality, up through various ways in which God could inspire someone about decisions in his own life, and would culminate in prophetic vision. In this section, the co-operative causality which is characteristic of Aquinas's metaphysics and whole theology of grace is very clear. The divine enables rather than suppresses the human.[68]

Having examined briefly the tongue as mediating the human spirit, and as an instrument of the mediation of the divine spirit, it may not seem completely strange to hear that Aquinas also offers an allegorical interpretation of the tongue as Christ himself. Aquinas claims that the verse about the tongue as a pen of a scribe can be read as God the Father speaking about Christ as the Son of God. This interpretation makes this verse a revelation of the Trinity.

Aquinas understands God to be one in being, but three in Person: Father, Son, and Holy Spirit. The Son, or second Person of the Trinity, eternally comes forth from the Father. As the One who first comes from the Father, Christ is the primordial "Word" of God, the first expression of the Father, in whom the Father knows himself and rejoices in divine bliss.[69] As eternal Word, the Son is primordial communication even before there is any created reality to receive any communication. As eternal Word, he is also the pattern through whom all creation comes to be made.[70] Aquinas holds that the order of the procession of creature is an image of the order of procession of the persons of the Trinity so that the world is intelligible because it reflects the Son, and it is good because it reflects the third Person of the Trinity, the Spirit (who is identified with the divine love).[71]

This identification of the Son with the Word is based on Scripture. The Gospel of John opens with, "In the beginning was the Word, and the Word was with God, and the Word was God" (John 1:1). The question of whether it is appropriate to speak of the Son as "tongue" is less clear. Aquinas warns that Augustine and Jerome do not like the application of these Psalm verses to Christ, while Pseudo-Dionysius approves of them.[72] In actual fact, Augustine acknowledges difficulties with this interpretation but accepts it. The concerns which Aquinas ascribes to Augustine seem to come from a misreading of Peter Lombard's evaluation of Augustine.[73] This suggests that Aquinas was not reading Augustine directly, but as quoted in Lombard's *Gloss*.

In Aquinas's explanation, the Son is called tongue in regard to communication outside of the Trinity. Christ is the Word in his coming forth from the Father, but as acting in creation, he is a tongue. This has a certain theological coherence. A person does not necessarily need his tongue to mediate his inner words to himself. He can form them in his mind, thinking over many ideas. It is only when he wants to speak to another that the words need to be articulated verbally using the tongue. Aquinas notes, "His proper operation is designated when he says, 'my tongue is the pen of a scribe.'"[74] Thus the tongue signifies Christ, as accomplishing the works of the Father in the created world. As a person speaks through his tongue, so the Father acts in the world through Christ.

One would think that, since a tongue is made of flesh, Aquinas would connect this text to the Incarnation, when the eternal Word took on human nature as Jesus Christ. Yet he applies it only to Christ as divine Word who speaks into the world both in creation and into human hearts. He makes a connection to the Incarnation only in the next verse where the Psalmist continues on to speak about Christ's humanity: "You are beautiful above the son of men."[75] Aquinas's desire to clearly and distinctly consider both Christ's divine and human natures may be the reason why he does not mention Christ's humanity in the earlier verse until he has talked his divinity. Nevertheless, the application of the tongue to Christ fits with Aquinas's overall Christocentric understanding of reality.

Conclusion

The books of Psalms, as a collection of songs, are inherently concerned with the action and meaning of the human tongue. Aquinas gives full attention to this dimension in his *Commentary on the Psalms*, organizing categories of sin, recognizing the freedom of virtue, and even offering a suggested Christological interpretation to the tongue. In doing so, Aquinas offers an enriching perspective to the study of media, if media is taken in the broad sense of anything which serves to bear and carry meaning between two or more other entities. Among these is the recognition that, because of the complexity of the human person, parts of the human person can themselves function as media. Further, while the tongue may not fit, strictly, all definitions of media or application of media theory, recognition of its mediatorial nature serves as a reminder that human life is profoundly communicative. It suggests that elements of media theory may be able to offer insight also into other aspects of human movement and psychology.

Finally, Aquinas offers a vision in which a hidden divine word echoes through all created media. If God himself is relational and the world is created through Christ as his tongue, then all created things partake in some way in this primordial communication. If God continues to inspire human minds with wisdom, then any act of mediating meaning is potentially a carrier of divine light. This may not be a vision all can accept, but perhaps it is one in which all can glimpse a profound possibility.

Notes

1 For example, "I will sing to the Lord" (Ps 12 (13):6 RSV), "Sing praises to the Lord, O you his saints" (Ps 29 (30):4) or "It is good to sing praises to our God" (Ps 146 (147):1).
2 See Jean-Pierre Torrell, *Saint Thomas Aquinas: The Person and His Work*, vol. 1 (Washington, DC: The Catholic University of America Press, 2005), pp. 147, 257–61.
3 Thomas Aquinas, *Commentary on the Psalms*. The Latin text (Psalms 1–5 Parma 1863; Psalms 52–4 Ucelli, 1880) can be found at: https://aquinas.institute/operaomnia/. Translations in this paper are my own. They are based on my work done for this edition.
4 See Thomas F. Ryan, *Thomas Aquinas as Reader of the Psalms* (Notre Dame, IN: University of Notre Dame Press, 2000), pp. 4–5.
5 *The Psalms I: 1–50*, Anchor Bible Commentary vol. 16, Mitchell Dahood (New York: Doubleday, 1997), xxix–xxxx. Also, "Psalms," in *The Oxford Companion to the Bible*, ed. Bruce M. Metzger (Oxford: Oxford University Press, 1993), p. 626.
6 Marcia L. Colish, "Psalterium Scholastocorum: Peter Lombard and the Emergence of Scholastic Psalms," *Speculum*, 67.3 (July 1992): 531.
7 Ibid., p. 531.
8 See Thomas F. Ryan, *Thomas Aquinas as Reader of the Psalms*, pp. 5–6.
9 See *The Psalms I: 1–50*, xxii; "Masorah," *Oxford Companion to the Bible*, 500–1; Aquinas's main text is the Gallican Psalter, as found in the Vulgate. He is, however, familiar with variants from different sources, including Jerome's *Juxta Hebraios*, the *Roman Psalter*, the Septuagint, and other Latin variation. See Thomas F. Ryan, *Thomas Aquinas as Reader of the Psalms*, pp. 17–19.

10 See Henri de Lubac, *Medieval Exegesis: The Four Sense of Scripture*, vol. 1, trans. Mark Sebanc (Grand Rapids, MI: Eerdmans, 1998), p. 142.
11 Albert the Great, "Super I Sententiarum," in *Opera Omnia Sancti Doctoris Alberti Magni*, vol. 29, ed. Maria Burger (Münster: Aschendorff), 1.1.5.
12 Thomas Aquinas, *Summa Theologia*, 1.1.10.co, ad 3.
13 See Aquinas, *Commentary on the Psalms*, Psalm 21 (22). Aquinas follows the Vulgate and Septuagint numbering of the Psalms, while most modern Biblical translations follow that based on the Hebrew. In notes which refer to Aquinas's text, the first number will refer to Aquinas's numbering, and the second to the Hebrew number. In notes which do not have reference to Aquinas, the single number is the Hebrew Psalm number. Excerpts from Aquinas's *Commentary on the Psalms* were prepared using the initial manuscript for my own translation of this work. See, Thomas Aquinas, *Commentary on the Psalms* (Steubenville, OH: Emmaus Academic Press, 2022). See also Gregory Vall's "Psalm 22: Vox Christi or Israelite Temple Liturgy," *Thomist*, 66.2 (2002): 175–200.
14 For an analysis of how Aquinas's acceptance of elements of Aristotle's anthropology gave importance to the senses and sensible objects, see "The Materiality of Sensation in the Art of the Late Middle Ages" by Martina Bagnoli in *Knowing Bodies, Passionate Souls: Sense Perceptions in Byzantium*, eds. Susan Ashbrook Harvey and Margaret Mullett (Washington, DC: Dunbarton Oaks Research Library and Collection, 2017), pp. 33–6.
15 For the way in which Aquinas holds the literal sense as foundational, see *The Study of the Bible in the Middle Ages*, ed. Beryl Smalley (Notre Dame, IN: Notre Dame Press, 1964), pp. 300–1.
16 *Summa*, 1.1.10.
17 Psalms, 5 (5), 9 (10), 11 (12), 14 (15), 15 (16), 21 (22), 30 (21), 33 (34), 34 (35), 36 (37), 38 (39), 44 (45), 49 (50), 50 (51), 51 (52), and 54 (55).
18 Psalms 2 (2), 10 (11), 16 (17), 17 (18), 18 (19), 24 (25), 26 (27), 27 (28), 32 (33), 35 (36), 40 (41) (*bilinguis,* double-tongued), and 41 (42).
19 Sagitta vulnerans lingua eorum, dolum locuta est. This text is used in the commentary on Psalms 21 (22), 34 (35), 36 (37); Lingua eorum gladius acutus. This text is used in the commentary on Psalms 5 (5), 10 (11), 13 (14), 14 (15), 34 (35), 35 (36), 49 (50), 51 (52). The Douay-Rheims text will be used as the basis of all the direct Biblical quotations because of its basis in a Latin Vulgate very similar to a text Aquinas used.
20 For example, in Psalm 34 (35).
21 To flatter, for example, in Psalm 5 (5); to hide plots; for example, in Psalms 13 (14) and 34 (35); to detract; for example, in Psalm 14 (15); to deceive; for example, in Psalms 35 (36) and 51 (52); to defraud; for example, in Psalm 49 (50).
22 For example, he does not use the Jeremiah verse equating the tongue with an arrow in Psalm 5 (6) or Psalm 10 (11), where Aquinas uses it, but he does introduce it in his commentary on Psalm 13 (14). See Hugh of St. Cher *Psalterium cum postilla*, vol. 2, Conrad Leontorius, (Basel 1504), p.20. Accessed online from Bayerische StaatsBibliotek: VD16 B 2582; https://www.gateway-bayern.de/.
23 Augustine does consider the arrows to signify the misuse of Scripture (*Enarrationes in Psalmos* on Psalm 10:3, PL 36:131) or the Apostles and their preaching (*Enarrationes in Psalmos* on Psalm 7:14 (18), PL 36:106). Peter Lombard also, in his commentary on Psalm 10:3 (11:2), interprets the arrows as possibly being heretics misusing Scripture, or people with evil intentions. Peter Lombard, *Gloss on the Psalms*, PL 191:148. Hugh of St. Cher gives the same interpretation (arrows as the misuse of Scripture) in the same place (on Psalm 10). See his *Psalterium cum postilla*, p. 20.
24 See Peter Lombard, *Gloss on the Psalms*, PL 191:371.
25 See, Aquinas, *Summa*, I.75.6.co; I.76.1.
26 See Martina Bagnoli"s "The Materiality of Sensation," pp. 33–6.
27 See Aquinas, *Summa*, I.78.3 and 4; I.84.6.
28 See Aquinas, *Summa*, I–II.22.1–3; I.82.3.
29 See Aquinas, *Summa*, I–II.61.2. For a further investigation of Aquinas's anthropology and understanding of the moral virtues, see, Romanus Cessario, *The Virtues, or the Examined Life*, (New York and London: Continuum, 2002); see also Aquinas, *Summa*, I–II.55.2.
30 For a recent affirmation of the importance of Aquinas's virtue theory in maintaining that virtue forms not merely the will but also patterns of thought and emotional response, see Romanus Cessario, "Sanctified Thought and Affection in Aquinas," *Thomist* 84.3 (2020): 467–80.
31 See Aquinas, *Summa*, II–II.62.3; I–II.65.2; also, Jean-Pierre Torrell, *Saint Thomas Aquinas: Spiritual Master*, vol. 2 (Washington, DC: The Catholic University of America Press, 2003), pp. 147, 352–6.

32 Aquinas, *Commentary on Psalms*, Psalm 36. Per gladium intelligitur omnis aperta facti persecution … Hic autem gladius est in vagina, quamdiu est in corde; sed quando profertur, est sicut jam evaginatus. Cavendum est ergo primum ut non habeamus eum. Secundo, et si haberetur, non evaginemus eum. Quia si tenetur in vagina, primo contrahit rubiginem, tandem tamen consumitur et tepescit odium et voluntas injuriandi.
33 See Aquinas, *Summa*, I–II.157.1. Some current psychological theories would agree with Aquinas that venting anger does not disperse it. See, for example, the New York Times Mary 8, 1983 article, "Venting Anger May do More Harm Than Good" by Jane E. Brody. https://www.nytimes.com/1983/03/08/science/venting-anger-may-do-more-harm-than-good.html.
34 Aquinas, *Commentary on the Psalms*, Psalm 34 (35). Aliquando enim aliquis opprimit … surreptione ex infirmitate: et hoc patet quod statim poenitet. Sed quando ex malitia opprimit, tunc gaudet se fecisse.
35 Aquinas, *Commentary on the Psalms*, Ps 49 (50). Si ex lapsu linguae aliquod inordinatum dicat, facilius portatur.
36 Cf. Aristotle, *Nicomachean Ethics*, 3.2, 111b; 5.6, 1134a.
37 Jas 3:2. Aquinas, *Commentary on the Psalms,* Psalm 49 (50). Si quis verbo non offendit, hic perfectus est vir.
38 Aquinas, *Commentary on the Psalms*, Psalm 9 (10). Et primo in corde … secundo de ore … tertio de opera.
39 Aquinas, *Commentary on the Psalms*, Psalm 38 (39). Alia ratio est, quia lingua est immediatum organum ad interiorem conceptum cordis explicandum. Unde quam cito verbum est in corde, est in lingua; et ideo oportet diligenter custodiri.
40 Aquinas, *Commentary on the Psalms*, Psalm 38 (39). Quod homo ponat custodiam cordi.
41 Ps 34 (35). Aquinas, *Commentary on the Psalms*, Psalm 34 (35). Praemeditatione.
42 Aquinas, *Commentary on the Psalms*, Psalm 15 (16). Cum exteriori gaudio prorumpit in laudem vocis.
43 See Aquinas, *Summa*, I–II.95.4; Aristotle, *Politics*, book 1, 1253a.
44 Ps 18 (19) 1, 3.
45 Aquinas, *Commentary on the Psalms*, Psalm 18 (19).
46 Aquinas, *Commentary on the Psalms*, Psalm 34 (35). Praemediatio … benedicam Domino.
47 Aquinas, *Commentary on the Psalms*, Psalm 5. Solus homo non potest bene gaudere de aliquo, sed quando amicos habet secum participes illius boni: et ideo dicit, "omnes …".
48 Psalm 50 (51):16. Libera me de sanguinibus, Deus, Deus salutis meae, et exsultabit lingua mea justitiam tuam.
49 Aquinas, *Commentary on the Psalms*, Psalm 50 (51).
50 See Aquinas, *Summa*, I.22.3, ad. 2.
51 See Aquinas, *Summa*, II–II.83.2.
52 See Aquinas, *Summa* I.9.1.
53 See Aquinas, *Summa* II–II.91.1.
54 Psalm 33 (34): Gustate et videte quoniam suavis est Dominus.
55 Psalm 33 (34):4: magnificate Dominum mecum.
56 Aquinas, *Commentary on the Psalms*, Psalm 33 (34). Experientia divinae bonitatis dicitur gustation.
57 For consideration of this sweetness in medieval sensation, see Martina Bagnoli, "The Materiality of Sensation," 36, 38. She connects the renewed interest in spiritual sweetness to both the influence of Aristotle's realist emphasis on the senses as mediating to the intellect as well as to renewed focus on the humanity of Christ.
58 Aquinas, *Commentary on the Psalms*, Psalm 33 (34). Securitas affectus.
59 For a description of this sort of knowledge and its situation within a medieval Dominican worldview, see the section on mystical experience in Sr. Albert Marie Surmanski, "The Experience of Eucharistic Beauty in Albert the Great's *De Corpore Domini*," *Nova et Vetera*, 17.3 (2019): 735–56.
60 Charles Burnett, "The Superiority of Taste," *Journal of the Warburg and Courtauld Institute* 54 (1991): 235. See also Martina Bagnoli, "The Materiality of Sensation," pp. 37–8.
61 Psalm 44 (45):2. Eructavit cor meum verbum bonum: dico ego opera mea regi. Lingua mea calamus scribae velociter scribentis.
62 Aquinas, *Commentary on the Psalms*, Psalm 44 (45). Eructatio ex nimia plenitudine, sive repletione procedit: in quo signatur quod ex abundantia devotionis et sapientiae loquitur … hujus editio Psalmi attribuitur cordi, ex cujus magna devotione est compositus … corde pronuntiat laudes Christi.

63 Aquinas's thought here is compatible with some of the insights in the document on divine revelation from the Second Vatican Council, *Dei Verbum*.

64 Aquinas, *Commentary on the Psalms,* Prologue quoting Psalm 44 (45). Lingua mea calamus scribae.

65 Aquinas, *Commentary on the Psalms*, Psalm 44 (45). Non intelligatur quod ex proprio hunc fecerim, sed auxilio spiritus sancti, qui utitur lingua mea, sicut scriptor utitur calamo. Et ideo principalis auctor hujus Psalmi est spiritus sanctus.

66 See Aquinas, *Commentary on the Psalms*, Psalm 44 (45).

67 See Aquinas, *Commentary on the Psalms*, Psalm 44 (45). In sacra Scriptura operationes metaphorice designantur per instrumenta vel membra quae sunt operationum principia; et sic per linguam et calamum operatio Dei designatur conveniens linguae et calamo. Operatio linguae est, quod per eam diffunditur sapientia cordis ad alios ...Deus ... loquitur, quando transfundit sapientiam suam in mentes rationales.

68 For more on this topic read Aquinas, *Summa*, I.22.4; I–II.110.3.

69 See Aquinas, *Summa*, I.34.1.

70 See John 1:3.

71 See Aquinas, *Summa*, I.45.6, co.

72 Cf. Pseudo-Dionysius, *Ad Titum*. PG 3:1103–4. Dionysius is not explicit in connecting the "tongue" to Christ, but speaks about word being formed in air – ie, the action of vocal chords and tongue, alluding to this Scripture text as speaking about the procession of the Son.

73 See, Lombard, *Ps.* PL 191:438; also See *Augustine, Enarrationes in Psalmos* on Psalm 44 (45); PL 36:496.

74 See Aquinas, *Commentary on the Psalms*, Psalm 44 (45). Propria operatio designatur cum dicit, lingua mea calamus Scribae.

75 Ps 44(45):3. Speciosus forma prae filiis hominum.

PART II

Interpretive Technologies – Viewing Culture and Society

PART II

Interpretive Technologies – Viewing Culture and Society

3

PAINTED, PRINTED, AND DIGITIZED

The Commemorative Images for the British "Worthies"

Anne Betty Weinshenker

The remarkable cycle of paintings conceived and commissioned by Owen McSwiny (1676–754) followed no iconographic tradition and did not initiate any.[1] Born in Ireland, McSwiny became an impresario at the Queen's Theater, Haymarket in London.[2] After having become unable to deal with his debts, he absconded to the Continent in 1713 and remained there for approximately the next twenty years. He spent time in France, the United Provinces, and Vienna and then settled in Italy, most of the time in Venice, before returning to England in about 1733 or 1734. During his self-exile, this enterprising and resourceful man (who has also not without reason been labeled "of dubious reputation"[3] and the like) devised a series of paintings and hired teams of artists from Venice and Bologna to execute them. They were completed over the course of the 1720s.[4] He planned twenty-four canvases for the group, although it appears that only twenty were carried out.

In about 1734 or 1735 McSwiny brought out a short pamphlet, entitled *To the Ladies and Gentlemen of Taste in Great-Britain and Ireland,* soliciting subscriptions for another of his projects, a series of prints reproducing the paintings.[5] They were to be created by artists in France and accompanied by what he termed "inscription plates," original half-title pages mainly designed by the up-and-coming François Boucher and Carle van Loo, with one by Pierre-Josse Perrot. The entire group was to be published as a collection titled *Tombeaux des Princes grands capitaines et autres hommes illustres, qui ont fleuri dans la Grand-Bretagne vers la fin du XVII et le commencement du XVIII siècle.*

McSwiny's advertising pamphlet also provides a considerable amount of information about his intentions and procedures for the series; he planned it to perpetuate "the remembrance of a set of British Worthies, who were bright and shining Ornaments to their country." Claiming to have fully determined the content of the canvases himself, he described them as providing "a succinct account of the most memorable transactions in the reigns of King William and Queen Mary, Queen Anne, and King George." He referred to the works as depicting "monuments," each intended as an allegorical commemoration of a major English political, military, or intellectual figure of the recent past. Some of their names continue to resonate: Isaac Newton, John Locke, Joseph Addison, and the Duke of Marlborough. Others, such as the Earls of Argyll, Godolphin, and Halifax, are now mainly found in historical texts.

DOI: 10.4324/9781003295082-6

The pamphlet specifies that every painting is to focus on an urn supposed to hold the remains of a deceased hero. Each of the compositions conforms to an arrangement whose principal feature is a classically derived or Baroque structure in a greater or lesser state of ruin. These serve as shelters, backdrops, and bases for the imagined funerary monuments centered in them, most of which are raised on high pedestals; the tombs are surmounted and, in some cases, flanked by statues. Around them is shown a staffage relating to the life and accomplishments of the dedicatee and engaged in viewing, discussing, or admiring the monument or in a variety of other relevant activities. According to the advertising leaflet, each canvas was completed by several different hands; text under the reproductive engravings and McSwiny's correspondence confirm that most of them were produced by three artists: one each for the figures, the architecture, and the landscape.

The majority of the "Worthies" celebrated in the paintings had firm Whig connections. Several had been involved in activities leading to or deriving from the Glorious Revolution of 1688 that deposed the Catholic King James II and replaced him with his daughter Mary, who was Protestant, and her husband, the Dutch William of Orange. The Whigs supported an increase in the authority of Parliament compared to that of the king and a Protestant, Hanoverian, succession to the throne. They roundly defeated the Tories, their political adversaries, in the general election of 1715. This outcome initiated a long period of Whig political domination under the leadership of Robert Walpole, who is regarded as the first prime minister of Great Britain.

Eleven of the paintings from the series were purchased by Charles Lennox, later the second Duke of Richmond. He was aged twenty when on his grand tour he met the enterprising McSwiny and became his main patron. After having received the canvases beginning in the mid-1720s[6] the Duke placed ten of them in the dining room of his country estate, Goodwood, and one in Richmond House, his townhome in London. The remaining paintings were probably purchased by Sir William Morice, his London neighbor.

The dining room at Goodwood seems to have been able to accommodate that many large works.[7] Such an area was generally semi-public, a place for gatherings of friends and family. The second Duke, who was involved in many cultural and political organizations and activities, must have had a substantial number of such occasions.[8] Covering a sizable part of the wall space, the ten colorful and imposing paintings would have been able to attract the attention of his guests. In commemorating the predominantly Whig heroes of the previous generation, they would be capable of communicating an affirmation of his adherence to the Whig political stance. Such a display would have been astutely strategic for Richmond, who was a great-nephew of the ousted King James II and whose father, the first Duke of Richmond, had been converted, albeit temporarily, to Catholicism.

Given the political supremacy of the Whigs, it seems highly likely that McSwiny expected to attract a large potential clientele, extending whatever gains he may have received from the sale of the canvases by bringing out the collection of prints a few years later.[9] His advertising pamphlet, where he referred to himself in the third person, advanced a more selfless motive for issuing the engravings: as this Collection of Paintings has been separated, and the greatest Part of it placed in the Gallery of an illustrious Nobleman, at too great a Distance from London to be frequently or conveniently seen, by the generality of People, he resolved to engrave the whole Work, that it might come into the Hands of many.[10]

His anticipation that there would be widespread interest in purchasing the engravings was probably fueled by the contemporary significant growth of print collecting.[11] McSwiny had personal ties to this practice: during most of his long sojourn in Venice, he lived in the *palazzo* of Joseph Smith, a wealthy English merchant and banker who was also an avid collector and dealer in art and precious commodities. McSwiny also had financial dealings with Smith and may have served as his agent in certain business transactions.[12] Smith's collections, apparently begun in the 1720s, came to include a very large number of prints gathered in albums. Among them were prints by or after Sebastiano and Marco Ricci and Canaletto, who were among the artists employed by McSwiny in those years to create paintings for the *Tombeaux* series.[13] Additionally, it seems likely that McSwiny would have been acquainted with Smith's closely associated colleague collector, the Venetian Count Antonio Maria Zanetti the Elder, who like him dealt in art and precious objects. The many albums of prints in Zanetti's collection might have provided further impetus for McSwiny to pursue the *Tombeaux* engravings project.[14]

Although McSwiny's prospectus states that there were to be twenty-four paintings, reproduced in the same number of engravings and accompanied by twenty-four inscription plates, ultimately a far smaller number of prints was created. The most complete collections of the *Tombeaux des princes* engravings include the majority of the following components: nine copies of tomb paintings, eleven inscription plates, a title page, a list of contents, and five pages of text, two eulogizing Isaac Newton and three in tribute to Charles Sackville, sixth Earl of Dorset. No known collection includes them all. McSwiny followed the common practice of promoting the sale of individual sheets by subscription, allowing the purchasers to assemble their prints in any order they chose.[15] This resulted in considerable variation in the contents and their ordering among the various known copies.

Completion of the project seems to have continued for several years. One of the inscription plates is dated 1736 and another 1737, while the title page on some copies carries 1741 as the year of publication. The fact that there exist sets carrying three different title pages makes it likely that there were several editions.[16] The existence of variations among the title pages suggests that sets may have been printed on different presses, possibly even in different countries; the copper plates to be printed would have been readily portable. McSwiny appears to have abandoned the project after 1741 for a variety of possible reasons.[17]

In producing the group of prints, McSwiny was employing a powerful technology: pictorial printmaking, the production of multiple original works of art rivaling the creation of unique hand-made works. Revolutionary in part because its products were less expensive to own and thus capable of more wide distribution, it had been practiced in Europe since the fifteenth century but was continuing to develop. The first instructional guide to the subject, the *Traité des manieres de graver en taille-douce* (treatise on intaglio techniques[18]) by the printmaker Abraham Bosse was published in 1645 in Paris. Its appearance may indicate a growing interest on the part of art lovers and collectors not only in connoisseurship but also in the technical processes required for the creation of printed images. In it Bosse fully details the steps for etching and engraving including selecting a copper plate, preparing it, compounding the coating needed for etching, devising instruments for incising the image onto it, and many other necessary printmaking studio skills, even including instructions for building a press. This manual was updated in the article "Gravure" in volume seven of the *Encyclopédie* published by Diderot and d'Alembert.[19] Its author, Claude-Henri Watelet, who had previously contributed the entry on "Estampe" to the fifth volume, acknowledges the assistance of the artist Charles-Nicolas Cochin the Younger, who had produced four of the prints for the *Tombeaux des princes*. The superior quality of French printmaking had long been recognized, and McSwiny, who was very knowledgeable about the contemporary art world, must have accordingly decided to employ French practitioners. He appears to have traveled twice to Paris in the early 1730s in connection with his project.[20]

Two categories, both appearing from early on, have often been distinguished in discussions of print history: original prints and reproductive prints.[21] An original print is designed to be finalized by means of a printmaking medium, be that woodcut, engraving, etching, or any other. A reproductive print translates an image previously created in any medium into one made by a printmaking process. Early reproductive prints copied drawings or other prints but by the seventeenth century were extensively employed to copy paintings.

Noteworthy for the high level of technical skill they display, the *Tombeaux* engravings fall into both categories. The copies of the paintings exemplify reproductive prints while the inscription plates are original works. Both types are scrupulously documented under the pictures. Each reproductive engraving carries the names of the artists who created the painting on the left below the image, e.g., for the Isaac Newton page: *J.B. Pittoni et D. et Jos. Valeriani Pinx.*, while on the right is found the credit for the engraver, e.g., *L. Desplaces Sculp.*; further to the right is *et D. M. Fratta delin.* (The significance of this last acknowledgment is discussed below.) A Latin excerpt from a classic text is located below each of the reproductive prints, adding further gravitas to the page.

The inscription plates state the name and contribution (in Latin) of the designing artist on the left and on the right provide the name of the engraver, e.g., on the Archbishop Tillotson plate: *F. Boucher invenit. et delin:* indicates that Boucher both designed and drew the image, and *N. De Larmessin Sculpsit.* documents the latter's contribution. All the prints carry the credit *Mac S.* at the bottom, centered for the inscription plates and on the right for the reproductive engravings.[22]

McSwiny employed Domenico Maria Fratta, an artist from Bologna, to make drawings of the paintings. There is a twofold explanation for this decision: the paintings, whether in England or in Venice, would be inaccessible to the Parisian engravers. The other motivation grew out of the technical requirements of the process: a picture directly copied onto the copper plate by incising (for engravings) or drawing (for etchings) would produce a printed image in reverse.[23] In order for the print to be correctly oriented, a drawn copy of the painting could be placed face down (and thus inverted) on the metal plate and transferred to it by pouncing. Fratta's known drawings are squared on their backs and have areas with pinpricks suggesting that method of transferal.[24] The fact that only two drawings for the *Tombeaux* are known suggests that the others might have been destroyed in the course of such use.

In the case of the *Tombeaux* prints, another stage was added to this process. Before shipping completed paintings to the Duke in England, McSwiny had copies made in *grisaille* (monochrome black, gray, and white); he called each a *Chiaro Scuro.* They seem to have been intended for his personal possession and were included among the paintings at the sale after his death.[25] It has been conjectured that they, rather than the original canvases, served as the images to be copied in the drawings.[26] This might have been expedient if the paintings had been sent to Richmond before the drawings were made. Further evidence that the *grisailles* played this role is found in a letter that McSwiny sent to Richmond stating that he brought a painter from Bologna "to do the Chiaro Scuro's, for the engraver..."[27] At about two and three-quarters feet high, the known *grisailles* would have been easier than the over 7-foot original paintings for Fratta to copy into his approximately 2-foot high drawings. Not depending on color for effect might additionally have matched the *grisailles* more compatibly with the black and white drawing and engraving media.

Employment of printmaking technology for the *Tombeaux* project, then, involved a multi-step process. All stages resulted in products that resemble one another, but each work has its own unique qualities. The reproduction of an image in a different medium in this way has appropriately been termed a "translation."[28] Comparison of any pair of those creations reveals the distinctive effects with which each iteration endows the image.

While most of the original paintings are now in public or private collections, fewer of the *grisaille* copies are known. Examining one of them in relation to the corresponding engraving reveals at least part of the transformation from the painted original to a graphic medium. This comparison is feasible in the case of the allegorical monument for Archbishop of Canterbury John Tillotson (1630–94). Although he only served in that capacity from 1691 until his death, he was the sole ecclesiastic included among the "worthies." A religious moderate, he was like most of the *Tombeaux* honorees a supporter of the Glorious Revolution of 1688. Similar to several of the others, he was a Fellow of the Royal Society, having been elected in 1672, the same year as Isaac Newton. He was close to William and Mary and to their successor, Queen Anne.

The painting of the allegorical tomb dedicated to him, completed by 1727, is by Giovanni Battista Pittoni for the figures, Canaletto for the architecture, and Giovanni Battista Cimaroli for the landscape. The original canvas, like the others in the series, substantiates McSwiny's claim that "the Harmony of the whole is so well preserv'd, that each Picture seems to be the Work of one great Master."[29]

Framed by chipped and cracked columns that have been slightly invaded by vegetation, an imposing mausoleum rises in a nearly profile view on the work's far left. Characteristically for the *Tombeaux* cycle, the imagery includes considerable attention to the statues depicted on the structure to communicate Tillotson's ecclesiastical role. Among them are figures that correspond to prescriptions in the *Iconologia* by Cesare Ripa, a manual of iconography widely used by artists that was first published in 1593 with many amplified later editions in the seventeenth and eighteenth centuries. Although a condensed English version appeared in 1709,[30] features in the Tillotson image correspond rather to the full Italian text; undoubtedly McSwiny would have been comfortable with written as well as spoken Italian. Directly related to Ripa's entries are the tomb's sculptures symbolizing Charity: a female figure holding a flaming heart and accompanied by three children, and Christian Faith, a female figure with a cross in her left hand and a chalice in her right. Hope, the third theological virtue, is represented by a statue of a woman holding an anchor and three plant stalks.[31]

An altar located in front of the monument and partly covered by a cloth displays appropriate accessories: a book, mitre, stole, crosier, censers, and ritual vessels. Acolytes carry others, including candlesticks. Wearing ceremonial garments, the sizable staffage of varying ages stands on the platform beneath the tomb. A prominently placed figure reading a book kneels, facing the altar.[32] The landscape stretches far into the distance, ultimately closed off by mountains. Architectural and sculptural remains occupy much of the mid-ground and background; among them are the remnants of an arcade, a steep pyramid, freestanding columns, a small exedra enclosing a multi-layered casket surmounted by statuary, and a pointed arch opening in a section of wall through which a giant is seen atop an entablature supported by two columns. These last elements allude to Gothic structural usage, appropriately associated with religion, to commemorate the archbishop.

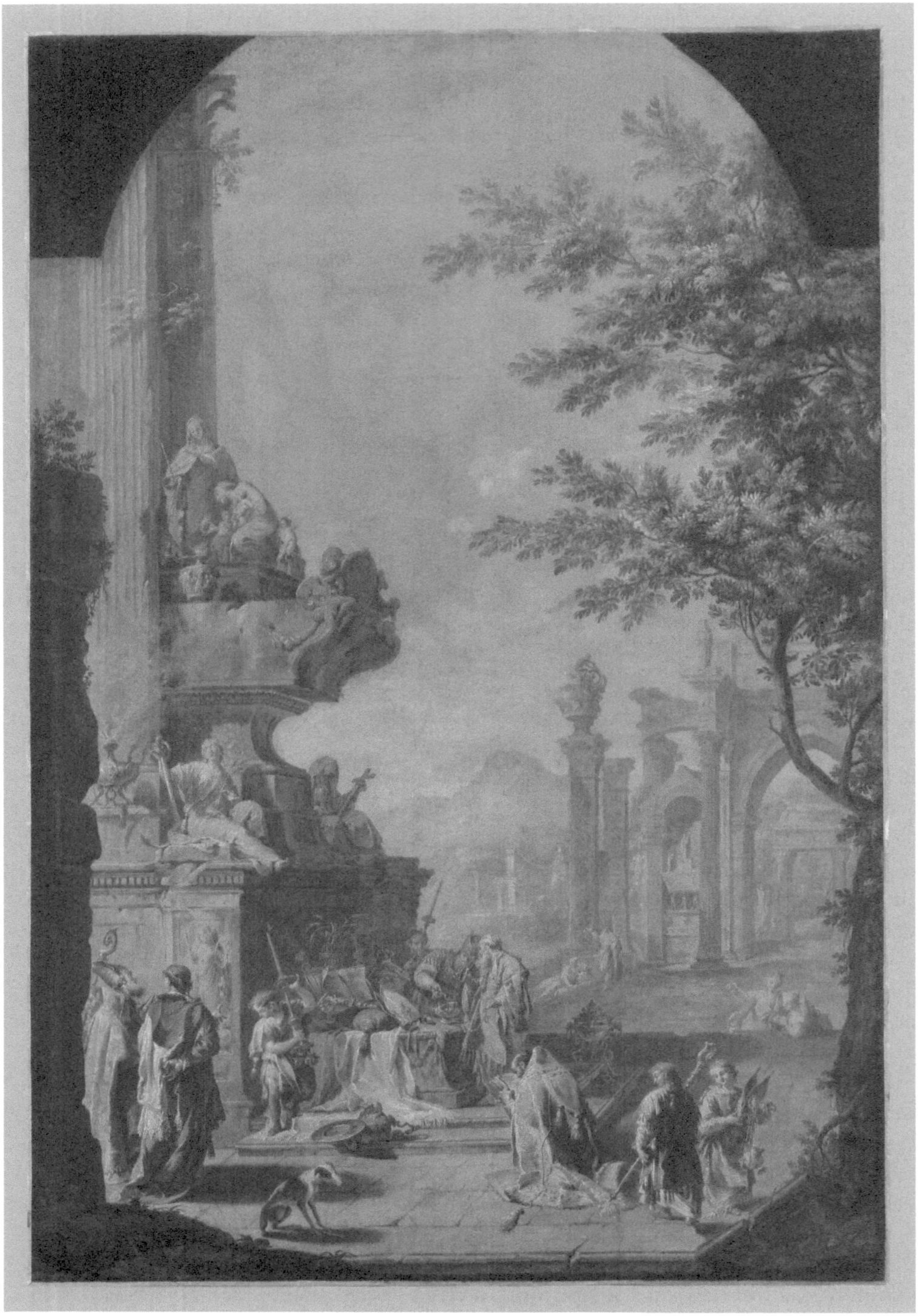

FIGURE 3.1 Allegorical Tomb of Archbishop Tillotson. Grisaille, oil on canvas. Paris, Muséedu Louvre.

The *grisaille* (Figure 3.1) is generally quite similar to the original painting but there are some surprising divergences. Among observable variations are the treatment of the statue group on top of the sepulcher: in the original composition the figure with the dove extends her left arm, holding her cloak out over the kneeling personification of Charity, but in the *grisaille* her left arm simply hangs down at her side. The forms and poses of the little girl statue behind Charity also differ in the two works. Tillotson's escutcheon, clearly visible on the extended front of the tomb in the painting, is absent from the *grisaille*. Other dissimilarities include the angle of the paving blocks, the smoke from the censer on the left, the shape and placement of tree branches and clusters of foliage, the mountains, and the clouds.

The most prominent difference is obviously the absence of color in the *grisaille*. Despite the identity of composition, the effects of the two works are strikingly dissimilar: the concentrated blue and gold of the clothing in the lower right of the painting capture the viewer's attention, while that emphasis is only approached but not duplicated in the *grisaille* by means of pronounced chiaroscuro. Although the mid-ground architectural elements in the painting are less tonally saturated than those in the foreground their distinct hue sets them off from their surroundings; in contrast, that area of the *grisaille*, with a minimal contrast of light and dark, seems to melt into its surroundings. The moods conveyed are different as well: the monochromatic painting delivers a quiescent, elegiac affect unlike the livelier impact of the original.

The relationship between the *grisailles* and the reproductive engravings seems in general to be a decisive element in McSwiny's employment of printmaking technology in the service of his commercial project. Yet for the *Tillotson* pair, although these two versions appear similar to one another they are not identical, and each has features closer to some in the original painting. Differences are again most noticeable in the perspective of the paving blocks and in the clouds and the foliage of the print, which do not faithfully mirror either those of the painting or the *grisaille* (Figure 3.2). Curiously, the statue group of Charity located on top of the tomb in the engraving is like that in the original painting but different from the image in the *grisaille*; in another instance Tillotson's armorial sign, absent from the *grisaille*, appears in the print as in the original painting. These are clearly observable and significant deviations distinguishing the engraving from the *grisaille*, and at odds with the conclusion that the drawings (and thus the engravings) were based on the *grisailles* rather than copying the original paintings. Perhaps the Tillotson print resulted from some circumstance that entailed an exception to the usual procedure.

Major variations between the engraving and the monochrome painting derive from the techniques adopted to create them. Painterly brushstrokes are visible in some areas, such as the tomb, of the *grisaille* as well as in the original painting. They are understandably absent from the much more linear print, which is in fact the product of both etching and engraving; the combination of these two intaglio processes was common at the time.[33] The evenly spaced, carefully parallel lines and regular, organized crosshatching seen in most areas of the image derive from the use of engraving technique and achieve the shadowed modeling while the freer, looser touches more typical of etching conjure the background mountains, the foliage, and the smoke as well as parts of the figures and of the statues.[34]

The Latin caption below the engraving also serves to distinguish it from all prior forms of the image. Copied from one of Tillotson's published sermons, it is his translation of a quotation from the Roman poet Persius.[35] Like the citations in Latin from Horace, Virgil, and Lucretius that McSwiny chose for placement under all the other reproductive prints it

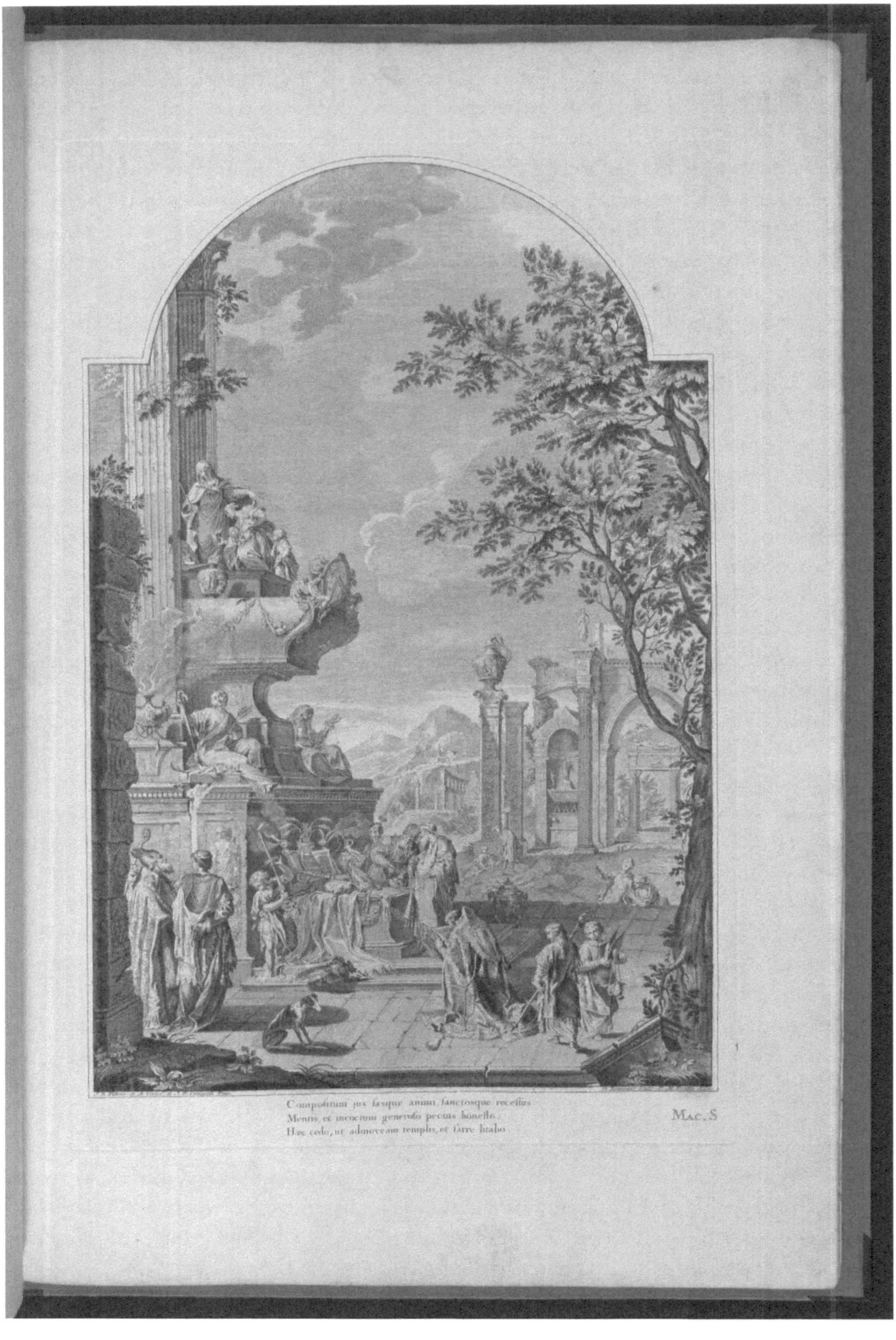

FIGURE 3.2 Allegorical Tomb of Archbishop Tillotson. Leaf 15 recto, Tombeaux des princes, grands capitaines et autres hommes illustres…. Engraving. Los Angeles, Getty Research Institute.

assumes an educated audience for the *Tombeaux* collection. Members of the nobility and the political and mercantile elite, undoubtedly his targeted addressees, would have appreciated the appropriately selected lines.

François Boucher designed the inscription plate that accompanies the Tillotson allegorical tomb as well as seven of the other ten half-title pages (Figure 3.3). Not reproducing any other images, the inscription pages fall into the category of original prints. McSwiny's advertising pamphlet states that they are to be "ornamented with emblematical figures"[36] but he does not explicitly claim credit for inventing them as he does for the original paintings. It seems likely that the procedure was nevertheless similar: McSwiny might well have stipulated the figures and objects for inclusion, which then were given form and composed by Boucher.

A combination of engraving for the major part of the image with etching in several details is employed for this print too. As with the other inscription pages, the plate for Tillotson reserves a large central open area for the name and title of the dedicatee. All of the symbolic elements revolve around it, forming a frame. At the apex a sacrificial lamb lies on an altar; beneath it the clouds shelter some very Boucheresque cherubs. Entwined in draperies, clouds, and architectural elements around the perimeter are assorted items of religious significance or clerical usage, including the Ark of the Covenant, grapes, and wheat of the sacrament, lilies, a set of candelabra, a smoking incense pot, a thurible, and a chalice. The symbols of the Evangelists: the angel of Matthew, the eagle of John, the lion of Mark, and the ox of Luke recline comfortably but alertly in the lower reaches of this border. Specific references to Tillotson show up in the mitre, crosier, and processional cross near the bottom. Also, there is a set of crossed keys. Although they commonly symbolize the papacy, they appear here to allude to the religious authority of the Archbishop of Canterbury.

I have come to realize that the utilization of digital techniques greatly facilitates conducting research that requires a comparison of the variant forms and details of a single image, as in the case of the *Tombeaux des princes*. Some time ago, while I was looking into eighteenth-century depictions of ruins, I came across illustrations of a few works from the *Tombeaux*; all of the paintings and the reproductive engravings from the series include representations of ruined or decaying structures. Intrigued by them, I consulted secondary sources and realized that I needed to view as many of the paintings as possible, which took me to museums in Washington, DC, Norfolk, Virginia, London and Birmingham, England, and Bologna as well as to the corporate headquarters of a bank in Bologna and to the British Embassy in Rome.

My reading made me aware of the existence of the series of engravings, but identified only three complete sets: in the British Library in London, the Bibliothèque Nationale in Paris, and the Biblioteca Marciana in Venice. Email correspondence with staff in those institutions furnished some description of their copies but no visual materials. I subsequently learned of three more sets in New York, one in the New York Public Library and two in the Pierpont Morgan Library, where I was able to see them.[37] They all had variant title pages and different ordering of the prints. I could examine them on-site, and it was possible to purchase some digital images. I then learned that the library of the Getty Research Institute in Los Angeles has a freely available copy online that includes all of the engravings and the accompanying five pages of text. Being able to access this resource provided invaluable assistance with my study: the images are high resolution, so that I can enlarge them greatly without losing definition. All their details are splendidly visible. I also later learned that the copy in the British Library has been digitized and is available to subscribers

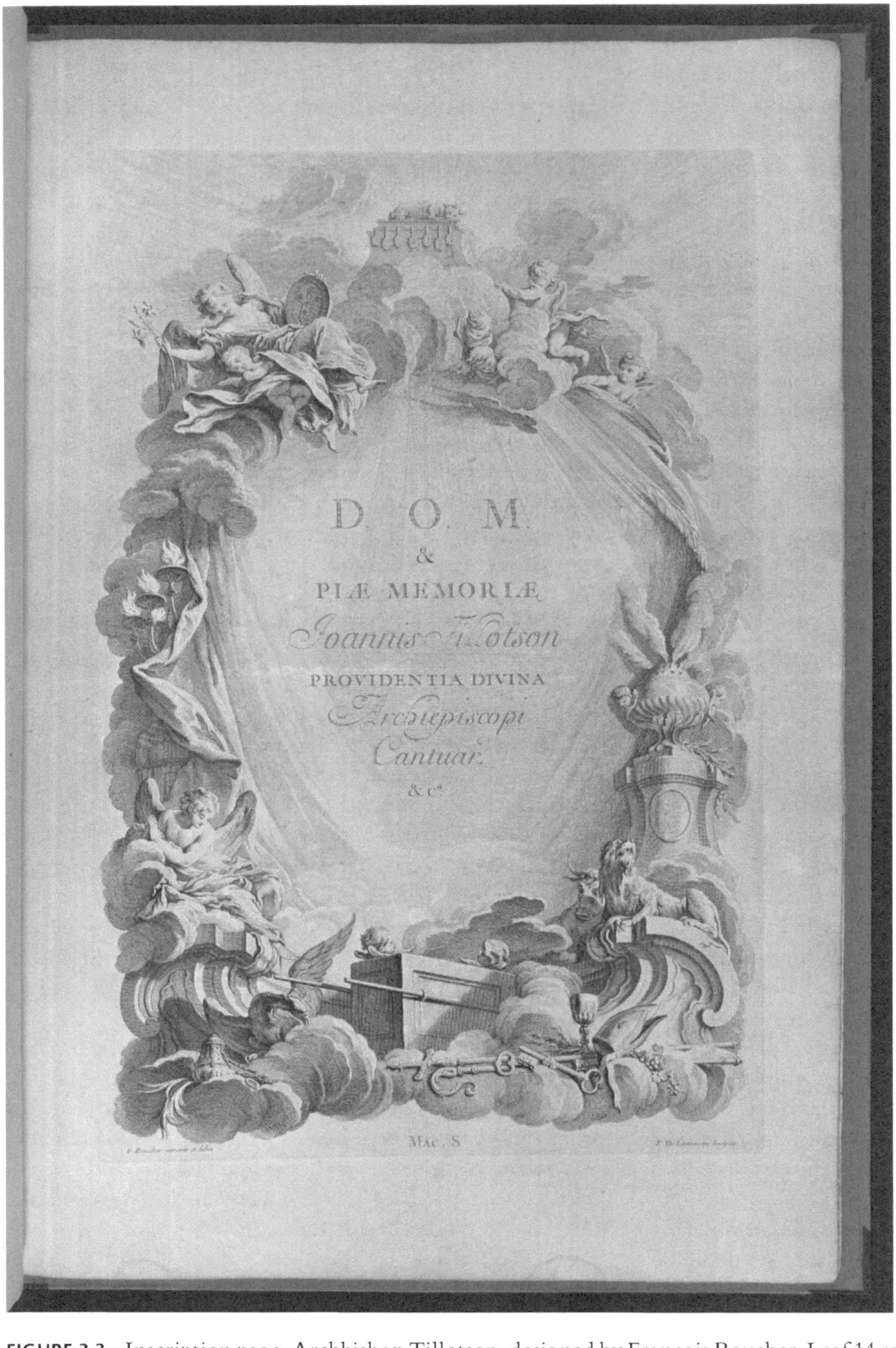

FIGURE 3.3 Inscription page, Archbishop Tillotson, designed by François Boucher. Leaf 14 recto, *Tombeaux des princes, grands capitaines et autres hommes illustres*.... Engraving. Los Angeles, Getty Research Institute.

to Eighteenth-Century Collections Online (ECCO). Online searching helped me to find digital images, widely varying in clarity, of many of the paintings and a few of the drawings and *grisailles*; email communications with museums and image repositories furnished more of them, enabling me to observe side-by-side comparisons with the electronic versions of the prints.

I prepared computerized lists and spreadsheets setting out the information I had gathered about the paintings: artists, subjects, approximate dates, and locations. I also made them for the reproductive engravings: locations of all the copies that I had found, as well as the presence or absence of inscription pages, their designers, engravers, contents and text pages, dimensions and orientations of the pages, and their ordering, types of title pages. When available, I included information and photographs of the actual tombs of the paintings' honorees as auxiliary material. Having all this data digitally organized enabled relationships between all the pictorial materials to become clearer and allowed me to draw conclusions about them.

I also benefited substantially from the availability of online primary textual sources, far greater in number than when I had conducted research in the past. Certainly, the gratifying experience of handling the original publications, turning their pages, and feeling their paper is not duplicated electronically, but its absence is compensated for by the convenience of utilizing high-resolution searchable digital versions. The *Iconologia* by Ripa, the treatise by Bosse, and the entries in the *Encyclopédie* were at my fingertips, saving hours of travel time and expense to visit library collections, and they were accessible at any hour. The ability to consult many secondary sources, such as publications on JSTOR, Project MUSE, and other databases, similarly greatly aided my study. Correspondence with editors and publishers, conducted online, also furthered the development and publication of my projects.

The various forms that the works of art of the *Tombeaux* cycle have assumed correspondingly impacted conditions of ownership and viewership. The twenty original paintings of the set were at the outset the property of two individuals, perhaps of a few more, to be seen and enjoyed by their circles of kinship and friendship. Employment of the technological methods available in his time allowed Owen McSwiny to multiply the numbers of works of art in the series created under his direction. Any number of individuals who might have been made aware of the existence of the prints would have been able to view, purchase, own, and display these original images. The ultimate acquisition of many of the paintings and prints by public collections enabled larger numbers of viewers to encounter and consider them. Although relatively limited in number, reproductions in print publications also distributed them more widely, but the technological innovations of the twentieth and twenty-first centuries have remarkably further extended their availability. The initiation and rapid expansion of electronic communications have been serving to remove the geographic restrictions that limited access to previous versions of these images. The possibility exists for them, or at least many of them, to be viewed and downloaded by individuals anywhere that digital connections exist. Printed versions can be produced for those who want to own physical copies.

The nature of the viewer's experience is necessarily far more diverse for those relying on electronic images than had been the situation in the past. As contemporary technology has expanded the opportunities for viewing the eighteenth-century originals and for possessing copies, it has provided functional but altered, even somewhat diluted, experiences. Online images vary greatly in clarity and in color (although the same is true for those in paper publications). Their dimensions are also strikingly unlike those of the original paintings and prints. A concentrated effort is needed in order to realize the full impression created by an over 7-foot tall painting, or even a 2-foot high engraving, that is being seen in a reproduction measuring only 5–10 inches on the screen. The assistance provided by being able to enlarge details digitally provides compensation for this drawback, an advantage essentially not available for the images in print publications. Large-scale projections of digitized works of art have also been created, introducing a form of public exhibition intended to reach increased numbers of viewers. Their potential has yet to be determined.

Notes

1 Major contributions concerning McSwiny's project include Barbara Mazza, "La vicenda dei 'Tombeaux des princes,'" *Saggi e memorie di storia dell'arte*, 10 (1976): 81–102; Francis Haskell, *Patrons and Painters* (New Haven, CT: Yale University Press, 1980), 287–91; George Knox, "'The Tombs of Famous Englishmen' as Described in the Letters of Owen McSwiny to the Duke of Richmond," *Arte Veneta*, 37 (1983): 228–35; W. G. Constable, *Canaletto* (Oxford: Clarendon, 1989), passim; Volker Adolphs, "Der Impresario als Auftraggeber, Owen McSwiny und die 'Tombeaux des Princes grands capitaines et autres hommes illustres,'" in *Venedigs Ruhm im Norden* (Hannover: Landesmuseum, 1991), 42–59; Xavier Cervantès, "'In Paint Each Hero's Glory Shown,'" in *Cartes, paysages, territoires*, ed. Ronald Shusterman (Bordeaux: Université Michel de Montaigne, 2000), 57–82.

2 On McSwiny, see T. D. Llewellyn, ed., *Owen McSwiny's letters, 1720–1744* (Verona: Scripta, 2009).

3 Joan Coutu, *Then and Now: Collecting and Classicism in Eighteenth-Century England* (Montreal: McGill-Queens University Press, 2015), 98; Judith Milhous and Robert Hume, "Heidegger and the management of the Haymarket Opera, 1713–17," *Early Music*, 27 (1999): 65–84.

4 Knox, *Tombs*, 228–30; Llewellyn, *McSwiny's letters*, 91–128.

5 *To the Ladies and Gentlemen of Taste in Great-Britain and Ireland*, fully presented in Llewellyn, *McSwiny's letters*, 373–6. For the assumed date: ibid., 44. The only known copy is in the British Library, London.

6 Llewellyn, *McSwiny's letters*, 95.

7 Most of them measure approximately 7.25 feet by 4.6 feet; Llewellyn, *McSwiny's letters*, 90, 109–13.

8 Earl of March, *A Duke and His Friends: The Life and Letters of the Second Duke of Richmond* (London: Hutchinson, 1911); Llewellyn, *McSwiny's letters*, 71–3.

9 He appears to have been in Paris in 1732, 1733, and 1734, a few years after the completion of the last painting of the series; Llewellyn, *McSwiny's letters*, 45.

10 Llewellyn, *McSwiny's letters*, 374. For a similar explanation of prints' usefulness: Rebecca Zorach and Elizabeth Rodini, "On Imitation and Invention: An introduction to the Reproductive Print," in Rebecca Zorach and Elizabeth Rodini, *Paper Museums: The Reproductive Print in Europe, 1500–1800* (Chicago, IL: Smart Museum, University of Chicago, 2005), 7 and Benedict Leca, "An Art Book and Its Viewers: The 'Recueil Crozat' and the Uses of Reproductive Engraving," *Eighteenth-Century Studies*, 38 (2005): 630.

In a related vein, prints have also provided valuable records of the appearance of works of art that are no longer extant or traceable; see Caroline Karpinski, "The Print in Thrall to Its Original: A Historiographic Perspective," *Studies in the History of Art*, 20 (1989): 101, https://www.jstor.org/stable/42620159. That purpose is served by the reproductive engraving from the *Tombeaux* of the allegorical tomb for Chancellor William Cowper, although a painted copy of the original also exists; Knox, *Tombs*, 234.

11 Antony Griffiths, "Print Collecting in Rome, Paris, and London in the Early Eighteenth Century," *Harvard University Art Museums Bulletin*, 2, no. 3 (Spring 1994): 37, 44.

12 Llewellyn, *McSwiny's letters*, 78.

13 Antony Griffiths, "The Prints and Drawings in the Library of Consul Joseph Smith," *Print Quarterly*, 8 (1991): 132–4, https://www.jstor.org/stable/41824637.

14 Griffiths, "Smith," 136–9; Griffiths, "Print Collecting," 45.

15 Tim Clayton, "Book Illustration and the World of Prints," in *The Cambridge History of the Book in Britain, V, 1695–1830*, eds. Michael Suarez and Michael Turner (Cambridge University Press, 2014), 230–2; Anne Betty Weinshenker, "McSwiny's Unique Projects: The *Tombeaux des princes*," *The Papers of the Bibliographical Society of America*, 110 (2016): 26.

16 Weinshenker, "McSwiny's," 6–13.
17 He received a minor government position in 1743; perhaps the security it provided, together with his aging, caused him to lose interest in the *Tombeaux* project; Llewellyn, *McSwiny's letters*, 47.
18 https://gallica.bnf.fr/ark:/12148/bpt6k108373v/f3.item. "Intaglio" refers to printmaking techniques, such as engraving or etching, in which the image to be printed is incised into the printing plate.
19 Claude-Henri Watelet, "Gravure," *Encyclopédie, ou dictionnaire raisonné des sciences, des arts et des métiers, etc.*, eds. Denis Diderot and Jean le Rond d'Alembert. University of Chicago: ARTFL Encyclopédie Project (Spring 2021 Edition), Robert Morrissey and Glenn Roe (eds.), http://encyclopedie.uchicago.edu/, 7: 877–90.
20 See note 9 above.
21 Karpinski, "Print in Thrall," 101–9; Zorach and Rodini, "On Imitation," 3–7.
22 McSwiny's name exists in variant spellings, one being "MacSwiny"; Llewellyn, *McSwiny's letters*, 15.
23 Zorach and Rodini, "On Imitation," 28, n. 59: "it was probably quite rare for an artist [printmaker] to work directly from the painted image."
24 Andrea Van Houtven, "Two Drawings by Domenico Maria Fratta for McSwiny's 'Tombeaux des Princes,'" *Master Drawings*, 37 (1999): 51.
25 Llewellyn, *McSwiny's letters*, 43.
26 Van Houtven, "Two Drawings," 53, n. 12; Llewellyn, *McSwiny's letters*, 43.
27 Llewellyn, *McSwiny's letters*, 200–2.
28 Michael Bury, "On Some Engravings by Giorgio Ghisi Commonly Called 'Reproductive,'" *Print Quarterly* 10 (1993): 4, https://www.jstor.org/stable/41824748.
29 Llewellyn, *McSwiny's letters*, 373.
30 *Iconologia: or, Moral Emblems*, by Caesar Ripa (London: Motte, 1709); see Hans-Joachim Zimmermann, "English Translations and Adaptations of Cesare Ripa's *Iconologia*: From the 17th to the 19th Century," *De zeventiende eeuw*, 11 (1995): 17–25.
31 *Iconologia di Cesare Ripa Perugino*, ed. Giovanni Zaratino-Castellini (Venice: Tomasini, 1645), 84–5, 201, 589–90, https://books.google.com/books?id=ocsQcOQLh5MC&pg=PA1&dq=ripa+iconologia&hl=en&sa=X&ved=0ahUKEwjf1q6w37PJAhVCGz4KHTXcARQQuwUIJz-AB#v=onepage&q&f=false.
32 A drawing study for this figure is in the Louvre: Giambattista Pittoni, "A Kneeling Bishop Reading," INV 18193, recto.
33 Abraham Bosse, *Traité des manieres de graver en taille-douce* (Paris, 1645), 3 states that he attempts to make etched lines look like those of engravings.
34 Zorach and Rodini, "On Imitation," 7; Leca, "An Art Book," 640–1.
35 Llewellyn, *McSwiny's letters*, 375.
36 Llewellyn, *McSwiny's letters*, 374.
37 Weinshenker, "McSwiny's," 3.

Bibliography

Bosse, Abraham. *Traicté des manieres de graver en taille douce* (Paris: Bosse, 1645). Kansas City, MO: Linda Hall Library.

Brown, Kathryn, ed., *The Routledge Companion to Digital Humanities and Art Hist*ory. New York: Routledge, 2020.

Griffiths, Antony. "The Prints and Drawings in the Library of Consul Joseph Smith." *Print Quarterly* 8, no. 2 (June 1991): 127–39. https://www.jstor.org/stable/41824637.

Griffiths, Antony. "Print Collecting in Rome, Paris, and London in the Early Eighteenth Century." *Harvard University Art Museums Bulletin* 2, no. 3 (Spring 1994): 37–58.

Karpinski, Caroline. "The Print in Thrall to Its Original: A Historiographic Perspective." *Studies in the History of Art* 20 (1989): 101–9. https://www.jstor.org/stable/42620159.

Knox, George. "'The Tombs of Famous Englishmen' as Described in the Letters of Owen McSwiny to the Duke of Richmond." *Arte Veneta* 37 (1983): 228–35.

Leca, Benedict. "An Art Book and Its Viewers: The 'Recueil Crozat' and the Uses of Reproductive Engraving." *Eighteenth-Century Studies* 38, no. 4 (Summer 2005): 623–49.

Llewellyn, T.D., ed., *Owen McSwiny's Letters, 1720–1744.* Verona: Scripta, 2009.

Van Houtven, Andrea. "Two Drawings by Domenico Maria Fratta for McSwiny's 'Tombeaux des Princes.'" *Master Drawings* 37, no. 1 (Spring1999): 47–54.

Weinshenker, Anne Betty. "McSwiny's Unique Projects: The *Tombeaux des princes.*" *The Papers of the Bibliographical Society of America* 110, no. 1 (2016): 1–30.

Zorach, Rebecca and Elizabeth Rodini, eds. *Paper Museums: The Reproductive Print in Europe, 1500–1800.* Chicago, IL: Smart Museum, University of Chicago, 2005.

4

MAPS, VIEWS, AND CHOROGRAPHIES

An Examination of the Depiction of Place and the Representation of Architecture in the *Civitates Orbis Terrarum (1572)*

Brittany Forniotis

When scholars seek to understand the appearance, urban situation, and significance of the monuments and institutions of medieval and early modern cities, they are often met with an absence of extant infrastructure, archaeological remains, or archival evidence.[1] One recuperative method to which scholars turn is the analysis of contemporary chorographic images that visualize the city, its architecture, and its culture.[2] Chorographies uniquely visualize cities and their immediate surrounds utilizing an elevated viewpoint, commingled visual perspectives, prominent and recognizable architecture, and a general disinterest in charting the navigability of the urban fabric. An excellent corpus of such images is the *Civitates Orbis Terrarum*, a six-volume atlas created by Georg Braun (1541–622) and Franz Hogenberg (1535–690) along with a team of engravers and cartographers. Published between 1572 and 1617, the volumes contain 546 views of cities from across the globe.[3] Because of their precise detail, the frequent use of labels, and their bird's-eye-view perspectives, the images of the atlas appear strikingly life-like, as though one could meander down the city streets to view the monuments as they were, or pass by on a boat and glimpse the same view.[4] However, the views in the *Civitates Orbis Terrarum* are not documentary evidence of the appearance of sixteenth-century cities, despite their tantalizing liveliness and the verisimilitude of their monuments to known remains. We must, then, rethink what the chorographies of the *Civitates Orbis Terrarum* offer (art) historians of the early modern world. Through an examination of the representations of hospitals in the first volume of the atlas (1572), I explore what can be gained from these chorographies for scholarship on architecture and the urban fabric. Hospitals make a productive case study, as monumental hospitals possess identifiable architectural features and were important to the communal life, and yet are not typically emblematic of medieval and early modern cities in the same way as cathedrals or palatial complexes. Rather than attempting to document cities as they were, Braun and Hogenberg and their colleagues made distinct visual choices in their chorographies to represent specific knowledges and advance visual arguments about cities. The chorographies present the world not as it was, but as Braun and Hogenberg wanted it to be known. To begin to disentangle these visual choices, I will first argue that the *Civitates Orbis Terrarum* is an atlas comprised

DOI: 10.4324/9781003295082-7

of chorographies, which are a type of city view that goes beyond abstracting the earth into navigable geographic coordinates in visualizing cities and their surrounds. Conceptualizing these images as chorographies, I will explore what the visual choices made by Braun and Hogenberg may have imparted to the viewer with a careful analysis of the representation of hospitals—major civic institutions in medieval and early modern cities.

Defining Chorography

Between maps and landscapes are intermediary representations of space called *chorographies*. As defined previously, chorographies are representations of cities and their immediate surroundings that utilize an elevated viewpoint, commingled visual perspectives, prominent and recognizable architecture like that of premodern monumental hospitals, and a general disinterest in charting the navigability of the urban fabric. These views vary in period and style, but were generally produced in Europe from the fifteenth century onward. Despite their localized production, a marked interest in intercontinental travel and exchange among Europeans resulted in the inclusion of urban sites from across the globe.[5] This study recognizes that chorographies deliberately abbreviate urban spaces to assign particular meanings to them. Thus, their uses as intellectual resources are contingent on the knowledge and biases of their creators.

Maps

The images in the *Civitates Orbis Terrarum* are frequently called maps, and I contend that chorographies are a type of map in the theoretical understanding of the concept, but are not synonymous with the common definition of maps. Maps are generally understood today as factual and objective two-dimensional representations of the earth used for navigation; however, scholars understand them as representations that express the worldviews and epistemologies of their creators.[6]

Theorists have probed the concept of "map" to produce definitions of the term that refute the understanding of a map as a direct replica of reality and instead consider them as tools for expressing ideological agendas.[7] For example, Christian Jacob theorized the map as "a symbolic mediation between humans and their spatial environment, but also between individuals who can communicate through this visual medium."[8] In Jacob's understanding, maps are a materialization of an intellectual framework that the creator constructs while trying to understand the world around them. From the physical world, to the eye, mind, and hand of the creator, to the physical or digital page, man's relationship with the environment is interpreted and reinterpreted. Even after its creation, the representation on the map continues to be interpreted in new ways by the viewer. Indeed, Denis Cosgrove agrees that while a map is the "spatial embodiment of knowledge" it is also a "stimulus to further cognitive engagements."[9] Mapmakers make theoretical knowledge about the three-dimensional world physical again in a two-dimensional form. Then, the viewer repeatedly engages intellectually with the map through the act of viewing, each time creating new knowledge for themself. Importantly, maps extend the abilities of the human body to form this knowledge about the world around them.[10] Cosgrove likens maps to tools that enhance vision, such as telescopes and microscopes. In maps, artists visualize the world at scales that are impossible to see with the naked eye, and that are often difficult to imagine. Artists can also bring disparate parts of the world together in a map or book of city views, as seen in the *Civitates Orbis Terrarum*, which offers images from Venice to Goa.

If maps are symbolic mediations between humans and space that stimulate cognitive engagements while enhancing human vision, then the images of the *Civitates Orbis Terrarum* and other chorographies like them are certainly maps. However, they are not maps in the practical sense—one cannot use these chorographies to navigate early modern cities on foot, on horse, or by boat. As we see in the *Civitates Orbis Terrarum* view of Toledo, only the streets in the foreground of the city are clearly articulated for the viewer (Figure 4.1). The further the eye proceeds into the background, the more closely together the buildings gather, until they become a mere suggestion of separate rooves at the horizon. The artist illustrates only the facades of the central cathedral and the fortified structure at the far right toward the horizon of the composition. This composition enhances our ability to see in that, through a clever concatenation of space, it allows for the impression of a complete visualization of the boundaries and surrounds of the city at once. The preciousness of its minute details beg for repeated, intense viewing, for one cannot take in the entire scene at a casual glance. Each reading imparts new impressions on the viewers and reshapes their understanding of Toledo through a compressed imagining of it.

In creating this view, the artists of the *Civitates Orbis Terrarum*'s "Toledo" mediate the human experience of spatial reality for the viewer. They offer a representation of the city that in many ways resembles it, particularly through its imaginings of monumental architecture,

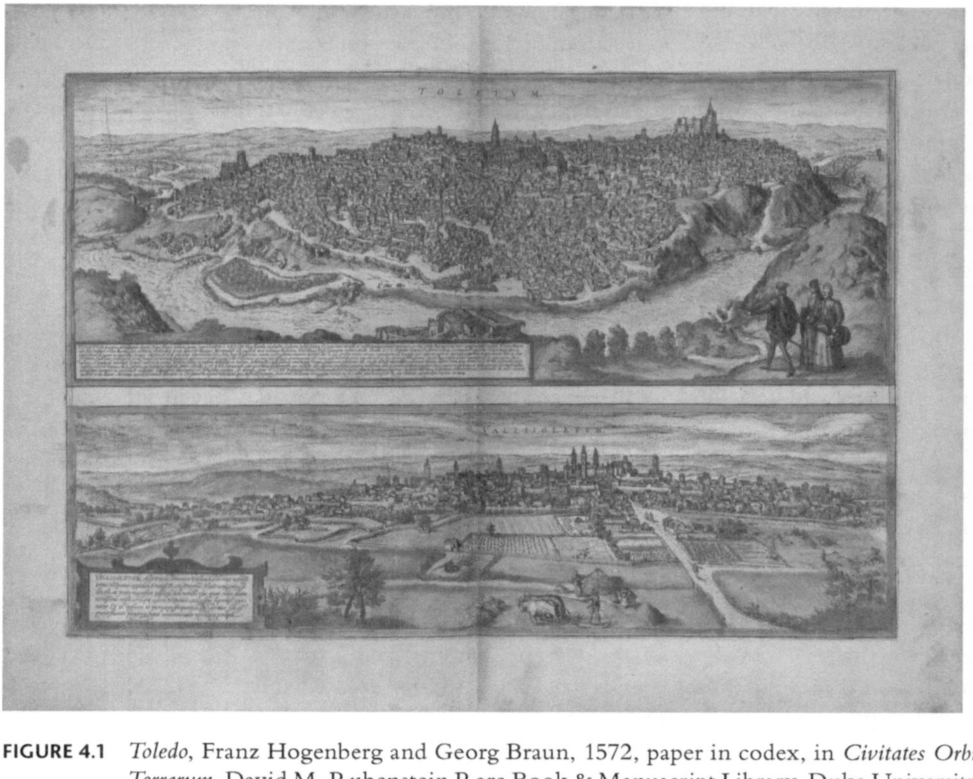

FIGURE 4.1 *Toledo*, Franz Hogenberg and Georg Braun, 1572, paper in codex, in *Civitates Orbis Terrarum*, David M. Rubenstein Rare Book & Manuscript Library, Duke University.

and yet it does not perfectly replicate it. In this way, the views of the *Civitates Orbis Terrarum* fit within theoretical understandings of "map," but not practical, twenty-first-century utilizations of the term. Because of this incongruity, chorography seems a more fitting description for the views of the atlas.

Theoretical Foundations of Chorography in Ptolemy

A common starting point for defining chorography resides in a passage of Claudius Ptolemy's cartographic treatise, *The Geography* (c.150 CE). Ptolemy neatly outlines the differences between geography and chorography. He writes that geography deals with "the whole known world together with the phenomena which are contained within" and that chorography treats the "smallest conceivable localities such as harbors farms villages river course and such like."[11] Geography shows "the known habitable earth as a unit in itself," whereas chorography deals "separately with the part of the whole, as if one were to paint only the eye or the ear by itself."[12] The part of the whole, as interpreted by early modern cartographers and humanists reading the fifteenth-century Latin translation of the text with renewed interest, referred to cities and their hinterlands.[13] Twentieth-century scholars of early modern cartography have since binarized Ptolemy's definitions of geography and chorography into oppositional terms that refer to rational science and creative art, respectively. Geography became the domain of measurements, mathematics, and the coordinate grid system, while chorography encompassed textual, visual, and symbolic renderings of place.[14] Modern scholars fabricated a dichotomy between methods and outputs that continues into modernity and continue to cite his separation of geography and chorography as foundational ideological frameworks for analyzing early modern representations of geospatial reality.[15]

However, this modern division is faulty in that it assumes geography and chorography to be oppositional, rather than adjacent or complementary. The superimposition of this supposed Ptolemaic dichotomy makes two critical false assumptions when used to categorize early modern geographic and chorographic works. First, it assumes that all representations of the earth are visual. Ptolemy's geography was widely known and studied as a *list* of geographic coordinates based on his own mathematic system for measuring the earth—that is to say, geography can be *textual*.[16] It was not until the late fifteenth century that artisans regularly made images to accompany the text; and indeed, the tenth-century Muslim cartographers who knew Ptolemy through Arabic translations and improvements did not rely on his theoretical knowledge or images therein to produce their own maps.[17] Furthermore, a long tradition of textual chorographies existed in medieval and early modern Europe, inclusive of poetry and exegetical travel writing.[18] Second, it assumes a firm division between science and art in visualizing the earth, as if geographic representations employing mathematics cannot be artistic and chorographic representations engaging with landscape do not incorporate complex techniques of perspective.

Indeed, as scholars such as Jesse Simon and Veronica della Dora make clear, the interest in Ptolemy has become an over-reliance on his definitions as explanations for why early modern artists and cartographers made geographic and chorographic images that look the way that they do. Jesse Simon argues that scholars have repeated and reified Ptolemy's privileging of geography as a scientific practice, as opposed to chorography, which they treat as an imprecise subdiscipline.[19] Simon analyzes the development of chorographic methods, rooted in Late Antiquity, to demonstrate that chorographies represent a rejection, not a loss, of geographic modes of representing space. Medieval and early modern mapmakers did not "lose" mathematical principles, but instead adopted an equally valuable alternative style that emphasized perception and experience in representing space.[20] Veronica della Dora demonstrates that European chorography had a long history prior to the fifteenth-century "rediscovery" of Ptolemy. She notes that cultural geographers like Denis Cosgrove overemphasized the connection between linear perspective, Ptolemy's cartography, and landscape in early modern representations of the environment.[21] Della Dora suggests that topography was the third category, along with geography and chorography, for representing the physical world. She argues that geography reduced the Earth to a set of geometrical points or coordinates and that chorography engaged with the formal qualities of localized regions, as seen in the views of the *Civitates Orbis Terrarum*. Topography, then, concerned itself with individual places and their location, or their place, and how they are remembered and used as memory tools.[22] Ultimately, chorographies and topographies are not mutually exclusive, and it is important to note that types of spatial representation exist outside of the Ptolemaic dichotomy of geography and chorography.

City Views

Early modern visual chorographies are synonymous in content with "city views," in which a city is the primary subject of an image. These views are not perfect replicas of cities, but construct that concatenate the monuments, thoroughfares, marketplaces, harbors, and gardens comprising the urban fabric into a representation of a city. In this way, several differentiating parts of the city are linked together into a whole, while others are omitted. As with maps, city views (and chorographies) can reveal what artists and/or their patrons find significant and wish to communicate about certain cities. Jessica Maier likens these views to portraits that fashion visual identities for cities—they present carefully considered representations of cities people who have never visited them.[23] Following Maier's logic, the artists and editors of the *Civitates Orbis Terrarum* thus fashioned identities for the cities they represented through their visual and textual choices. These choices include documenting, reimagining, or obfuscating monuments; expanding or collapsing public areas, such as town squares; and strategically labeling the contents of the views. Manipulations of the urban fabric in city views, as in chorographies, visualize a constructed version of the city that is meaningful to their creators and audiences.

A Case Study in Choice-Making: Hospitals Depicted in the *Civitates Orbis Terrarum*

To analyze the meaning-making visual choices that the creators of the *Civitates Orbis Terrarum* made while visualizing cities in a chorographic atlas, I turn to their depictions of hospitals and their architecture across the first volume of the series. Hospitals, as noted previously, work well as an architectural standard for examining the visual strategies implemented in chorographies. They range in scale and monumentality, both within and between early modern cities, with some institutions occupying donated residences in quiet urban neighborhoods and others located within grand, purpose-built edifices in the central square. These institutions were central to communal life in early modern European cities because of their commitment to the charitable care of the poor, elderly, and generally unprovided for members of society, and their bolstering of the reputations and religious experience of their elite patrons. Many of the largest hospitals also served the general public through the operation of pharmacies, baths, and gardens, in addition to their employment of people living both in the city and in the countryside estates that supported their work.

Further, hospitals were constructed on a large scale from at least the sixth century in the cities of Europe, North Africa, and Central Asia, thus they appear throughout the views of the *Civitates Orbis Terrarum*. Across the diverse cultures of the region, patrons built hospitals to care for the physical and spiritual wellbeing of their communities, hosting a variety of guests and strangers in a collective effort to heal the body and soul.[24] However well-known certain hospitals, such as the Ospedale di Santa Maria Nuova in Florence or the Hospital Complex of Sultan Süleymaniye in Istanbul, became their architectural forms did not come to represent cities in the way that major cathedrals and royal residences might. Thus, while hospitals are frequently depicted in premodern chorographies and maps, they are not a requisite for representing a city. As Maier's concept of city portrait makes clear the depiction of a monumental cathedral, like the Notre Dame in Paris, identified the city as itself while simultaneously symbolizing the religious community and elite patronage involved in its function and construction. A view of Paris in which one could not identify the Notre Dame would be unlikely to be recognized as Paris by those not intimately familiar with the minor monuments' urban landscape. Because their inclusion and realism are not necessary to identify a cityscape, the appearances of hospitals are subject to artistic choice in the way that other monuments are not. Hospitals, as minor monuments whose inclusion are not required to mark a city as itself and yet hold economic, social, and religious significance and possess unique architectural forms, then allow scholars to comprehend the documentary and polemic qualities of chorographies like those in the *Civitates Orbis Terrarum*.

In what follows, I identify and examine four strategies of hospital representation in the first volume of the *Civitates Orbis Terrarum*. Each chorography examined visualizes a prominent city, densely populated with buildings and residents from a range of socioeconomic backgrounds who might seek services at the various hospitals located therein. Despite what scholars such as John Henderson and Ahmed Ragab have made clear about the importance of hospitals in urban communities, the atlas' artists utilized different methods for representing the cities and hospitals in these views.[25] First, as seen in the view of Milan, the artists overemphasize a prominent quarantine hospital situated outside of the city walls, in a mode that highlights the externality of the minor monument to the community and deemphasizes the other monuments in the view. Then, as observed in the view of Florence, the artists relegate all minor monuments into the background of the view, such that hospitals are curiously absent, despite their historical prominence in the community. The third strategy, which the artists deploy in the view of Istanbul, subsumes hospitals within the larger religious complexes they often inhabit. A final strategy the artists of the atlas implement is depicting monumental hospitals as prominent and central to their communities; however, in a singular fashion.

Milan

The *Civitates Orbis Terrarum* view of Milan depicts the city encased within crest-shaped defensive walls and a moat that seems to divert the Ticino and Adda Rivers to wrap deftly around the city (Figure 4.2). At the pinnacle of the view is the indomitable Castello

Sforzesco (c. 1450), the ducal seat of the ruling Sforza family. The dense medieval city fans out from the grounds of the castle, and between this urban core and defensive walls is a register of pastoral estates. Outside the walls, the view shows fields and forests, and a large, courtyarded structure with its own moat that rivals the Castello Sforzesco in size. In fact, this fortress-like structure depicts the Lazzaretto di Milano, a hospital built outside of the city walls to treat plague victims in the late fifteenth century. In the view of Milan, the engravers highlight the Lazzaretto through its comparatively enormous structural size on the map and its singularity: it is the only edifice outside of the defensive wall.

But why depict the Lazzaretto in this way? Surely, there were other structures lying outside of the walls of Milan in the sixteenth century. And it seems unlikely that the size of the hospital actually outstripped the massive Duomo di Milano (c. 1386), here seen in the middle of the map (labeled "Il Duomo") or the Castello Sforzesco. Perhaps this documentary discrepancy is merely an issue of competing perspectives, as one might note that the horse-drawn carriage just to the left of the cartouche in the bottom-right corner of the view is also inordinately large given the size of the buildings within Milan's walls and the minute trees surrounding the out-lying fields. Although the mixed perspective of the view—categorical of chorographies—plays a role here, a more profitable line of thinking considers the representation of the Lazaretto in light of the heightened significance of plague hospitals in the late-sixteenth century.

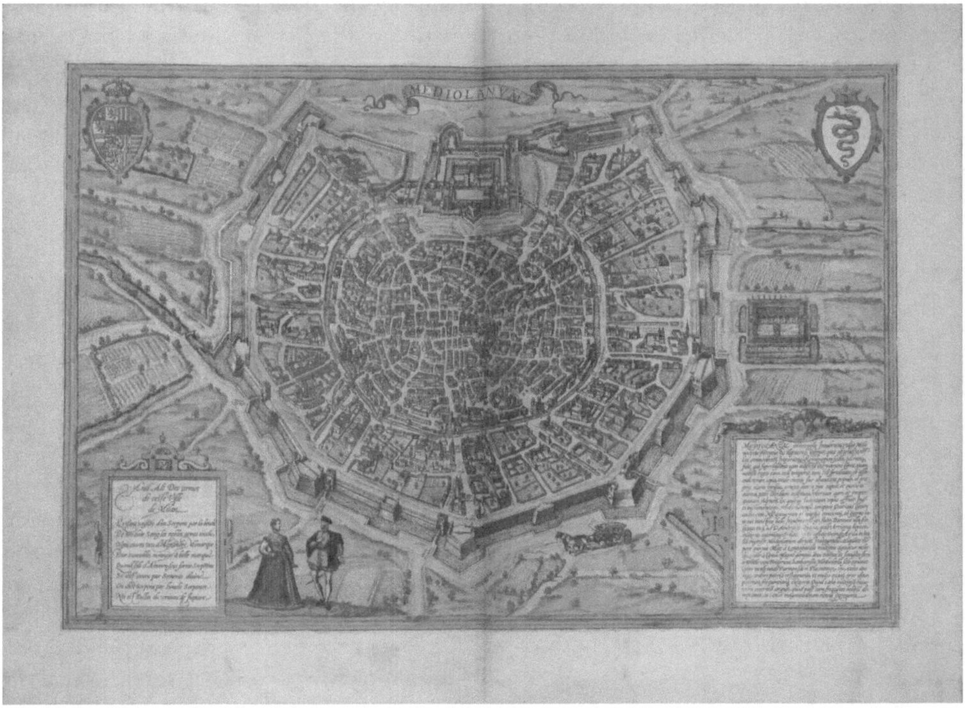

FIGURE 4.2 *Milan*, Franz Hogenberg and Georg Braun, 1572, paper in codex, in *Civitates Orbis Terrarum*, David M. Rubenstein Rare Book & Manuscript Library, Duke University.

Milan enacted aggressive legislation to contain the plague and its victims in the early fifteenth century.[26] Prior to Sforza's rule, the Visconti established a permanent health commission to oversee the administration of local hospitals, ultimately leading to the establishment of the Lazzaretto di Milano in the mid-fifteenth century.[27] The commission and the hospital grew out of an earlier tradition of managing the sick which relied on their expulsion from the city. Left largely untouched by the Black Death proper, Milan enacted a reactionary expulsion policy during a later outbreak of plague in 1374.[28] The sick were sent to live beyond the city walls in make-shift huts or in camps in the surrounding woods. In 1400, working under the supervision of Duke Giangaleazzo Visconti, the health commission established two temporary extramural *lazzaretti* to segregate the infected in more humane conditions.[29] The Lazzaretto di Milano and its complex functionally replaced these remote temporary structures in the mid-fifteenth century and continued to house plague victims in the incessant recurrences of the plague that swept through the city until the eighteenth century.

To decode the inflated scale of the Lazzaretto, we can compare it to the Ospedale Maggiore, a renowned courtyarded hospital built in 1456, which blends into the urban fabric as one of many red-roofed structures found in the *Civitates Orbis Terrarum*'s Milan.[30] At a glance, the viewer cannot make out the Ospedale Maggiore, but has no difficulty spotting the Lazzaretto looming over the hinterlands of the city. Interestingly, the Ospedale Maggiore is labeled as a "Hospital," but the Lazzaretto carries the label "Gregorio," for a church originally located near the structure. The prominence of the fortress-like *lazzaretto*, its walls in parallel with those of the city, suggests a tension between the city and the extramural hospital. Its size and solitude endow it with a visual pride-of-place in this engraving of the city; the *lazzaretto* is both included in this representation of the city of Milan and yet, decidedly apart from it in a way in which the Ospedale Maggiore, a renowned general hospital known across Europe for its progressive architectural design, is not. The artists of the atlas rendered the Lazzaretto in such a way that clearly distinguishes it from other structures that severed similar purposes, resulting in its perceived prominence to the viewer unfamiliar with the city of Milan.

Florence

Florence is a particularly interesting case study for the depiction of hospitals, as the city had at least sixty-eight premodern hospitals distributed throughout the heart of the medieval city.[31] Yet the view in the *Civitates Orbis Terrarum* does not indicate their presence or the presence of secondary monuments within the city. In the congested scene, the two halves of the city, split by the Arno River, are crowded with densely packed buildings. No visual indication exists of streets or public squares inside the walls of the city proper, and the lack of legend or labels throughout the composition further inhibits the identification of major hospitals-cum-monuments such as the Ospedale degli Innocenti (Hospital of the Innocents, c. 1419), designed by the famed architect, Filippo Brunelleschi (1377–446). One can easily identify the iconic dome of the Duomo di Firenze (1296–436) and façade and tower of the Palazzo Vecchio (1299–314), both of which tower over the cityscape and signal the dominance of the Medici family, the most well-known patrons and inhabitants associated with of both architectural projects. The artists of the chorography imagine a Florence disconnected from the immense medical community materialized within its walls. Instead, they characterize the city through well-known architecture connected to the power of the Medici.[32]

Istanbul

Another chorography in the *Civitates Orbis Terrarum* in which one might expect to see hospitals is the view of Istanbul (Figure 4.3). The development of hospitals in Istanbul stretches back to at least the twelfth century, with the construction of the Pantokrator Monastery (1126) and its accompanying hospital patronized by Empress Irene of Hungary (1088–134) and husband Emperor John II Komnenos (1118–43) (now the Zeyrek Mosque).[33] Both Byzantine and Ottoman rulers built hospitals in the city: Mehmed II (1432–481) built the Fatih Mosque Complex, inclusive of a major hospital, begun in 1463 on the site of the Church of the Holy Apostles in what is now the Fatih district of the city; similarly, Suleiman the Magnificent (1494–566) commissioned Mimar Sinan (c. 1488/1490–588) to construct the Süleymaniye Mosque Complex in 1550.[34] Like those of the Fatih and Süleymaniye Mosque Complexes, hospitals that were part of larger religious complexes were common in premodern cities. These charitable structures often featured worship spaces, schools, bathhouses, and soup kitchens. In Muslim communities, hospitals and comparable institutions required endowment documents called waqfiyya (s. waqf) to legally ensure their functionality after the death of their patron. Waqfiyya typically endowed the institutions with land or shops to fund the often detailed wishes of their patrons, which could include paying physicians' salaries, providing for Qur'anic reciters or madrasa students, or offering alms for the poor.[35] Endowed complexes contributed to the development of cities by bringing in cash and goods from the surrounding lands, employing residents in their many enterprises, and benefitting the spiritual wellbeing of their illustrious patrons.

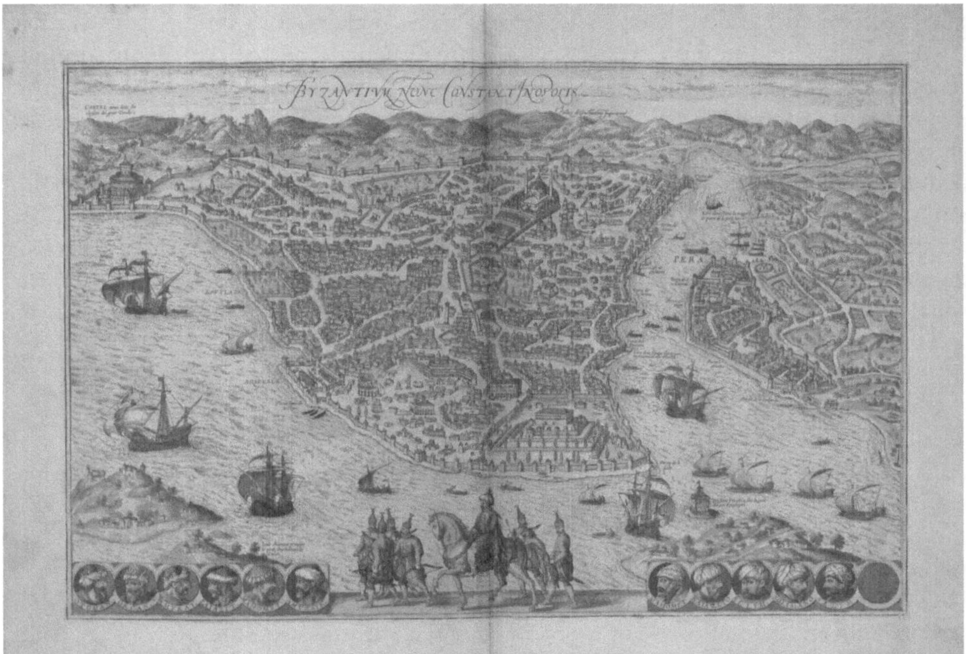

FIGURE 4.3 *Istanbul/Byzantium now Constantinople,* Franz Hogenberg and Georg Braun, 1572, paper in codex, in Civitates Orbis Terrarum, David M. Rubenstein Rare Book & Manuscript Library, Duke University.

Despite their significance across the diverse cultural groups of the city, in the view of Istanbul, no clearly identifiable free-standing hospitals are documented. Instead the hospitals of the city are subsumed into the iconography of the religious structures they accompany, as in the Fatih Hospital, or are not documented at all. The composition of the view of Istanbul favors that of Milan, rather than the highly compressed view of Florence, so one can clearly identify the representations of monuments, streets, and houses. The Pantokrator Hospital, by then the Zeyrek Mosque, the Fatih Mosque Hospital, and the Süleymaniye Hospital are all located near one another in the Fatih district of the city, which is represented in the upper right area of the walled portion of Istanbul. Yet the only monuments identified in this part of the view are the "Almaratro" (the Italian name for the Fatih mosque complex), the seat of the Orthodox Patriarchate "Patriarchato", and a theater, "Theatro."[36] Although the *Civitates Orbis Terrarum* view of Istanbul dates to roughly a century after the beginning of Ottoman rule, it seems that Braun and Hogenberg chose to largely omit the Ottoman presence in the city and to perpetuate information found in older views.

Across the chorography of Istanbul, the references to the built environment of its Ottoman rulers remain few. While their portrait busts frame the party of soldiers crossing the bottom of the picture plane and the Fatih Mosque Complex clearly resembles an Ottoman religious structure with its forest of blue domes, the Italian labels adorning the view and the latinized monuments resist the political reality of the city. The following four monuments alert the reader to Turkish life in the city: the Turkish cemetery at Pera ("Sepulture de Turchi"), the terraced Topkapı Palace ("Seraglio Nouo habita el gran Turcho"), the Ottoman Treasury ("Castel nouo doue sta eltesoro del gran Turcho"), and the double-walled Old Palace ("Seraglia Vechio").[37] The remainder of the labels and structures represented on the view refers to churches, cathedrals, and ancient Roman monuments, such as columns and theaters. Visually, the church spires, protruding columns, and languishing ruins evoke the trappings of Rome—to which Constantinople has often been compared—rather than presenting a new portrait of the city inclusive of the slate-blue domes of Ottoman mosques and palaces that populated Istanbul in the late-sixteenth century.[38] Perhaps, the illustrators exclude the hospitals because they do not meaningfully contribute to the presentation of Istanbul as a mirror of Rome in the way that ancient ruins and medieval churches do. At least in the case of the Fatih Mosque Complex, the hospital technically exists in the view, but it does not receive the same treatment as the hospitals in Milan, for example.

Lisbon

Finally, the view of Lisbon offers the fourth way in which hospitals are represented in the *Civitates Orbis Terrarum*. The composition of this view initially offers the viewer large swaths of tan beach and harbor to embark their mental journey; however, the buildings quickly join forces and prevent the viewer from identifying pathways through the urban fabric. As the buildings of the city rise up the hills of the background, several accessible pockets offer the eye relief from the multitude of roofs. Beyond the portside structures, few monuments are distinct enough for the viewer to immediately recognize. In fact, the view, much like Florence, is completely devoid of labels indicating buildings and regions of the city. The main focal points of the sweeping vista of Lisbon are the well-outfitted ships parading past the coast and the towers of the large fortified buildings at the highest elevation of the city just to the right of the middle of the image.

Despite the spatial compression across large swaths of the city, the view of Lisbon offers the viewer at least one monumental hospital: the Hospital Real de Todos-os-Santos (All Saints Royal Hospital, built between 1492 and 1504). This structure is visible in the center of the city and it is depicted as a rectangular building with two cruciform courtyards. In the center of the hospital's courtyards is a large chapel, complete with a massive tower on the east end. The grand staircase of the entrance opens onto a large public square, with people meandering about. This detail is key: the Hospital Real's position as the face of the only public square portrayed in the view makes its importance to Lisbon clear. Public squares were the heart of public life in medieval and early modern cities, and their use as gathering places for the people dates to at least ancient Roman forums.[39] That the monumental hospital comprises part of the public square indicates its significance in Braun and Hogenberg's imagining of the city. Here, the hospital is at the community's nucleus.

However, without a standardized iconography to indicate "hospital" in the represented architecture of the structure, the uninformed viewer might not identify this building as a hospital. The artists of the *Civitates Orbis Terrarum* visualize churches and cathedrals with soaring steeples topped by crosses and often attempt to recreate the actual features of iconic cathedrals, such as with the dome and façade of the Duomo in Florence. Similarly, the artists represented the Fatih Mosque Complex as an amalgamation of its iconographic architectural features—the slender minarets, the slate-blue field of small domes, and the crescent moons symbolic of Islam. Early modern hospitals lack such iconographic architecture, except perhaps the prominent, central courtyards. As courtyards are not unique to hospitals, the viewer is left to make a critical inference about what the large double court-yarded building in the center of Lisbon represents. In the constructed imagining of the city, the architecture of a prominent medical institution becomes indistinguishable from a government or palatial building.

Conclusion

From this examination of the nature of chorographic views, and the representation of buildings such as hospitals therein, scholars seeking information on premodern cities may make the following conclusions. Despite the high level of architectural detail and life-like impressions artists provide of the cities in their chorographies, they are not replicas of reality. Instead, it is productive to conceptualize chorographies as concatenated representations of urban regions that martial specific knowledges of far-flung cities to create visual arguments. Therefore, it is not advisable to consider them as evidence for architectural change over time for either monuments or for the layout of the urban fabric. What can be learned from such chorographies, then, is how their creators, like Braun, Hogenberg, and their associates for the *Civitates Orbis Terrarum*, wanted to present the world around them. In the view of Milan, we perhaps see latent trauma or fear of past and future bubonic plague outbreaks made physical in the foreboding presence of the Lazzaretto di Milano.[40] The Florentine view suggests a crowded, unnavigable city, where the Medici overlords firmly rule. Braun and Hogenberg's view of Istanbul reveals an uncomfortable relationship between European viewers and the Ottomans who ruled the city. The creators only cede the Ottomans the foreground—the represented architecture of the city remains in the hands of the Europeans. Finally, in Lisbon, the unlabeled monuments blend together, clarifying the difficulty of identifying specific architecture in chorographies. Chorographies describe cities and their hinterlands much like portraiture describes a sitter. For historians, they do not provide documentary evidence, but rather illuminate the ways in which premodern people understood the world around them.

Notes

1 I would like to extend my sincerest gratitude to Philip J. Stern, Ph. D., Edward Triplett, Ph. D., Rosalind Rothwell, Samantha Schmidt, Andrea C. Snow, Ph. D., and the organizers and participants of the Ohio State University Medieval and Renaissance Graduate Student Association's Graduate Student Symposium in 2021, who all provided feedback and commentary on this project. Additionally, I would like to thank the editors of this volume for including my work.

2 Though not discussed in detail in this paper, the chorographies in the *Civitates Orbis Terrarum* often feature conversant figures in detailed regional costuming or miniature figures engaging in labor. Or, as in the view of Istanbul later discussed, the image includes framed portrait busts of the Ottoman rulers, with the final frame left empty.

3 For more on the history of such atlases, the circumstances of the facture of the *Civitates Orbis Terrarum*, and the symbolic nature of perspectival points, see Petruţa Năiduţ, "A Book of Cities: Mapping Urban Space in Braun and Hogenberg's Civitates Orbis Terrarum (1572–1617)," *American, British and Canadian Studies* 34, no. 1 (2020): 8–25.

4 Schmidt notes that Braun and Hogenberg established the following generic convention in the *Civitates Orbis Terrarum*: a focus on "urban (rather than the more common rural) centers and commercial points of entry…" Benjamin Schmidt, *Inventing Exoticism: Geography, Globalism, and Europe's Early Modern World*, Material Texts (Philadelphia: University of Pennsylvania Press, 2015), 107.

5 For more on the European interest in visualizing the geography outside of the continent, see Schmidt, *Inventing Exoticism*.

6 Britta Ricker, Menno-Jan Kraak, and Yuri Engelhardt, "The Power of Visualization Choices: Different Images of Patterns in Space," in *Data Visualization in Society*, eds. Martin Engeresten and Helen Kennedy (Amsterdam: Amsterdam University Press, 2020), 409; Charles W. J. Withers, *Placing the Enlightenment: Thinking Geographically about the Age of Reason* (Chicago: University of Chicago Press, 2007), 13.

7 Tamara Bellone et al., "Mapping as Tacit Representation of the Colonial Gaze," in *Mapping Crisis: Participation, Datafication and Humanitarianism in the Age of Digital Mapping*, ed. Doug Specht (University of London Press, Institute of Commonwealth Studies, 2020), 29; Benjamin Schmidt, "Mapping an Empire: Cartographic and Colonial Rivalry in Seventeenth-Century Dutch and English North America," *The William and Mary Quarterly* 54, no. 3 (1997): 578.

8 Christian Jacob, *The Sovereign Map: Theoretical Approaches in Cartography throughout History*, ed. Edward H. Dahl, trans. Thomas Conley (Chicago: University of Chicago Press, 2006), 8.

9 Denis Cosgrove, "Introduction: Mapping Meaning," in *Mappings*, ed. Denis Cosgrove (Chicago: The University of Chicago Press; Reaktion Books, 1999), 2.

10 Ibid.

11 Claudius Ptolemy, *The Geography*, trans. & ed. Edward Luther Stevenson (Mineola: General Publishing Company, 1991), 25.

12 Ibid.

13 Anthony Grafton, *New Worlds, Ancient Texts: The Power of Tradition and the Shock of Discovery* (Cambridge, MA and London: The Belknap Press of Harvard University Press, 1992), 49.

14 David Woodward, *Maps as Prints in the Italian Renaissance: Makers, Distributors & Consumers*, The Panizzi Lectures (London: British Library, 1996).

15 Much of the previous scholarship on chorography takes interest in this binary and looks for places in the history of city views where art and science meet; for example, in the use of optical tools to create the multiple perspectives of chorographies. For more see, Filippo Camerota, "Looking for an Artificial Eye: On the Borderline between Painting and Topography," *Early Science and Medicine* 10, no. 2 (2005): 263–85.

16 See Books Two through Eight in Ptolemy, *The Geography*.

17 Naomi Miller, *Mapping the City: The Language and Culture of Cartography in the Renaissance* (London and New York: Continuum, 2003). For more on Muslim cartography see Karen C. Pinto, *Medieval Islamic Maps: An Exploration* (Chicago: University of Chicago Press, 2016).

18 For more on textual chorography, see Margaret Small, "Displacing Ptolemy? The Textual Geographies of Ramusio's Navigazioni e Viaggi," in *Mapping Medieval Geographies: Geographical Encounters in the Medieval West and Beyond: 300–1600*, ed. Keith Lilley (Cambridge: Cambridge University Press, 2013), 152–72.

19 Jesse Simon, "Chorography Reconsidered: An Alternative Approach to the Ptolemaic Definition," in *Mapping Medieval Geographies: Geographical Encounters in the Latin West and Beyond, 300–1600*, ed. Keith Lilley (Cambridge: Cambridge University Press, 2014), 23–44.

20 Ibid.

21 Veronica della Dora, "Topia: Landscape before Linear Perspective," *Annals of the Association of American Geographers* 103, no. 3 (2013), 688–9.

22 Ibid, 689.

23 Jessica Maier, "A 'True Likeness': The Renaissance City Portrait," *Renaissance Quarterly* 65, no. 3 (2012): 711–52.

24 John Henderson, *The Renaissance Hospital: Healing the Body and Healing the Soul* (New Haven: Yale University Press, 2006), 85–187.

25 Ibid; and Ahmed Ragab, *The Medieval Islamic Hospital: Medicine, Religion, and Charity* (New York: Cambridge University Press, 2015).

26 David Michael D'Andrea, *Civic Christianity in Renaissance Italy: The Hospital of Treviso, 1400–1530* (Rochester: University of Rochester Press, 2007), 101.

27 D'Andrea notes the date as 1450, while Janet Stevens Crawshaw marks it as 1448 in Jane L. Stevens Crawshaw, "The Renaissance Invention of Quarantine," in *The Fifteenth Century XII: Society in an Age of Plague*, eds. Linda Clark and Carole Rawcliffe, vol. XII (Woodbridge and New York: The Boydell Press, 2013), 163; D'Andrea, *Civic Christianity*, 10.

28 Crawshaw, "The Renaissance Invention of Quarantine," 164.

29 Ann Carmichael, "Contagion Theory and Contagion Practice in Fifteenth-Century Milan," *Renaissance Quarterly* 44, no. 2 (1991): 216–7.

30 Henderson, *The Renaissance Hospital*, 85; Antonio di Piero Averlino, *Treatise on Architecture; Being the Treatise by Antonio Di Piero Averlino, Known as Filarete.*, trans. John R. Spencer, Yale Publications in the History of Art 16 (New Haven: Yale University Press, 1965), vol. 2, 54–7; 138–40.

31 Henderson, *The Renaissance Hospital*, Appendix, 341–55.

32 A clear connection between the authors and the Medici family is, as of yet, unknown; however, this area may prove a fruitful vein of further research.

33 For more on the Pantokrator hospital, see Timothy S. Miller, *The Birth of the Hospital in the Byzantine Empire* (Baltimore: Johns Hopkins University Press, 1997).

34 See, Gülru Necipoğlu, *The Age of Sinan: Architectural Culture in the Ottoman Empire* (Princeton: Princeton University Press, 2011).

35 Amy Singer, "Giving Practices in Islamic Societies," *Social Research* 80, no. 2 (2012): 350. Also Necipoğlu, *The Age of Sinan*, and Ragab, *The Medieval Islamic.*

36 Maurice Cerasi, "The Urban and Architectural Evolution of the Istanbul Di̇vanyolu: Urban Aesthetics and Ideology in Ottoman Town Building," *Muqarnas* 22 (2005): 207; tentatively identified as the Pammakaristos Church.

37 As of the publication, it is unclear why the Topkapı Palace and the treasury are noted as separate buildings.

38 Though Greek colonies populated the site since at least 650 BCE, the founding of the city of Constantinople recoded the gateway to the Black Sea. Because of the transfer of the seat of imperial power, late antique and medieval scholars conceptualized Constantinople as "the New Rome." Indeed, Constantinople grew into the mantle of prestige and power that this epithet proffered over the next thousand years.

39 For more on public squares and perspective, see Marvin Trachtenberg, *Dominion of the Eye: Art and Power in Early Modern Florence* (Cambridge, UK: Cambridge University Press, 1997).

40 For more on the relationship of plague hospitals and collective trauma, see Brittany Forniotis, "Out of Sight, Out of Mind: Italian Lazzaretti and Collective Trauma in Fourteenth- and Fifteenth-Century Italian Cities," *Comitatus* 52 (2021): 137–63.

Bibliography

Ballon, Hillary, and David Friedman. "Portraying the City in Early Modern Europe: Measurement, Representation, and Planning." In *The History of Cartography, Volume 3, Cartography in the European Renaissance*, edited by David Woodward, 680–704. Chicago: University of Chicago Press, 2007.

Bellone, Tamara, Salvatore Engel-Di Mauro, Francesco Fiermonte, Emiliana Armano, and Linda Quiquivix. "Mapping as Tacit Representation of the Colonial Gaze." In *Mapping Crisis: Participation, Datafication and Humanitarianism in the Age of Digital Mapping*, edited by Doug Specht, 17–38. London: University of London Press, Institute of Commonwealth Studies, 2020.

Berggren, J. Lennart, and Alexander Jones. *Ptolemy's Geography: An Annotated Translation of the Theoretical Chapters*. Princeton: Princeton University Press, 2000.

Camerota, Filippo. "Looking for an Artificial Eye: On the Borderline between Painting and Topography." *Early Science and Medicine* 10, no. 2 (2005): 263–85.

Carlton, Genevieve. *Worldly Consumers: The Demand for Maps in Renaissance Italy*. Chicago: University of Chicago Press, 2015.

Carmichael, Ann. "Contagion Theory and Contagion Practice in Fifteenth-Century Milan." *Renaissance Quarterly* 44, no. 2 (1991): 213–56.

Casey, Edward S. *Representing Place: Landscape Painting and Maps*. Minneapolis: University of Minnesota Press, 2002.

Cerasi, Maurice. "The Urban and Architectural Evolution of the Istanbul Di̇vanyolu: Urban Aesthetics and Ideology in Ottoman Town Building." *Muqarnas* 22 (2005): 189–232.

Comes, Mercé. "Cartography in the Late Middle Ages." In *Ibn Khaldun: The Mediterranean in the 14th Century Rise and Fall of Empires*, 1:210–21. Seville: Fundación El legado andalusì; Fundación José Manuel Lara, 2006.

Cosgrove, Denis. "Introduction: Mapping Meaning." In *Mappings*, edited by Denis Cosgrove, 1–23. Chicago: The University of Chicago Press; Reaktion Books, 1999.

———. *Geography and Vision: Seeing, Imagining and Representing the World*. 2nd ed. London; New York: I.B. Tauris; Palgrave Macmillan, 2008.

Crawshaw, Jane L. Stevens. "The Renaissance Invention of Quarantine." In *The Fifteenth Century XII: Society in an Age of Plague*, edited by Linda Clark and Carole Rawcliffe, XII:161–74. Woodbridge and New York: The Boydell Press, 2013.

Crone, Gerald R. "Review of Theatrum Orbis Terrarum. A Series of Atlases in Facsimile." *The Geographical Journal* 130, no. 4 (1964): 577–8.

D'Andrea, David Michael. *Civic Christianity in Renaissance Italy: The Hospital of Treviso, 1400–1530*. Rochester: University of Rochester Press, 2007.

Dora, Veronica della. "Topia: Landscape before Linear Perspective." *Annals of the Association of American Geographers* 103, no. 3 (2013): 688–709.

Edson, Evelyn, and Emilie Savage-Smith. *Medieval Views of the Cosmos*. Oxford: Bodleian Library, 2004.

Fiorani, Francesca. *The Marvel of Maps: Art, Cartography and Politics in Renaissance Italy*. New Haven: Yale University Press, 2005.

Forniotis, Brittany. "Out of Sight, Out of Mind: Italian Lazzaretti and Collective Trauma in Fourteenth- and Fifteenth-Century Italian Cities." *Comitatus* 52 (2021): 137–63.

Frangenberg, Thomas. "Chorographies of Florence: The Use of City Views and City Plans in the Sixteenth Century." *Imago Mundi* 46, no. 1 (1993): 41–64.

Grafton, Anthony. *New Worlds, Ancient Texts: The Power of Tradition and the Shock of Discovery*. Cambridge, MA and London: The Belknap Press of Harvard University Press, 1992.

Henderson, John. *The Renaissance Hospital: Healing the Body and Healing the Soul*. New Haven: Yale University Press, 2006.

Jacob, Christian. *The Sovereign Map: Theoretical Approaches in Cartography throughout History*. Edited by Edward H. Dahl. Translated by Thomas Conley. Chicago: University of Chicago Press, 2006.

Kahlaoui, Tarek. *Creating the Mediterranean: Maps and the Islamic Imagination*. Vol. 119. Handbook of Oriental Studies, Section one, The Near and Middle East. Boston and Leiden: Brill, 2018.

Koeman, Cornelius, Gunter Schilder, Marco van Egmond, and Peter van der Krogt. "Commercial Cartography and Map Production in the Low Countries, 1500–ca. 1672." In *The History of Cartography, Volume 3, Cartography in the European Renaissance*, edited by David Friedman and David Woodward, 1296–383. Chicago: University of Chicago Press, 2007.

Landau, David, and Peter Parshall. *The Renaissance Print: Ca. 1470–1550*. New Haven: Yale University Press, 1994.

Maier, Jessica. "A 'True Likeness': The Renaissance City Portrait." *Renaissance Quarterly* 65, no. 3 (2012): 711–52.

Miller, Naomi. *Mapping the City: The Language and Culture of Cartography in the Renaissance*. London and New York: Continuum, 2003.

Miller, Timothy S. *The Birth of the Hospital in the Byzantine Empire*. Baltimore: Johns Hopkins University Press, 1997.

Năiduţ, Petruţa. "A Book of Cities: Mapping Urban Space in Braun and Hogenberg's Civitates Orbis Terrarum (1572–1617)." *American, British and Canadian Studies* 34, no. 1 (2020): 8–25.

Necipoğlu, Gülru. *The Age of Sinan: Architectural Culture in the Ottoman Empire*. Princeton: Princeton University Press, 2011.

Nuti, Lucia. "The Perspective Plan in the Sixteenth Century: The Invention of a Representational Language." *The Art Bulletin* 76, no. 1 (1994): 105–28.

Pinto, Karen C. *Medieval Islamic Maps: An Exploration*. Chicago: University of Chicago Press, 2016.

Ptolemy, Claudius. *The Geography*. Edited and translated by Edward Luther Stevenson. Mineola: General Publishing Company, 1991.

Ragab, Ahmed. *The Medieval Islamic Hospital: Medicine, Religion, and Charity*. New York: Cambridge University Press, 2015.

Ricker, Britta, Menno-Jan Kraak, and Yuri Engelhardt. "The Power of Visualization Choices: Different Images of Patterns in Space." In *Data Visualization in Society*, edited by Martin Engeresten and Helen Kennedy, 407–424. Amsterdam: Amsterdam University Press, 2020.

Schmidt, Benjamin. "Mapping an Empire: Cartographic and Colonial Rivalry in Seventeenth-Century Dutch and English North America." *The William and Mary Quarterly* 54, no. 3 (1997): 549–78.

———. *Inventing Exoticism: Geography, Globalism, and Europe's Early Modern World*. Material Texts. Philadelphia: University of Pennsylvania Press, 2015.

Schulz, Juergen. "Jacopo de' Barbari's View of Venice: Map Making, City Views, and Moralized Geography before the Year 1500." *The Art Bulletin* 60, no. 3 (1978): 425–74.

Simon, Jesse. "Chorography Reconsidered: An Alternative Approach to the Ptolemaic Definition." In *Mapping Medieval Geographies: Geographical Encounters in the Latin West and Beyond, 300–1600*, edited by Keith Lilley, 23–44. Cambridge: Cambridge University Press, 2014.

Singer, Amy. *Charity in Islamic Societies*. Themes in Islamic History. Cambridge: Cambridge University Press, 2008.

———. "Giving Practices in Islamic Societies." *Social Research* 80, no. 2 (2012): 341–58.

Small, Margaret. "Displacing Ptolemy? The Textual Geographies of Ramusio's Navigazioni e Viaggi." In *Mapping Medieval Geographies: Geographical Encounters in the Medieval West and Beyond: 300–1600*, edited by Keith Lilley, 152–72. Cambridge: Cambridge University Press, 2013.

Stillo, Stephanie E. "Putting the World in Its 'Proper Colour': Exploring Hand-Coloring in Early Modern Maps." *Journal of Map & Geography Libraries* 12, no. 2 (May 3, 2016): 158–86.

Stone, Jeffrey C. "Timothy Pont and the Mapping of Sixteenth-Century Scotland: Survey or Chorography?" *Survey Review* 35, no. 276 (2013): 418–30.

Talbert, Richard J. A., and Richard Watson Unger, eds. *Cartography in Antiquity and the Middle Ages: Fresh Perspectives, New Methods*. Leiden: Brill, 2008.

Trachtenberg, Marvin. *Dominion of the Eye: Art and Power in Early Modern Florence*. Cambridge, UK: Cambridge University Press, 1997.

Withers, Charles W. J. *Placing the Enlightenment: Thinking Geographically about the Age of Reason*. Chicago: University of Chicago Press, 2007.

Woodward, David. *Maps as Prints in the Italian Renaissance: Makers, Distributors & Consumers*. The Panizzi Lectures. London: British Library, 1996.

PART III

Proximity – The Earthly and Divine Spheres

5

ARS COMBINATORIA

Deciphering the Earthly and the Divine in the Medieval World and Beyond

Beatrice Bottomley and Arianna Dalla Costa

Introduction

How do pre-modern theories of language and signs interact with early modern theories of semiotics and cryptography, which would later be foundational in the development of computer science? What reflections do these theories offer on writing, or more broadly language, as technology? This essay examines these questions through the development of a technique – the combination of symbols through rotation – and its manifestation in three textual objects: Llull's *ars combinatoria,* Alberti's cipher disk, and the *zā'irja.*

In his 1466 treatise *De componendis cyfris,* Leon Battista Alberti (1404–72 CE) described a cipher disk, which was made up of two concentric disks attached by a common pin. The disks could be rotated in relation to one another in order create a system of polyalphabetic substitution that would encode messages according an unpredictable law of correspondence. Alberti's cipher disk was revolutionary among the cryptographic methods of his time. David Kahn traces the inspiration for the cipher disk back to the *ars combinatoria* of Ramon Llull (1232–316 CE).[1] The *ars* took the form of a paper machine operated by rotating three concentrically arranged circles to create combinations of a symbolic alphabet. Llull claimed that these combinations would show all possible solutions to questions concerning any discipline, from astrology to law to medicine. Lllul's *ars combinatoria* not only served as a source of inspiration for Leibniz's 1666 *Dissertatio de arte combinatoria* (Dissertation on the Combinatorial Art), but also piqued the interest of Pico della Mirandola, Giordano Bruno, and Agrippa von Nettesheim. In tracing the potential sources of inspiration for Llull's *ars*, scholars have suggested the *zā'irja* as a model for the Llullian device. The historian Ibn Khaldūn (1332–406 CE) describes the *zā'irja* as a diagrammatical representation of the universe used as a divinatory device. Consisting of a series of concentric circles, often enclosed in a square and divided by twelve rays, the *zā'irja* enabled the diviner to derive answers to questions in rhymed verse.

At the basis of these three objects is the production of combinations of symbols through rotation. By briefly outlining these three textual objects and the contexts of their production and usage, we hope to open up the discussion to the 'mechanization' of thought and

DOI: 10.4324/9781003295082-9

reality through systems of symbols, the potential benefits and pitfalls of attempting to trace transmission and reception, and shifting approaches to the production and communication of information through linguistic, visual, and material means.

Ramon Llull's *Ars Combinatoria*

Ramon Llull (1232–316 CE) was a Catalan intellectual, missionary, and mystic, who is known for having developed what Leibniz later called the *ars combinatoria* – a technique which Llull re-elaborated in his many works throughout his whole life.[2] What we know about Llull's life we learn from his *Vita coetanea*, an autobiography that he dictated to the monks of the Chartreuse of Vauvert in Paris.[3] Although this work does not cover every period of Llull's life, we do Llull was born into an aristocracy in Majorca, and whilst he got married and had a child, he received a vision of the crucifix at the age of thirty, which made him decide to dedicate his life to the service of Christ. In particular, one way in which he intended to dedicate his life to the Christian cause was 'to write a book, the best in the world, against the errors of the unbelievers'.[4]

His efforts culminated in the *Ars compendiosa inveniendi veritatem,* which he composed in 1274. In this book, he describes for the first time his combinatory art and shows how to use it in the disciplines of philosophy, theology, medicine, and jurisprudence. It was first and foremost, however, a missionary tool. Disillusioned by the methods used by his contemporaries in the *disputationes* to convert Jews and Muslims, he created a new system in an attempt to convert non-believers. Rather, than basing his arguments on the Bible, the Fathers of the Church, or the works of his contemporary theologians, he drew from a set of premises that are shared by the three religions of the book, which include, for example, the existence of God and His attributes. The religious basis of the universal grammar utilised in the *ars* was found by Llull in the meditative practices of Christian contemplatives. They addressed God in their prayers with what is known as the 'names of God', which Llull referred to as 'virtues' or 'dignities'.[5] These names are the common language that the three religions share and the basis from which conversion can take place.

However, the *Ars compendiosa inveniendi veritatem* is not the only text in which Llull elaborates his system. Scholars have divided Llull's production of the *ars* into two phases. The first of which is the Quaternary Phase,[6] which includes the *Ars compendiosa inveniendi veritatem* (mentioned above) and the *Ars demonstrativa* (c.1283). The second phase, known as the Ternary Period,[7] includes the *Ars inventiva veritatis* (1290), the *Tabula generalis* (1292–4), the *Ars generalis ultima* (1305–8), and finally the *Ars brevis* (1308). The second phase in his production was sparked by the cold reception of the *ars* by Parisian students, who found it unwieldy to operate. The episode of Llull's first visit to Paris is described in the *Vita coetanea*:

> Having lectured on this Commentary [on the *Ars demonstrativa*] in Paris, and having observed the attitude of the students there, he returned to Montpellier, where he once again wrote and lectured on a book, this one entitled the *Ars inventiva veritatis.* In this book, as well as in all others he wrote from then on, he used only four figures, eliminating — or rather disguising, because of the weakness of human intellect which he had witnessed in Paris — twelve of the sixteen figures that had formerly appeared in his Art.[8]

This abridged version of the *Ars generalis ultima* features in the *Ars brevis,* which we examine in this essay.

It is interesting to note that Llull calls his system an 'art' which in Latin (*ars*) is a synonym of the Greek *techne*. In this way, the *ars* is a practical tool for producing and organising thought. This technique builds on fundamental notions common to Christian, Jewish, and Islamic theology. As such, someone who uses the technique should not need to refer to external textual sources. The *ars* uses a limited set of principles in order to investigate an illimited number of topics and thus can be considered 'compendious'. It is also 'general', as it can be applied to any discipline or subject, in addition to being 'inventive', like Aristotelian dialectic, and 'demonstrative'.[9] The *ars* is formed of five different components. The three foundational components are the 'terms', 'figures', and 'alphabet'. The 'terms' are basic concepts used in this system, such as the attributes of God: goodness, greatness, and so on. The 'figures' are graphic devices that show relationships between terms. The 'alphabet' is made up of letters assigned to terms or to the aforementioned figures. Finally, two other components guarantee the functioning of the *ars* – these are the conditions and the procedure for answering questions and supporting demonstrations. Of these five components, the 'figures' have acquired the most popularity, due to the originality of their form. These can be grouped into five types: circular non-rotating figures (*rotae*), triangular figures, circular rotating figures (*volvelles*), tables, and elemental figures. All of these components can be found in each version of the *ars* in different formations. In the following paragraphs, we will focus on how the components are organised in the *Ars brevis*.[10]

An 'artist' is someone who has learnt by heart the procedure through which a coherent sequence of prepositions can be developed in order to ask and answer questions. The system of the *Ars brevis* is comprised of the following components. There are nine Latin letters – B C D E F G H I K; each of which corresponds to the fundamental terms of the *ars*. Each letter stands for six different terms that belong to six different groups, which are the absolute principles (goodness, greatness, eternity/duration, power, wisdom, will, virtue, truth, and glory), the relative principles (difference, conformity, opposition, beginning, middle, end, superiority, equity, and minority), the questions (if, what, from what, why, how much, of which kind, when, where, how and with what), the subjects (God, angel, heaven, man, imaginative, sensitive, vegetative, elemental, and instrumental), the virtues (justice, prudence, fortitude, temperance, faith, hope, charity, patience, and pity), and the vices (avarice, gluttony, luxury, pride, sloth, envy, anger, falsehood, and inconstancy).

The syntax of this system is expressed through four figures; the first two of these figures are illustrated below. Their function is not symbolic nor magical, they simply show how the terms of the *ars* are grouped.[11] In this way, they act as a tool for learning and memorising.[12] The first figure is called 'A' and indicates God and every other being of reality. This is the figure of the divine names (*dignitates*). It is a circle divided into nine sections, which correspond to the nine *dignitates*, which are expressed with the nine Latin letters (Figure 5.1). According to Llull, this figure is the ideal foundation for general combinatory calculations. The nine divine names are linked by lines that indicate the convertible identity between all the principles. The artist has to find valid conjunctions between terms and avoid false ones. The second figure is called 'T' and is formed by three equilateral triangles enclosed in a circle, which is divided into nine sections that correspond to the nine relative principles. Each triangle links three letters of the alphabet forming triplets of terms (Figure 5.2). The third figure was formed from the composition of the first and second figures. It was a table with the cells displaying the nine terms of the *ars*, which were paired and expressed by letters in thirty-six combinations. The fourth figure encapsulated all of the previous ones. It was made of three concentric circles, of which the largest was fixed and the other two are movable. Each circle was divided into nine sections containing a letter of the alphabet, which corresponded to the term. Combinations of these letters were produced by rotating the two inner circles, thus offering numerous permutations of the terms.

Scholars in the past have identified Llull's system with a form of logic.[11] However, Llull himself differentiated his method from that of logic and similar disciplines.[12] As we indicated earlier, unlike in logic, the symbols in the *ars* refer to constants, not variables. These constants are absolute principles through which reality can be investigated and the truth demonstrated. Moreover, as Marta Romano suggests, in writing the *Ars Brevis* Llull's ambition was to create a universal *mathesis* – in other words, a re-elaboration of the knowledge of reality as a complete encyclopaedia. Llull's system offers a technique that reproduces mental processes as a material and graphic device.[13] Graphic representation enables the simultaneous observation and manipulation of concepts and thus brings to the fore the relationships between them. In this way, the visual aspect offers an alternative approach to the production of knowledge. Although Llull's figures offer an original graphic form, which had a great

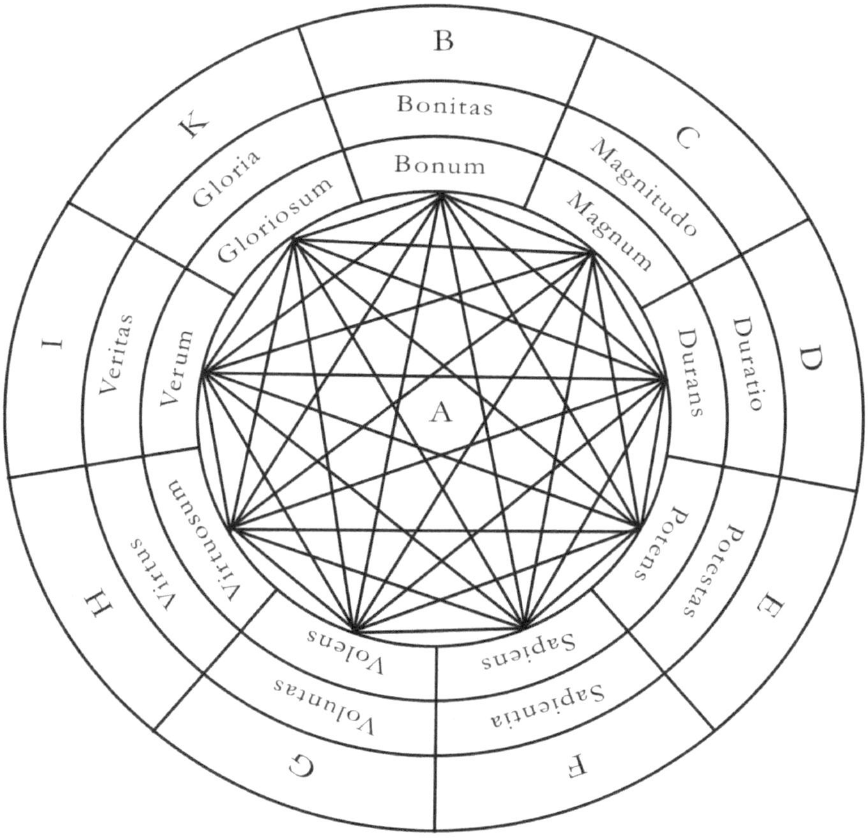

FIGURE 5.1 'A' illustrates all the possible combinations of the divine names (*dignitates*).

influence on later thinkers, the use of diagrammatic illustrations to expound theoretical ideas was by no means particular to his work. It was, in fact, characteristic of the Middle Ages. Both abstract ideas and scientific systems were expressed formally through diagrams.[14]

After Llull's death, his system was widely circulated in the fourteenth and fifteenth centuries. With the introduction of printing in the sixteenth century, the diffusion of Llull's *ars*, and the interest in it, spread widely.[15] Agrippa's commentary of the *Ars brevis* was printed several times.[16] Giordano Bruno wrote numerous commentaries on the *ars*.[17] After reading these commentaries, in addition to Llull's own works, Leibniz published his *De arte combinatoria*.[18] Llull's *ars* sparked the interest not only of the key scholars of the Renaissance but also inspired other practices and techniques, including those developed within the pseudo-Llullian alchemical tradition.[19] These offshoots from the *ars* differ in purpose and application from the Llull's original missionary intentions. However, this does not mean that Llull's visionary project failed, rather he did, indeed, develop a universal system that could be applied to many different disciplines.

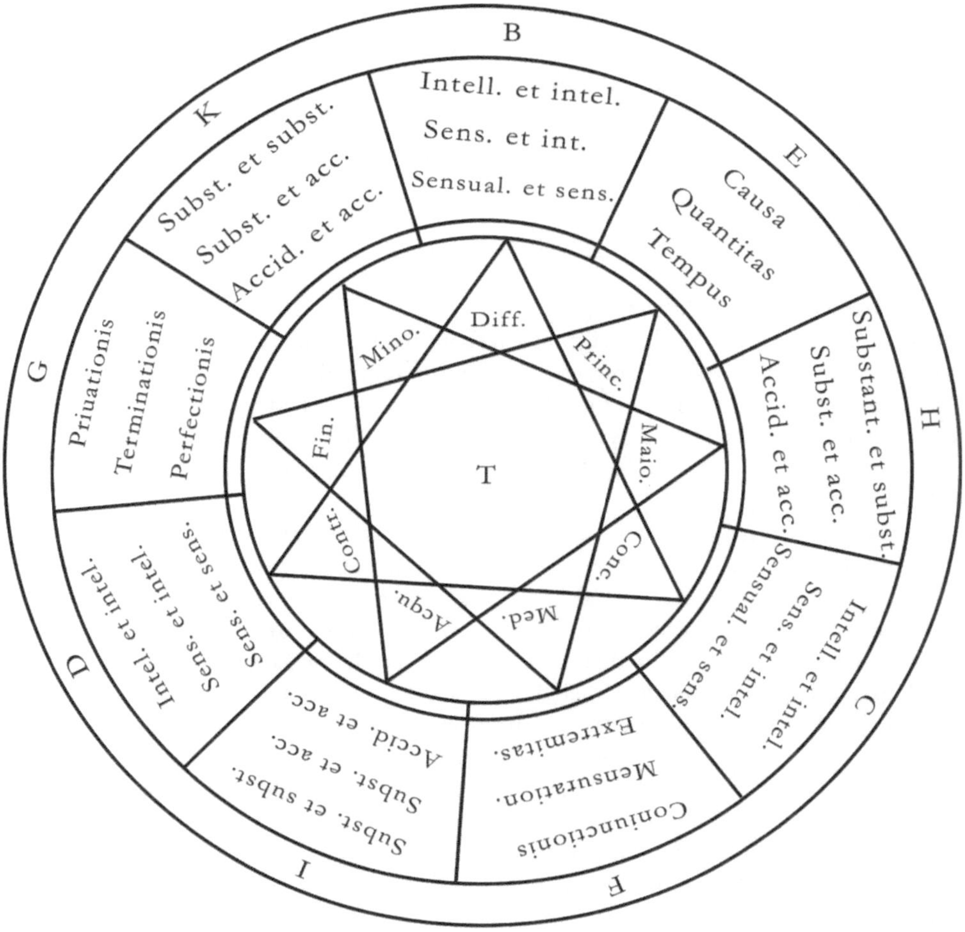

FIGURE 5.2 'T' employs three equilateral triangles to combine triplets of terms.

Leon Battista Alberti's Cipher Disk

Among the Renaissance figures that were inspired by Llull's *ars*, some scholars have included Leon Battista Alberti (1404–72 CE). Born into a Florentine family, Alberti was educated in law in Bologna. However, he also became known as an architect, writer, painter, musician, humanist, mathematician, cryptographer, linguist, and philologist. He embodied the ideal of the 'Renaissance man', for his almost universal abilities, and wrote on a wide range of topics, both in prose and poetry.

Among his lesser-known works is the short treatise *De componendis cyfris,* in which he elaborates a system for encryption that uses a rotating device with letters inscribed on its circumference. Khan suggested that Llull's *ars* served as the inspiration for Alberti's device.[20] However, this hypothesis was supported by scant evidence. Recently, the discovery of a Llullian codex, the *De quadratura et triangulatura circuli*, in the library of Alberti has sparked new interest in this hypothesis.[21] Despite this new finding, the relationship between Llull's system and Alberti's cipher disk remains unclear. Furthermore, other possible sources of inspiration for Alberti's device have been suggested.[22]

Alberti wrote *De componendis cyfris* in 1466 following a conversation with his friend Leonardo Dati, apostolical secretary of Pope Paul II. During a walk in the Vatican Gardens, Dati complained about the inadequacy of existing methods of encryption and suggested to Alberti that, given his interdisciplinary expertise, he develop a new technique.[23] In addition to giving a critical overview of the available methods of encryption, he underlines that in order to develop a cipher, 'It is necessary to consider the function that letters have in writing and what writing itself consists of'.[24] He then demonstrates how numerical relations between vowels and consonants can be used to both encipher and decipher a text.[25]

In *De componendis cyfris,* Alberti suggests that, 'a cipher should be defined as a method for writing secretly by means of arbitrarily chosen signs, the meaning of which has been agreed on between the two correspondents, so as to be unintelligible to others'.[26] He proposes a device called a *formula* that enables the separation of the form of a letter or number from its received content and produces a dynamic recombination between the two. Only someone who owns the same device is able to derive this new relationship between form and content and thus decrypt a message.

Alberti's *formula* is made of two concentric disks, which are attached by a pin that serves as a common axis.[27] Each disk contains a ring divided into twenty-four sections, which he calls *domicilia.*[28] The sections in the outer disk, which is fixed, contain the letters of the alphabet in uppercase and in the usual sequence, written in red ink. The inner disk, which is movable, contains the encrypted alphabet in lowercase letters, written in black ink, and ordered randomly. The mobile disk includes twenty-three letters and the sign '&'. Whilst in the external disk, 'H', 'K', 'Y', and '&' are substituted by '1', '2', '3', and '4' in a smaller size in black ink. The correspondents choose a shared index letter, which can be taken from the capital letters of the stationary disk or lower letters of the movable disk (Figure 5.3). This index letter determines the relative position of disks, and thus the system of substitution. The letter corresponding to the index should be communicated and changed every few words. In this way, Alberti proposes a polyalphabetic system of encryption – in other words, the encryption key changes multiple times in the same message following unpredictable laws of correspondence. This offered the most solid method of encryption of its time and is the first recorded model of polyalphabetic code in Europe. Alberti describes it as, 'the most occult and convenient method of writing'.[29]

> It is my wish that this essay be preserved by our friends and not allowed to fall into the hands of the general public, divulging a matter that is best reserved for the use of statesmen in extremely important undertakings.[30]

This final request with which Alberti concludes his treatise on cryptography, as Augusto Buonafalce has rightly noticed, has been mostly honoured. While the studies on the surviving manuscripts show that the *De componendis cyfris* was circulated among secret service agencies in Rome, Florence, Venice, Paris, and London, there is scant evidence of the actual use of the text. It seems that the text remained unknown to cryptologists, who independently recreated the system that Alberti had produced. Most scholars focused on other parts of Alberti's wide production, and thus his cipher disk did not achieve recognition until the twentieth century. He has been celebrated as the father of modern Western cryptography, despite the fact that the evolution of cryptographic techniques does not seem to have been affected by the *De componendis cyfris* in any major way.[31]

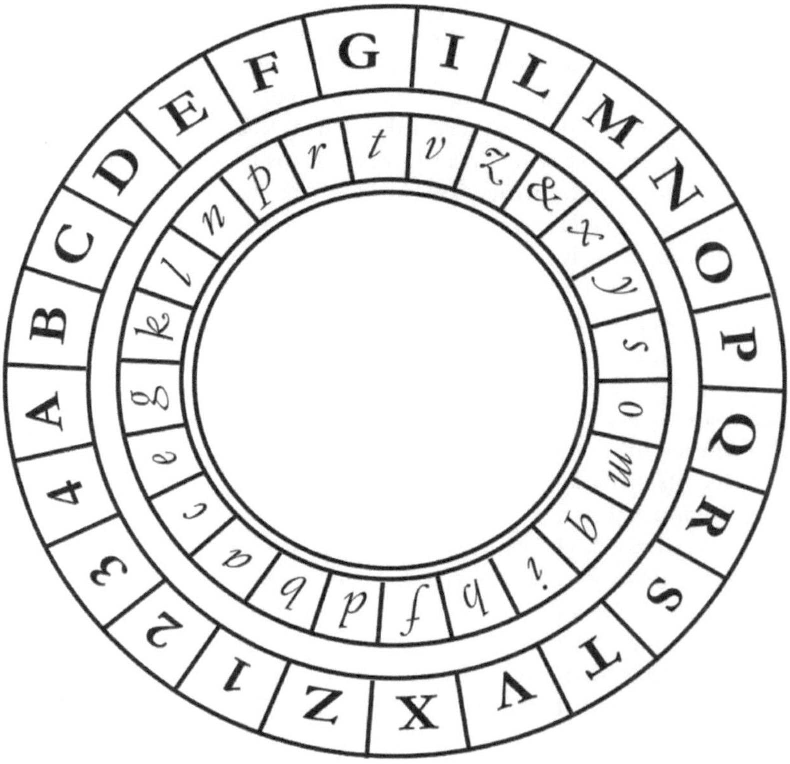

FIGURE 5.3 Alberti's cipher disk is made of two wheels are attached by a pin. This allows the inner disk to rotate while the outer one remains fixed.

Alberti underlines the importance of considering the function that letters have in writing, in addition to what writing itself consists of. Underpinning this reflection is the question of how one navigates between form and content in the production of meaning.[32] Alberti's cipher disk separates the forms of the letters from their content in order to disguise meaning. This interest in the form and composition of letters could possibly be linked to Alberti's curiosity in typography, which was in its infancy in Europe at that time.[33] Alberti drew not only on the form and content of letters, but also employed their correspondence with numbers. This alpha-numerical approach is something that we will encounter in our next textual object: the *zā'irja*.

The *Zā'irja*

As we mentioned above, some scholars have traced the inspiration for Alberti's cipher disk to Llull's, which has itself been linked to the Islamic and Jewish intellectual traditions. Both Dominique Urvoy and David Link suggest that the model for Llull's *ars* can be found in the *zā'irja*.[34] As Anne Regourd notes, the *zāʾirja* (or *zāyirja*) can refer to both a diagrammatic representation of the universe (*zāʾirja al-ʿālam*) and the science underlying this representation (*ʿilm al- zāʾirja*).[35] The astrologer Abū Maʿshar (787–886 AD) uses the term *zāʾirja* to refer to a horoscope – in other words, a diagram that displays the positions of the celestial bodies at a given time.[36] Other contemporary astrologers do the same, including Sahl Ibn Bishr (c.786–845 AD).[37] The *zā'irja* as a divinatory technique and textual object is described in various sources, namely, Ibn Khaldūn's *Muqaddima* (Introduction to History), and (Pseudo) al-Būnī's *Shams al-maʿārif al-kubrā* (The Major Sun of Knowledge), in addition to (Pseudo) Ibn ʿArabī's *Kitāb uṣūl al-ʿuqūl* (Book of the Foundation of Intellects).[38] Here, we will principally draw on the descriptions of the *zā'irja* in Ibn Khaldun's *Muqqadima* and (Pseudo) al-Būnī's *Shams al-maʿārif.*

In his vast *Muqqadima,* Ibn Khaldūn lays down some of the key principles that shape his historiographical approach, from his theorisation of political power to the division of sciences. Ibn Khaldūn places particular importance on empirical observation and a critical approach to sources. In this way, we should consider his detailed descriptions of the *zāʾirja* as the work of an observer, rather than a practitioner. Ibn Khaldūn examines the *zāʾirja* in two different sections of the *Muqqadima*: first, in his discussion of the various types of human beings who have supernatural perception and, second, in his description of the various sciences. Ibn Khaldūn describes the *zāʾirja* as a technical principle for the 'discovery of the supernatural'.[39] He ascribes its invention to al-Sabtī (d.ca.1205 or 1298 CE). However, this attribution is the subject of much debate.[40]

The form of the *zāʾirja* is a large circle that encloses other concentric circles, which contain the celestial spheres, the elements, different types of beings, and various sciences. Each circle is divided into sections, the areas of which represent, among other things, the signs of the zodiac. Chords are the lines dividing each section that run to the center of the circles Along each chord is a set of letters that have a numerical value. Some are *zimām* numerals, which were used by government officials and accountants in the Maghreb. Others are ordinary *ghubār* numerals.[41] Inside the *zāʾirja*, between the circles, are found the names of the sciences and subject areas of the created world, for example, medicine or warfare.[42] On the other side of the same page is a table with many squares. Some of which are filled by letters. The *zāʾirja* is surrounded by verses of poetry.[43] Ibn Khaldūn ascribes one of these verses to al-Wuhayb (d.1131 AD), which he suggests is key to the employment of the *zāʾirja:*

A weighty question you have got. Keep, then, to yourself
Remarkable doubts have been raised and can be straightened out with due diligence.[44]

As with many other divinatory techniques, to use the *zāʾirja* one must first ask a question. In order to derive the answer, one writes down the question in unconnected letters of the Arabic alphabet. The astrological ascendant of that moment should also be determined. The chord of the *zāʾirja* that borders the sign of that ascendant is chosen. One notes down all the letters and the numbers on that chord and converts the numbers into letters.[45] The results are entered into the table. The letters are divided by certain intervals called 'cycles' (*dawr*, pl. *adwār*). From each cycle, the letter at the end is removed. The result is a series of unconnected letters, which are used to form a verse of poetry that responds to the question (in the same metre as the verse quoted above).[46] Ibn Khaldūn describes a number of other methods, which all differ from one another. However, they often share the same basic components: the conversion between numbers and letters, the employment of an astrological framework, and the production of an answer in poetry. Sometimes the table is used to calculate the elemental relations and powers of the letters.[47] These methods appear complex and are often difficult to follow (at least for the authors of this chapter). As Ibn Khaldūn points out

> many an operation with numbers, which are the clearest things in the world, is difficult to grasp, because the relations are difficult to establish and intricate. This is the case to a much greater degree here, where the relations are so intricate and strange.[48]

However, for those who can master this technique, 'it is thus obvious that it is from the relations existing among data that one finds out the unknown from the known'.[49]

This emphasis on employing the relations between symbols is also present in *Shams al-maʿārif al-kubrā*, a grimoire that is attributed to al-Būnī (d.1225 or c.1232 CE). In fact, Ibn Khaldūn does make references to al-Būnī and we can note a number of parallels between the methodologies described by these two texts.[50] *Shams al-maʿārif* exists in three redactions; a short, a medium, and a long version. The authorship of these different redactions is ambiguous.[51] Noah Gardiner argues that the longer version – *Shams al-maʿārif al-kubrā* – which is our focus for this essay, is in fact the product of one, or more, early modern compilators.[52] It potentially draws on works by al-Būnī, in addition to other thinkers.[53]

Unlike in Ibn Khaldūn's *Muqqadima,* no description or diagram of the *zāʾirja* is included in this edition of *Shams al-maʿārif al-kubrā,* or the limited number of manuscripts that we were able to consult.[54] In some instances, the description of the methodology differs from that of Ibn Khaldūn. For example, in the first procedure reported in *Shams al-maʿārif,* one fragments the name of the seeker and mixes it with the letters of the question. The letters are converted into numerals, which are used to determine a poetic metre. The letters are then arranged according to this metre in order to produce an answer.[55] Other methods described in the text also employ fragmentation and combination in order to derive answers. However, they include the operation of magic squares[56] or astrological components.[57]

In this way, the *zāʾirja* employs the correspondences not only between letters and numbers, but also between letters and elements, in addition to celestial bodies. The emphasis is not placed on separating the form of the letter from its content, but rather attributing additional content to that form. In other words, the same set of letters takes on new levels of signification. This signification does not only have a semantic value, but also connects the letters to concrete aspects of reality, which enables them to have an operative aspect. The *zāʾirja* produces information as verse, not as a combination of symbols, and thus still adheres to the linguistic norms and stylistic modes of Arabic literary culture. Like in Llull's *ars*, the graphic aspect of the *zāʾirja* situates the user within a cosmological framework. Rather than following the traditional orientation of writing from top to bottom, the text included in the *zāʾirja* is organised along the circular and radial lines of the diagram. In this way, although this device does not have moving parts, rotation is one of its innate qualities. The user needs to turn the page around or physically move around it in order to read each section. Rotation is also implied by the cyclical disposition of the signs of the zodiac and the celestial bodies. Unlike Llull's *ars*, the *zāʾirja,* like most divinatory practices, is a tool for the investigation of everyday matters, in addition to more abstract questions. *Shams al-maʿārif al-kubrā* mentions that seekers ask about love and health, among a variety of questions.[58]

Anna Akasoy and Alexander Fidora highlight that many comparisons between Llull's work and specific texts – or, in this case, specific textual objects – belonging to the Islamic intellectual tradition have scant evidence to back up a direct link.[59] Although a number of parallels strongly suggest the possibility of influence, this question is open to discussion. Another comparison that has been drawn is between Llull's *ars* and certain elements of the Jewish Kabbalistic tradition.[60] Giovanni Pico della Mirandola (1463–94 CE) saw an affinity between the *ars* and a form of kabbalah that was chiefly concerned with the combination of letters of the alphabet that represent the names of God, in addition to their use in achieving ecstatic experiences. Both practices are referred to by Pico as *revolutione alphabetaria.*[61] Whilst the *ars* is a method through which one may obtain *scientia* (wisdom), ecstatic kabbalah focuses on reaching a state of prophecy or mystical union. Llull was in contact with many important Jewish figures living in Barcelona, including the Kabbalist Rabbi Solomon Ibn Adret (1235–310 CE).[62] It is likely – but not proved beyond doubt – that Llull was influenced by the Jewish intellectual tradition in his formulation of the *ars*. However, Saverio Campanini also suggests that another perspective is possible; that is to say, Llull's *ars* may have itself influenced kabbalistic currents in the second half of the thirteenth century.[63]

Conclusion

These textual objects – Llull's *ars combinatoria,* Alberti's cipher disk, and the *zāʾirja* – bring together graphic, material, and linguistic aspects. From the graphic perspective, their diagrammatic nature enables the user to observe symbols simultaneously and thus infer relationships between them. As Sybille Krämer has noted, diagrams enable the human mind to make comparisons between dissimilar elements and recognize patterns among them.[64] Whilst in Alberti's cipher disk, the emphasis is placed on the relationship between form and content, which is internal to the symbols, Llull's *ars* and the *zāʾirja* bring the external relationships between symbols to the fore. The material aspect of these textual objects permits these relationships to be manipulated through rotation. It is through the circular movement, which is both an implicit and explicit feature, that the creative function of these objects is realized. The creative process of the cipher disk is grounded in a semantic approach to language. Whereas Llull's *ars* and the *zāʾirja* draw not only on the semantic signification of symbols but also their correspondence to concrete features of reality, which confers upon these techniques an operative aspect. Llull's *ars,* as a tool of conversion, and the *zāʾirja,* as a form of divination, both seek to reveal information. Inasmuch as Llull's system employs a symbolic alphabet in order to subvert the ambiguity of language, and thus produce a universal system to communicate and organize knowledge, Alberti's cipher disk exploits ambiguity in order to conceal information and thus render it private.

Scholars have often heralded these textual objects as precursors of techniques found in modern informatic science. As we have seen in this essay, although tempting, it is difficult to draw direct lines of transmission among these objects, their creators, and later innovations. Nevertheless, examining these three textual objects together offers interesting reflections on shifting approaches to visuality, materiality, and language in the production and communication of information. As we have seen, these processes are entrusted to paper machines, whose mechanisms are, to a certain extent, self-sufficient systems, in as far as they operate according to internal principles. However, at the heart of such operations is the externalization of thought and its being processed through manipulation, which brings together the human hand and the machine.

Notes

1 David Khan, Preface to Leon Battista Alberti, *A Treatise on Ciphers*, eds. by D. Khan and A. Buonafalce (Milan: Tipografia Galimberti, 1997), X.

2 Gottfried Wilhelm Leibniz writes the *Dissertatio de arte combinatoria* in 1666. It is an extended version of his first doctoral thesis. In this work, he addresses what Llull had called his *Ars magna* as 'combinatory art'.

3 For the edition of the *Vita coetanea* see 'Ramon Llull, *Vita Coetanea (A Contemporary Life)*, ed. and trans. by A. Bonner (Barcelona: Tamesis, 2010).'

4 *Vita Coetanea*, SW I 15.

5 The divine names also feature in the Jewish kabbalistic tradition, see Marla Segol, *Word and Images in Medieval Kabbalah* (New York: Palgrave Macmillan, 2012), 133. They are also a key component of *ʿilm al-ḥurūf*, 'science of letters', an Islamic discipline that examines the operative function of letters and numbers, see 'Toufic Fahd, 'Ḥurūf ('Ilm al-)' in Kate Fleet, Gudrun Krämer, Denis Matringe, John Nawas, Devin J. Stewart, and Everett K. Rowson (eds.) *The Encyclopedia of Islam III* (Leiden: Brill, 1971), 595.

6 Named as such because the elements of the combination are articulated in groups of four.

7 With a reduction to combinations of groups of three.

8 From Anthony Bonner, *The Art and Logic of Ramon Llull – A User's Guide* (Leiden: Brill, 2007), 5.

9 J.M. Ruiz Simon, 'Quomodo est haec ars inventiva? (L'art de Llull i la dialèctica escolàstica)', in *Studia Lulliana* 33 (1993), 77–98, 77–78.

10 A very clear explanation of the various components of the Art can be found in Anthony Bonner, *The Art and Logic of Ramon Llull* (Leiden: Brill, 2007), 21–5.

11 For example, in Paolo Rossi, *Clavis universalis: arti della memoria e logica combinatoria da Lullo a Leibniz* (Bologna: Il Mulino, 1983).

12 'It should be clear that this Art and logic and metaphysics in a certain sense deal with the same thing, since the intention of each is to encompass all things; nevertheless, it differs from the other two in two ways: in its manner of considering it subject matter, and in the manner in which it is based on principles. Metaphysics considers things exterior to the mind insofar as they concern their reason for being (*prout conveniunt in ratione entis*); logic, however, considers things according to their existence in the mind, since it deals with those intentions which follow on their being intelligible things, that is to say, genus, species, etc., and also about those things involved in the act of reason, such as syllogisms, consequences, etc.; but this Art, as the highest of all human sciences, considers being indifferently according to one mode or another. Whence it follows that they differ in their manner of considering the subject matter (*ex parte subjecti*).' - see *Introductoria Artis demonstrativae* in Bonner, *The Art and Logic of Ramon Llull* (2007), 18–19.

13 M.M.M. Romano, 'Introduzione', (2002), 27.

14 For more information on the various typologies of diagrams used in the Middle Ages, see Michael Evans, 'The Geometry of the Mind', in *Architectural Association Quarterly*, 12.4 (1980), 32–55. Some of the most renowned medieval authors who made extensive use of images and diagrams in their works are the Italian theologian Joachim of Fiore (1135–202 CE), whose *Liber figurarum* contains

a most interesting and unique set of diagrammatic figures, see Marjorie Reeves and Beatrice Hirsch-Reich, *The Figurae of Joachim of Fiore* (Oxford: Claredon Press, 1972); and the author of the encyclopedic *Liber floridus*, Lambert of Saint-Omer (c.1060–125), see Albert Derolez, *The Making and Meaning of the Liber Floridus: A Study of the Original Manuscript Ghent: University Library MS 92* (London: Harvey Miller, 2015).

15 Among the scholars who commented on Llull's work, we find, among others, Cusano, Bessarione, Pico, Lefevre d'Etaples, Bovillus, and Bernard de Lavinheta. - see Rossi, *Clavis Universalis. Arti della memoria e logica combinatoria dal Lullo a Leibniz* (1983), 63.

16 Henricus Cornelius Agrippa, "Tabula abbreviata commentariorum Artis Inventivae", in *Commentaria in Artem Brevem Raymundi Lulli* (Cologne: Joannis Soter, 1531) (first edition).

17 Giordano Bruno, *De compendiosa architecturaet complemento Artis Lulli* (Paris: Aegidius Gorbinus, 1582); Giordano Bruno, *De lampade combinatoria lulliana* (Wittemberg: Georgius Nigrinus, 1587); Giordano Bruno, *De specierum scrutinio et lampade combinatoria Raymundi Lullii* (Prague: Georgius Nigrinus, 1588). For further information on the reception of Llull in Bruno see Francis A. Yates, "The Art of Ramon Llull. An Approach to It Through Llull's Theory of the Elements", in *Journal of the Warburg and Courtauld Institute*, 17 (1954), 115–73. This has been republished in *Llull and Bruno. Collected Essays* (London: 1982), vol. I, 9–77.

18 Gottfried Wilhelm von Leibniz, *De arte combinatoria* (Lipsiae: apud Joh. Simon. Fickium et Joh. Polycarp. Seuboldum in Platea Nicolaea, literis Spöreliansis, 1666).

19 See Michela Pereira, *The Alchemical Corpus Attributed to Raymon Lull* (London: Warburg Institute, 1989). From the same author 'Un lapidario alchemico: il *Liber de investigatione secreti occulti* attribuito a Raimondo Lullo. Studio introduttivo ed edizione', in *Documenti e studi sulla tradizione filosofica medievale, Rivista Internazionale per lo Studio del Medioevo Latino*, I, 2 (1990), 549–603; 'Filosofia naturale lulliana e alchimia. Con l'inedito epilogo del *Liber de secretis naturae seu de quinta essentia*', in *Rivista di Storia della Filosofia*, 41.4 (1986), 747–80.

20 D. Khan, 'Preface', X.

21 See Bertolini, *Censimento*, Premessa, tome I, cit., VIII–IX. in Niccolò Galimberti, 'Il *De componendis cyfris* di Leon Battista Alberti tra crittologia e tipografia', in *Subiaco, la culla della stampa* (Rome: Iter Edizioni, 2010), 137.

22 For example, Buonafalce cites some potential classical sources, including Ovid, Aulus Gellius, and Suetonis, whom all made references to ciphers and concealed messages. These sources could have given Alberti the rudiments of cryptography, although they did not necessarily determine the form of the device. (See A. Buonafalce, 'Introduction', in Alberti, *Treatise on Ciphers*, XVIII).

23 Leon Battista Alberti, *A Treatise on Ciphers* (Milan: Edizioni Galimberti, 1997), 4.

24 Alberti, *Treatise on Cciphers*, 5.

25 Alberti, *Treatise on Ciphers*, 6.

26 Alberti, *Treatise on Cciphers*, 5.

27 Alberti had previously described a similar device – also called a formula. – in *Trivia senatoria*. It was made up of three concentric disks, each with six words on their circumferences. With their rotation, the disks produced a great number of different triplets of concepts, which could provide the basis for an argument. Buonafalce argues that this device takes inspiration from Llull's *ars*.

28 It is interesting that Alberti uses the *domicilia* in this context. It usually found in texts on astrology and astronomy.

29 Alberti, *Treatise on Ccyphers*, 18.

30 Alberti, *Treatise on Ciphers*, 22.

31 A. Buonafalce, 'Introduction', in Alberti, *Treatise on Cyphers*, XV.

32 On the use of characters and writing ciphers, Alberti writes 'The meaning they will assume will indeed be arbitrary, not based upon the resemblance between signs and nature, such as those carved on the ancient Egyptian obelisks, but rather determined by convention by the men who devised the cipher. Whatever the convention, single signs many represent single letters, or syllables, or words or even whole sentences' (Alberti, *Treatise on Ciphers*, 14).

33 This is well documented in N. Galimberti, 'Il *De componendis cyfris* di Leon Battista Alberti tra crittologia e tipografia' (2010), 167–240.

34 Dominique Urvoy, *Penser l'Islam. Les resupposes Islamiques de l' 'art' de Llull* (Paris: Vrin, 1980), 111 and 162; David Link, 'Scrambling T-R-U-T-H: Rotating Letters as Material Form of Thought', in *Variantology 4 – On Deep Time Relations of Arts, Sciences and Technologies in the Arabic-Islamic World and Beyond* (Cologne: Verlag der Buchhandlung Walther Koenig, 2010), 216.

35 Anne Regourd, 'Traditions and Practices in the Medieval Islamic World', in Matthias Heiduk, Klaus Herbers, and Hans-Christian Lehner (eds.) *Prognostication in the Medieval Period* (Berlin: De Gruyter, 2021), 473.

36 Charles Burnett and Keiji Yamamoto translate *zā'irja* as both horoscope and chart, see 'Abū Ma'shar, *On Historical Astrology*, ed. and trans. by K. Yamamoto and C. Burnett (Leiden: Brill, 2000), vol. I, 493.'

37 Edward S. Kennedy and David Pingree, *The Astrological History of Māshā'allāh* (Cambridge, MA: Harvard University Press, 1973), 131.

38 When discussing *Kitāb uṣūl al-'uqūl,* Regourd refers to BnF Arabe 2684, ff. 91r and 98r, and BnF Arabe 2694, ff. 2r and 12v. BnF Arabe 2684 is a seventeenth-century composite manuscript, which includes a number of texts that describe the *zā'irja* and are attributed to various authors. BnF Arabe is a sixteenth-century manuscript, which is now attributed to Yaḥyā ibn 'Abd al-Wāḥid al-Khayyāṭ, rather than Ibn 'Arabī. In the past, *Kitāb uṣūl al-'uqūl* was ascribed to Ibn 'Arabī'. However, this attribution has recently been challenged. A manuscript of *Kitāb uṣūl al-'uqūl* is kept at Princeton Library, in addition to a number of works that describe *zā'irja.* A survey of these various sources would be an interesting subject for future investigation. For the purpose of this essay, we have had to limit ourselves to early modern descriptions of a technique with premodern origins.

39 Ibn Khaldūn, *The Muqaddimah*, ed. and trans. F. Rosenthal (New York: Bollingen, 1958), vol. I, 238. Elsewhere Ibn Khaldūn suggests that the *zā'irja* does not belong to the realm of the supernatural, see vol. I, 244. Rosenthal based his translation on a number of manuscripts, which he describes in detail, see vol. I, lxxxxvii. He notes the variation among texts, but underlines that some of these are corrections and additions made by Ibn Khaldūn himself during his lifetime.

40 For a summary of this debate, see A. Regourd, 'Traditions and Practices in the Medieval Islamic World' (2021), 475. Even the identity of al-Sabtī has been a subject of discussion.

41 For further description of the numerical systems, see Ibn Khaldūn, *The Muqaddimah*, ed. and trans. F. Rosenthal (New York: Bollingen, 1958), vol. III, 197.

42 Ibn Khaldūn, *The Muqaddimah*, vol. I, 239.

43 For images of the *zā'irja*, see Link, 'Scrambling T-R-U-T-H' and 'Ibn Khaldūn, *The Muqaddimah*, vol. III, end pocket.

44 Ibn Khaldūn, *The Muqaddimah,* vol. I, 240.

45 The correspondence between letters and numerals is determined by *taksīr*, 'fragmentation', a technique that breaks words down into their constituent letters and calculates their numerical and elemental values. Ibn Khaldūn attributes this technique to *as-sīmiyā'*, which he describes as a sister science to *al-kīmiyā'*, 'alchemy', see Ibn Khaldūn, *The Muqqadimah*, vol. III, 182.' A*s-sīmiyā'* is concerned with the operative function of letters and numbers; Ibn Khaldūn offers contrasting views on the legality of its practice, see vol. III, 179 and vol. III, 182.

46 Ibn Khaldūn, *The Muqaddimah*, vol. I, 242.

47 Ibn Khaldūn, *The Muqaddimah*, vol. III, 214.

48 Ibn Khaldūn, *The Muqaddimah*, vol. I, 244.

49 Ibn Khaldūn, *The Muqaddimah*, vol. I, 244 (Moreover, In the chapter on Algebra, Ibn Khaldun describe algebra as 'a craft through which it is possible to discover the unknown from known data, if there exists a relationship between them' – Ibn Khaldūn, *The Muqaddimah*, III, 124).

50 Ibn Khaldūn refers to al-Būnī, possibly referencing *Shams al-ma'ārif*, see Ibn Khaldūn, *The Muqqadimah*, vol. III, 177.

51 Noah D. Gardiner, PhD diss. *Esotericism in a Manuscript Culture: Aḥmad al-Būnī and His Readers through the Mamlūk Period* (University of Michigan, 2014), 31.

52 In this essay, we have examined the most recent edition of *Shams al-ma'ārif al-kubrā,* published by *Maktaba Jumhurriya Maṣr* in 2005. The edition is a reprint of an earlier edition made by 'Abd al-Qādir al-Adhamī; it is not clear which manuscripts he used. Despite the doubt surrounding the authenticity of *Shams al-ma'ārif al-kubrā*, it remains a hugely popular work up to this day.

53 Gardiner, *Esotericism in a Manuscript Culture* (2014), 36.

54 These include BnF MS Arabe 2652 and BnF MS Arabe 2653.

55 Aḥmad al-Būni, *Shams al-ma'ārif al-kubrā, 'The Major Sun of Knowledge'*, ed. 'Abd al-Qādir al-Adhamī (Cairo: Maktaba Jumhurriya Maṣr, 2005), 354.

56 Al-Būni, *Shams al-ma'ārif al-kubrā*, 354.

57 Al-Būni, *Shams al-ma'ārif al-kubrā*, 254.

58 Al-Būni, *Shams al-ma'ārif al-kubrā*, 355.
59 Anna Akasoy and Alexander Fidora, 'Ibn Sab'īn and Raimundus Lullus - the Question of the Arabic Sources of Lullus' Logic Revisited', in Anna Akasoy (ed.) *Islamic Thought in the Middle Ages* (Leiden: Brill, 2008), 459.
60 In this essay we will not be able to describe in detail any of the diagrammatical representations of the Jewish Kabbalistic tradition. For further studies on this topic see Marla Segol, *Word and Image in Medieval Kabbalah* (London: Palgrave Macmillan, 2012) and Giulio Busi, *Qabbalah visiva* (Turin: Einaudi, 2005).
61 Saverio Campanini, 'Una fonte trascurata sul rapporto tra *qabbalah* e combinatoria lulliana in Pico della Mirandola: il commento alle preghiere di Yehudah Ibn Malka', in *Studia Lulliana*, 55 (2015), 83–127.
62 Moshe Idel, 'Ramon Lull and Ecstatic Kabbalah', in *Journal of the Courtauld and Warburg Institutes*, 51 (London: 1988), 170–4.
63 S. Campanini, 'Una fonte trascurata sul rapporto tra *qabbalah* e combinatoria lulliana' (2015), 90.
64 Sybille Krämer, 'Epistemology of the Line, Reflections on the Diagrammatical Mind', in *Studies in Diagrammatology and Diagram Praxis*, ed. by Olga Pombo and Alexander Gerner (London: College Publications, 2010), 13–38, 23–4.

Bibliography

Manuscripts

Paris, BnF Arabe 2684
Paris, BnF Arabe 2694

Primary Sources

'Abū Ma'shar. *On Historical Astrology*. Edited and translated by Keiji Yamamoto and Charles Burnett. Leiden: Brill, 2000.
Aḥmad al-Būni. *Shams al-ma'ārif al-kubrā, 'The Major Sun of Knowledge'*. Edited by 'Abd al-Qādir al-Adhamī. Cairo: Maktaba Jumhurriya Maṣr, 2005.
Giordano Bruno. *De compendiosa architecturaet complemento Artis Lulli*. Paris: Aegidius Gorbinus, 1582.
Giordano Bruno. *De lampade combinatoria lulliana*. Wittemberg: Georgius Nigrinus, 1587.
Giordano Bruno. *De specierum scrutinio et lampade combinatoria Raymundi Lullii*. Prague: Georgius Nigrinus, 1588.
Gottfried Wilhelm von Leibniz. *De arte combinatoria*. Leipzig: Joh. Simon. Fickium et Joh. Polycarp. Seuboldum in Platea Nicolaea, 1666.
Henricus Cornelius Agrippa. 'Tabula abbreviata commentariorum Artis Inventivae'. In Joannis Soter (ed.) *Commentaria in Artem Brevem Raymundi Lulli*. Cologne: Joannis Soter, 1533.
Ibn Khaldūn. *The Muqaddimah*. Edited and translated by Franz Rosenthal. New York: Bollingen, 1958.
Leon Battista Alberti. *A Treatise on Ciphers*. Edited by David Khan and Augusto Buonafalce. Milan: Tipografia Galimberti, 1997.
Leon Battista Alberti. *A Treatise on Ciphers*. Milan: Edizioni Galimberti, 1997.
Ramon Llull. *Arte Breve*. Edited and translated by Marta M.M. Romano. Milan: Bompiani, 2002.
Ramon Llull. *Vita Coetanea (A Contemporary Life)*. Edited and translated by Anthony Bonner. Barcelona: Tamesis, 2010.

Secondary Sources

Akasoy, Anna and Alexander Fidora. 'Ibn Sab'īn and Raimundus Lullus – the Question of the Arabic Sources of Lullus' Logic Revisited', 433–458. In Anna Akasoy (ed.) *Islamic Thought in the Middle Ages*. Leiden: Brill, 2008.
Bonner, Anthony. *The Art and Logic of Ramon Llull – A User's Guide*. Leiden: Brill, 2007.
Busi, Giulio. *Qabbalah visive*. Turin: Einaudi, 2005.

Campanini, Saverio. 'Una fonte trascurata sul rapporto tra *qabbalah* e combinatoria lulliana in Pico della Mirandola: il commento alle preghiere di Yehudah Ibn Malka', 83–127. In *Studia Lulliana*, 55, 2015.

Carruthers, Mary. *The Book of Memory. A Study of Memory in Medieval Culture*. Cambridge: Cambridge University Press, 1990.

Carruthers, Mary and Jan M. Ziolkowski. *The Medieval Craft of Memory. An Anthology of Texts and Pictures*. Philadelphia: University of Pennsylvania Press, 2002.

Derolez, Albert. *The Making and Meaning of the Liber Floridus: A Study of the Original Manuscript Ghent: University Library MS 92*. London: Harvey Miller, 2015.

Evans, Michael. 'The Geometry of the Mind', 32–55. In *Architectural Association Quarterly* 12.4, 1980.

Galimberti, Niccolò. 'Il *De componendis cyfris* di Leon Battista Alberti tra crittologia e tipografia', 167–240. In Comitato Subiaco, la culla della stampa (ed.). Rome: Iter Edizioni, 2010.

Gardiner, Noah D. (PhD diss.) *Esotericism in a Manuscript Culture: Aḥmad al-Būnī and His Readers through the Mamlūk Period*. University of Michigan, 2014.

Idel, Moshe. 'Ramon Lull and Ecstatic Kabbalah', 170–4. In *Journal of the Courtauld and Warburg Institutes*, 51, 1988.

Kennedy, Edward S. and David Pingree. *The Astrological History of Māshā'allāh*. Cambridge, MA: Harvard University Press, 1973.

Krämer, Sybille. 'Epistemology of the Line' Reflections on the Diagrammatical Mind', 13–38. In *Studies in Diagrammatology and Diagram Praxis*. Edited by Olga Pombo and Alexander Gerner. London: College Publications, 2010.

Link, David. 'Scrambling T-R-U-T-H: Rotating Letters as Material Form of Thought', 215–66. In Siegfried Zielinski and Eckhard Furlus (eds.) *Variantology 4 – On Deep Time Relations of Arts, Sciences and Technologies in the Arabic-Islamic World and Beyond*. Cologne: Verlag der Buchhandlung Walther Koenig, 2010.

Pereira, Michela. 'Filosofia naturale lulliana e alchimia. Con l'inedito epilogo del *Liber de secretis naturae seu de quinta essentia*', 747–80. In *Rivista di Storia della Filosofia*, 41.4, 1986.

Pereira, Michela. *The Alchemical Corpus Attributed to Raymon Lull*. London: Warburg Institute, 1989.

Pereira, Michela. 'Un lapidario alchemico: il *Liber de investigatione secreti occulti* attribuito a Raimondo Lullo. Studio introduttivo ed edizione', 549–603. In *Documenti e studi sulla tradizione filosofica medievale, Rivista Internazionale per lo Studio del Medioevo Latino*, I, 2, 1990.

Reeves, Marjorie and Beatrice Hirsch-Reich. *The Figurae of Joachim of Fiore*. Oxford: Claredon Press, 1972.

Regourd, Anne. 'Traditions and Practices in the Medieval Islamic World', 468–84. In Matthias Heiduk , Klaus Herbers and Hans-Christian Lehner (eds.) *Prognostication in the Medieval Period*. Berlin: De Gruyter, 2021.

Rossi, Paolo. *Clavis universalis: arti della memoria e logica combinatoria da Lullo a Leibniz*. Bologna: Il Mulino, 1983.

Segol, Marla. *Word and Images in Medieval Kabbalah*. New York: Palgrave Macmillan, 2012.

Urvoy, Dominique. *Penser l'Islam. Les présupposés Islamiques de l' 'art' de Llull*. Paris: Vrin, 1980.

Yates, Francis A. 'The Art of Ramon Llull. An Approach to It through Llull's Theory of the Elements', 115–73. In *Journal of the Warburg and Courtauld Institute*, 17, 1954.

6

"IT'S LIKE I'M ACTUALLY THERE!"

Jumbotrons, Liveness, and the *Corpus Christi*

Katharine D. Scherff

The altarpiece is an essential part of the Medieval Paschal celebration and one that I have argued in previous work is also a virtual medium and technological apparatus. As part of the liturgical program, the altarpiece reflected the theological significance of the altar, the place where the Eucharist is prepared. For many art historians, this imagery has largely existed within the symbolic realm. Eucharist-centric and corpus-centric imagery were quite common in Northern European and Iberian altarpieces from the fourteenth to sixteenth centuries as the rise of sacramental gaze and emphasis on the *real presence* within the Eucharist grew in popularity in the fifteenth and early sixteenth centuries. Conversely, I argue that altarpieces, like Robert Campin's *Entombment*, known as *The Seilern Triptych* (c. 1425), with corpus-centric imagery, are an example of "altar screens" that mediatize the unseen much like the oversized screens we call jumbotrons that facilitate the live viewing experience at sporting and other live performances (Figure 6.1). Within a culture subjugated by mass media, conventional assessments position the live and mediatized in opposition to each other, as if rivals, where one dominates the other.[1] That is, the value of attending a live event versus its mediatization through recordings or television, for example. I dispute this supposition and argue that the live and the mediatized are complements that function in concert to create unique media. It is this very premise that I build my argument around supporting the altarpiece as not only a reenactment of the true presence but a live mediatized broadcast of transubstantiation which is then visually relayed as the incarnate or embodiment of the eucharistic celebration.

Medieval Mass and Live Performance

"Live performance" traditionally refers to a play, a musical concert, or a kind of exhibition, in real-time, performed before an audience. The meaning of live performance changes and evolves in the same way that technology, social constructs, and media shift and develop. Live television, live radio, and live streaming concerts have permeated our understanding of what "live" is. Live performance is wrapped in magic and esteem as we often place

DOI: 10.4324/9781003295082-10

value and primacy in witnessing an event firsthand. The excitement of the multisensorial happening is all too enticing for the viewer who wishes to have a singular experience. Eric Bogosian bemoans the mediated, describing the value of live theater performance as:

> medicine for a toxic environment of electronic media mind-pollution... Theater clears my head because it takes the subtextual brainwashing of the media madness and SHOUTS that subtext out loud...Theater is ritual. It is something we make together every time it happens. Theater is holy. Instead of being bombarded by a cathode ray tube we are speaking to ourselves. Human language, not electronic noise.[2]

It is clear here that Bogosian finds value in the happening – "every time it happens" and places an inherent value within live performances' ability to create community, as "it is something we make together." He connotes an agency of the live performance/audience paradigm. A similar sentiment arises when Bogosian's thoughts are put within the context of the medieval mass – a type of live performance. The Eucharistic celebration comes with a cacophony of sensorial experiences. In its very construction, it displaces time and space, suspending the toils and turmoil of the day-to-day. It was the "medicine" for those who suffered and there is an innate reverence of adoration and auspicious majesty associated with the mystic practices – an intoxicating "ritual" – "something we make together every time it happens" – "holy." Eleanor Bloomfield describes the medieval mass as "ritual...a staged performance deliberately intended to provoke a response in its congregation, which, in dramatic terms, can be considered as its audience."[3] As Thora Brylowe and Stephen Yeager so astutely observe in the introduction of their recent edited volume, *Old Media and the Medieval Concept*, the Middle Ages are the "mediating times."[4] The Medieval mass was the ultimate mass media filled with modes of reaching the mass audience.

The *Corpus Christi*

The centerpiece of the mediating medieval mass was the altarpiece. Altarpieces often made metaphorical or direct references to the body of Christ. Sequential illustrations of Christ's passion, including Crucifixion, Deposition, and Entombment narratives, were popular in the fifteenth and early sixteenth centuries. When linked together in succession, the imagery creates a sequential visual narrative that guides meditation.[5] Demonstrating "mystical devotion,"[6] intense contemplation of the flesh of the body of Christ in late medieval piety shaped the imagery both as narrative and allegory devoted to Christ's Passion and *corpus*. Models of these panel paintings include Petrus Christus' *Lamentation* (ca. 1450 now on view at the Metropolitan Museum of Art)[7] a follower of Hugo van der Goes, *Descent from the Cross* in the parish of Asteley, England (sixteenth century – St Mary the Virgin), from the Burgos School *Crucifixion with Christ Carrying the Cross and the Lamentation* from the Galilee Chapel (early sixteenth century – Durham Cathedral). These narratives reinforce the contemplation of salvation found only within the *corpus christi*. Though the Eucharist was rarely a topic of homilies in the early Middle Ages, a homily from the twelfth-century *Orrmulum* corresponds between the account of Jesus's birth in the Gospel Luke and meditations on the flesh of Christ.[8]

> And because he was made human to give people on earth his holy flesh and blood, true bread to their souls, therefore he chose that same town to be born in that is called

> Bethlehem because it signifies that house in which bread is made and that is Christ's church, for Christ's flesh and blood is hallowed in his church, there to become the bread of life to all servants of Christ.[9]

In the fifteenth century, transubstantiation and the Eucharist became a large focus of Christian devotion because Christian piety and the urge to be close to the Eucharist largely informed the content of panel imagery.[10] Sitting on the altar, the altarpiece constructed a central axis between the altar and altar imagery, thereby fusing with the representation of the *corpus christi* and the Eucharist. Campin's *Seilern Triptych* illustrates this focus on the saving flesh of Christ. A deceased Jesus is placed in his tomb from which he will be resurrected in three days. His resting tomb is a holding place to stage the preparation of the most holies. Ready to receive the *corpus* the tomb is the altar on which a Paschal supper is prepared. The reenactment of Christ's death in the image concretely merged the centrality of Christ's flesh and sacrifice with that of transubstantiation and the altar. Therefore, a mimetic parallel takes place. As the *corpus* is prepared within the panel, the bread and wine are also prepared upon the church altar. This relational imagery, addressing the metaphorical body of Christ, illustrates a tension between illusion and reality – what is real or live and what is simulation, a concept that we will return to.

The exploration of this concept is represented in the popular late medieval devotional imagery of the Man of Sorrows and Mass of St Gregory. The former archetype contrives a personal connection between the suffering of Jesus and the Christian viewer. This fosters a level of immediacy through which the viewer can access the viewed through pious meditation. Though this devotional image varies in composition, it is often conceived as an icon. The Metropolitan Museum of Art in New York has an exceptional collection of this visual troupe including Israhel van Meckenem's *Christ as the Man of Sorrows between Two Angels* (Figure 6.2).[11] The early fifteenth-century engraving illustrates a half-length portrait with a nude Christ revealing the stigmata in his right hand while gesturing with his left hand to the spear wound in his side described in the Gospel of John. Flanked by weeping angels, Jesus is seated on his tomb, referencing the site of Resurrection. The figures are positioned close to the foreground, even with its splendid Gothic interior, there is a discernable lack of spatial depth. This compressed field encourages a devotional focus on the mourning and suffering exhibited. The visual expression of pain and grief was meant to illicit piety from the viewer. Israhel van Meckenem's engraving the *Mass of Saint Gregory* (ca. 1480) celebrates and recreates the vision of the dead Christ by Pope Gregory the Great (d. 604) (Figure 6.3). During mass, the Man of Sorrows thus refutes the skepticism of the Real Presence in the Eucharist. Both compositional styles emphasize Christ's death, suffering, and living salvation. A remarkable alignment further cements the spatial immediacy of the *corpus christi* prepared on the altar imagery and the Eucharist prepared on the altar *mensa*. In the central panel of the *Seilern Triptych*, Christ is laid upon the sarcophagus slab shrouded in linen much like the corporal cloth placed on the altar during the Eucharistic celebration. This analogous imagery actualized the most sacred moment of the mass. The tomb is positioned for the viewer, as described by Shirley Blum, as "the altar supporting Body and Blood of the dead Christ."[12] This convention reinforces the spatial relationship in the analogous imagery of the *Mass of Saint Gregory*, where Christ rises from the tomb that is delivered to the altar.

These representations between the altar and the *living flesh* are visually tethered as they put Christ's body and blood in direct relationship with the altar. These images, and others like it, reinforce the role of the Church as the mediator between the divine and penitent, where the eucharist plays a tangible role as the in-between space and bridge tying these two parties together. Lamentation, Entombments, and other *corpus*-centric narratives were commonly represented with great diversity throughout the late Middle Ages in Northern Europe, Spain, and Italy. In the Northern countries, however, this imagery was more prominently featured in central narratives. Simon Marmion's *The Lamentation of Christ* (ca. 1473), Petrus Christus' *Lamentation* (ca. 1450), Robert Campin's *Seilern Triptych* (ca. 1410–5), Rogier van der Weyden's *Entombment of Christ* (ca. 1450), Hans Memling's *Adriaan Reins Altarpiece* (ca. 1480), and many more outline the correlation between the imagery that is broadcast on the altar panel and the ritual actions unfolding in the live performance at the altar. The miracle of the mass is then mediatized and projected onto a screen and tethering the material altar with that which is viewed on the altarpiece. This is grounded in the liveness of the representation.

The screen

The liveness of altar imagery is not uniquely medieval. Initially, the concept of liveness conjures the magic of live performance, the energy, the sensations, and the *aura* (borrowing from Walter Benjamin) that relates to *live* media events. In many instances liveness has been given primacy over the mediated setting the two in opposition, where live theater performance is heralded – the finery threatened to be tarnished by the cheap mass production of television, film, and the like. If we can return to Bogosian's lamentation quoted earlier, it is clear that he values the happening, the moment, and the "live-ness" that many associate with live events. He describes the concept in a romantic sense of community, language, and ritual. However, film and theater have a deeply rooted relationship. The development of early cinema was largely modeled after theatrical practice. A. Nicholas Vardac, author of the seminal 1949 work *Stage to Screen*, noted the parallels between cinematic and theatrical characteristics. Most are noted in the stock melodrama:

> This form required the presentation of a series of stage pictures for the development of the narrative, managed either through a continuous flow of these pictorial episodes in a single line of action, or, more frequently, depending upon a cross-cutting or flash-back between parallel lines of action, and employing methods of scene changing analogous to the film dissolve or the fade-out and fade-in.[13]

In 1992, Steve J. Wurtzler challenged this earlier precept where the live is considered outside of the representation of liveness.[14] This misconception then gives primacy to the live as the real over the mediatized or reproduced.[15] He challenges the binary opposition by positioning media in terms of its relation to the audience. Wurtzler submits a chart in which two various kinds of events are positioned according to spatial and temporal paths. From Wurtzler's chart, two categories of representations emerge that are neither purely live nor purely recorded, materialize: (1) those in which performance and audience are spatially separated but temporally co-present ("live" television or radio) (2) those in which performance and audience are spatially co-present but elements of the performance that are pre-recorded (lip-synched or stadium replays on video displays). Liveness is not absolute, it is "simultaneously live and not-live."[16] Though radio and television are more akin to the ontology of liveness than theater or film, despite the fact that television ceases to be "live."[17]

In September of 1927, the first "television" system broadcast was a straight-line by Philo Farnsworth. Though this breakthrough was a major headline in 1928, a straight-line was not mass marketable, therefore, few owned a television. It was not until the 1930s and RCA television broadcast signaling that the phenomenon began to catch on. The 1936 summer Olympic Games in Berlin were televised by Telefunken and the BBC aired King George VI's coronation on May 12, 1937.[18] By the 1940s, twenty-three television stations were actively broadcasting with the American-based National Broadcasting Company (NBC), Columbia Broadcasting Company (CBS), and the DuMont Television Network broadcasting from New York.[19] The 1950s was considered the golden age of "live" television. Though live broadcast is older than television, the televisual experience was born from the very idea of live. Philip Auslander observed that "the fact that television can "go live" at any moment to convey sight and sound at a distance in a way no other medium can remains a crucial part of the televisual."[20] Television was created to foster the experience of immediacy, bringing world events right into the home in a way that the theater and film never could. Auslander further observes that through the historical relationship of theater and film "television colonize[d] liveness."[21] Middle-class families now had more access than ever to live performances. Turning their suburban homes into theaters, on-screen productions of plays, ballet, and opera could be pumped into their living rooms, like the American Broadcasting Company's (ABC) broadcast of Gian Carlo Menotti's opera, *The Telephone*, first broadcast in 1956.[22] The NBC president, Lenox R. Lohr (1891–968), described the utilitarian feature of television as "broadcasting events exactly when and as they happen."[23] Interested in the sociology surrounding televisual liveness, Jane Feuer, posited that the fundamental concept of the television medium was its inextricable link to the live.[24] However, liveness, in reality, is a descriptive term, one inferring ritual, simultaneity, transmission, and reception.[25] Where the concept of a "live broadcast" or "live television" was only distinguished after the invention of pre-recorded content, the point in which it became necessary to make the distinction between a live or prerecorded transmission.[26]

Philip Auslander builds on the televisual through the paradigm of live and mediated performance in his 1999 publication *Live Performance in a Mediatized Culture*. In point, television is a hybrid – live and prerecorded material.[27] Here there is an integral relationship between live and mediatized performance. Auslander perceptively notes that since the invention of electric amplification, sound has been mediated.[28] And, for that matter, live performance in more recent history is mediated further using video projection screens, or more colloquially named – *jumbotrons*. One milestone in the history of music listening is marked by the invention of the gramophone. As McLuhan describes media as the extension of man, through this extension we also lament loss or amputation.[29] Through the audio recording of music one's aural experience is then divorced from the visual. Fortunately, this new listening media did not render the visual experience of a live musical performance irrelevant. When listening to music the imagination can run free, as the nineteenth-century impressionist composers connoted, conjuring images in our heads. Divorced from the visual, the human mind's projections of images are formed by the imagination. This phenomenon was harnessed and intensified through large video projections at live performances. "The seeds of the contemporary concert screen were planted in the mid-1960s, with light shows and pulsing, psychedelic oil-and-liquid stage effects. By the late 1970s, projected images and films were part of the progressive rock concert repertoire."[30] From here, the effects have evolved and transformed. Sporting, events, contemporary rock concerts, and even the Metropolitan opera utilize large viewing screens to amplify the live visual experience for its audience. This "simultaneous" broadcast of the events unfolding on stage or on the field is accepted by spectators as the authentically live. The audience is not moved to contemplate the authenticity of the projection of the simulcast, even with all its instant replays, scrolling statistics, and even English subtitles translating operatic arias at the bottom of the screen. The "live" stream on the video screen remediates the televisual experience of watching a live event at home. Jay David Bolter and Richard Grusin observed this phenomenon where in "the representation of one medium in another."[31] Just as early film modeled live performance, live events now incorporate the televisual experience.[32]

In a period without electronic *jumbotrons*, however, this may seem implausible. As discussed earlier, the Middle Ages were indeed the mediating ages. It was a mediatized culture projecting, reproducing, and broadcasting the unseen through media. That is not to say, of course, that the Medieval audience was not a consumer of the live as well. The mass itself satiated the desire for immediacy. The live performance of the mass was an essential part of this closeness. In *Religion and Culture in Germany, 1400–1800*, Robert Scribner notes that "for laypeople, Christ was first made present by an act of 'sacramental seeing.'"[33] Scribner highlights the primacy of seeing the live elevation of the host, and visually consuming the Eucharist as "sacramental seeing." By seeing the host through the mass or in veneration the viewer could extend the sacramental gaze, prolonging the immediacy. The representation of the Man of Sorrows archetype perfectly demonstrates this phenomenon where transubstantiation is the live and the imagery above is the mediatized representation. In the same way that jumbotrons reproduce the live action on the stage, the altarpiece broadcasts what is seen and unseen, closing the distance between the penitent and the divine.

Pious Action

Why do we make altarpieces or any ritual imagery? Walter Benjamin describes the emergence and proclivity of mass culture in terms of overcoming distance.

> The desire of contemporary masses to bring things "closer" spatially and humanly, which is just as ardent as their bent toward overcoming the uniqueness of every reality by accepting its reproduction. Every day the urge grows stronger to her hold of an object at very close range by way of its likeness, its reproduction.[34]

When the Fourth Lateran Council in 1215 codified transubstantiation, it also stipulated the yearly consumption of the Eucharist inaugurating a new ritual – after consecrating the Eucharistic wafer, the priest would raise it high above his head for all to see. The *elevatio* of the Eucharist – lit by candles and announced by ringing bells – became the climax of each Mass. As people in the Middle Ages generally received Communion only once a year (around Easter), seeing the consecrated host became a substitute. Indeed, it was not unusual for the layperson to run from church to church to see as many Elevations as possible.

The 1215 Council elucidations, including the *elevatio* and changes in the position of the celebrant, are often cited as the more prominent catalysts in the rise of the altarpiece.[35] Despite its liturgical associations and Eucharistic references, the altarpiece is not a liturgical object.[36] It is clear the Medieval person was fixated on the sensorial gaze for the very act of viewing is an act of worship.[37] Scribner described the visual experience as a "pious action."[38] Common forms of visual fixation are found in images like the Man of Sorrows discussed earlier. Scriber more specifically notes the Man of Sorrow imagery inscribed with such text as "*ecce homo*" – behold the man – the very words with which Pontius Pilate presented Christ to his accusers.[39] This *imago pietatis* is cemented as indexical objects demanding active seeing. Behold the miracle! Behold action! As Pilate pushed Christ toward the masses, the *corpus christi* in the altarpiece also cements the visual reality of space and satiates the desire for closeness. Eucharistic imagery treated the faithful to a clearer demonstration or vision of Christ's True Presence in the Host. As stated in my introduction, this imagery has largely existed within the symbolic realm and altarpiece imagery like the *Seilern Triptych* is regarded as a reenactment of the mass ceremony.[40] The revelation of seeing the *corpus christi* – beholding the man, the flesh, the miracle – is a revelation of action. Would this then leave Eucharistic imagery in the realm of the live or simulation?

Imago and Symulachrum

By the fourteenth century, the concept of *symulachrum* was firmly established in German lay literature and is later examined in French theology. By this point in the High Middle Ages, *simulacrum* was understood to be the representation of the ephemeral.[41] This precept differs from the *imago dei* – "painted images and the sign of the ideal and the divine."[42] Assaf Pinkus suggests that this difference is a matter of semiotics.[43] He posits that "*imago* is a self-contained image, striving to reveal truth that is external to the viewer,"[44] whereas the *simulacrum* may only produce "an effect of resemblance."[45] This simulation of a true model, then, reinforced the medieval construct that believing is seeing and seeing is believing. Though Assaf Pinkus applies these concepts to three-dimensional sculpture, the ephemeral divine participation is exactly what is emphasized.

The term simulacrum comes from the Latin *simulacrum – likeness, or semblance.* As Pinkus inferred, *imago* and *simulacrum* are often interchangeable in classical and Medieval text. It refers to the representation or imitation of a thing. The essence and ontology of simulacrum have been of philosophical and theoretical debate since antiquity. Simulation is argued by many to be false or a parody and therefore a perversion of the real. For Plato and Aristotle, the philosophical debate of simulacra was directly linked to the real and the many orders of simulation. Through the metaphor of puppets producing shadows on a cave wall the very concept of simulacra is unpacked in The Allegory of the Cave.[46] Plato explored many aspects of the metaphor from the puppets which represented what was outside the cave and the shadows on the cave wall which are then a simulation of the puppets. The puppets were a primary simulation whereas the shadows were the second-order simulation of the real world outside. Aristotle discussed simulation through mimesis, a representation like Plato's shadows dancing along the cave wall. For Aristotle, mimesis was the representation of nature, of reality. As a natural part of life, Aristotle claimed that there is a natural pleasure in mimesis therefore humans have an innate inclination toward mimesis.[47] It is through mimesis that the real becomes apparent to us; it is how we learn about the real. It is not, as it is for Plato, a hindrance to our perception of reality.

The twelfth-century scholar William of Conches (d. 1154) commented on Plato's *Timaeus*, *Glosae super Timeum.* Sharing in Aristotle and Plato's assertion that stimulation is directly linked to the real, Conches associated positive meaning with *imago* and *simulacrum* because of their ability to reveal the truth. William divides the imago and simulacrum as the *imago/imagines* – the painted image, and the *simulacrum* – the three-dimensional representation. Following William's logic, Pinkus aligns his own discussions of the two principles with this understanding, though William tends to blur the boundaries and even exchange one for the other.[48] Paraphrasing Plato, William draws upon a comparison where he typifies simulacrum as "of the divine wisdom" (*hic mundus divine sapentie simulacrum dicitur*) and the imago "of the world of ideas" (*exemplum*) and eternal.[49] In his analogy, he aligns the temporal birth of Christ with that of the perfect immutable *imago* – the Almighty God, whose existence fostered the human understanding of the ephemeral and the mutable through *simulacra*, because there is only one perfect *imago* – Christ himself.[50]

Popular medieval simulations are notable in imitations of Jerusalem or the Holy Sepulcher, erected inside European churches.[51] This practice was quite common in France and Germany. The Sepulcher at the Cathedral of Magdeburg was a permanent stone replica that stood from the thirteenth to the nineteenth centuries.[52] As described in the fifteenth-century *Visitatio Sepulchri* from the Magdeburg Cathedral, a Paschal play was performed that may have incorporated the created Holy Sepulcher.[53] Similar to the relationship between the altar and altar imagery, Christ's spatiotemporal presence within the Holy Land tethered God to a time and place. Kathryn Blair Moore noted a church father's perspective on this connection between time and space, "Augustine's notion of material signs as providing the primary means for knowing a transcendent God correlated with the larger paradoxical relationship of the earthly and heavenly Jerusalem."[54] In this instance, this is a pure simulation as it is the action of pretending – the imitation and reenactment of a historical model. I use the qualifier "pure" here to emphasize Pinkus's point in *Sculpting Simulacra in Medieval Germany*. In his concluding chapter, he asserts that the representational modes one encounters in the Middle Ages are charted upon a kind of sliding scale, a spectrum between extremes.[55] This summation then blurs the boundaries between *imago* and *simulacrum* constructing a versatile lens through which to evaluate sacred imagery.

St Bonaventure (d. 1274) saw that the beauty of the form was the beauty of God, tethering the penitent viewer to the divine.

> From these two first steps, by which we are led by hand to gaze upon God in (His) vestiges as after the manner of the two wings descending about the feet (of the Seraphim), we can gather, that all creatures of this sensible world lead the spirit (*animum*) of the one contemplating and tasting (*sapientis*) (them) into the eternal God, for the reason (*pro eo*) that of that First Principle most powerful, most wise and best, of that eternal Origin, Light, and Fullness, of that, I say, Art efficient, exemplary (*exemplantis*) and ordering (*ordinantis*) there are shadows, resonances (*resonantia*) and pictures, there are vestiges, likenesses (*simulacra*) and spectacles divinely given to us as first premises of a syllogism (*proposita*) and signs to survey God (*ad contuendum Deum*); which, I say, are exemplary and/or rather exemplified (*exemplata*), proposed to minds still rough and sensible, to be transferred through the *sensibles*, which they see, to the intelligibles, which they do not see, as through signs to things signified (*signata*)."[56]

For many Church fathers, the image was viewed as problematic.[57] As Medieval scholars are keenly aware, visual techniques were encouraged and regularly harnesses to aid in memory and sensual mediation. This is evident in the abundance of the fourteenth- and fifteenth-century materials including tabernacles, cult statues, prayer cards, and the spectacular large, winged altarpieces generated in the north of Europe which reinforce the Medieval desire to access the divine. These types of devotional paraphernalia though were necessary teaching aids or mnemonic devices they so easily crossed into the realm of idolatry.[58] Even Saint Bonaventure remarked an unease toward simulacrum:

> Moreover desire is principally for that which most moves it. However that moves most which loves most; however to be blessed is loved most; however to be blessed is not had except through the best and last end: therefore human desire seeks after (appetit) nothing except because (it is) the Most High Good, and/or because it is for That, and/or because it has come likeness to It. So great is the force of the Most High Good, that nothing can be loved by a creature except through a desire for It, which (creature) thereby (tunc) fails and errs, since it accepts a likeness and imitation (simulacrum) in place of the Truth (pro veritate)."[59]

Many modern theorists have shared in Bonaventure's trepidation. In his 1981 publication *Simulacra and Simulation*, Jean Baudrillard defined simulacra as a "copy" or "imitation" of the real which inevitably would defraud the viewer into a perception of the world which was wholly a corrupted truth and therefore false.[60] Auslander describes simulation as "recreations of performances that never took place, representation without referents in the real."[61] Alternatively, Peter Dronke maintained that *imago* and *simulacra* have "essential cognitive function, that they are ways of showing what cannot be said, ways of leading the mind to imitations at the limits of its efforts at intellectual understanding."[62] Scholars, and this author, have waded through the ambivalence, contradiction, and, in many instances, disdain for the simulation. I concur with Dronke and add that, additionally, the *imago* and *simulacrum* are not in a binary opposition, but, rather, complementary. In *Art Forgery: The History of Modern Obsession* (2012), Lenain Thierry describes the merits of simulacrum in his summary of Deleuze.

> A copy has nothing to do with a simulacrum in that it leaves the privilege of the original perfectly intact. It is positioned at its side or behind it, never in its place. The copy does not hide its status as an object coming only second with respect to the original and derives from an intention to acknowledge or even enhance the prestige of the object-in-chief.[63]

Imago and simulacrum are co-present, along a spectral line or even parallel to each other. Perhaps it does, as Pinkus asserts, lay on a spectrum or perhaps the "altar screen" in its relationship to the altar is *something else entirely*.

The Body of Christ is the temporal sacrifice of the living flesh. The unique matter of the Eucharist is that the substance of the bread still appears to have all the qualities of its former self, though miraculously it is transformed into the living flesh of Christ. However, as one of my dear colleagues often jokes "Jesus doesn't just *walk* into the church."[64] Though this is said in jest, there is a point made here. Jesus, in full corporeal form, does not enter the church, march down the nave, and surrender to the congregates his body for ritual consumption.

This, of course, is the miracle of the sacrament – in essence the bread changes, yet there is no change in empirical appearance. The substance is transubstantiated beyond comprehensible reality. It is fashioned into something entirely new – the incarnation or the embodiment of Christ. Suzannah Biernhoff outlines the Medieval premise of embodiment in her discussion of the "body" and "flesh" in *Sight and Embodiment in the Middle Ages* (2002).[65] Here, she posits that "human corporeality was not homogenous and stable," where the material and spatial nature of the body operates along a spectrum. As the human body was the embodiment of original sin, the body of Christ was the embodiment of salvation. St Augustine discussed this duality in terms of the inner and outer man who are presented in the same opposition as Adam and Christ. Where one is the "earthly man" and the other "the heavenly man" – the very "image and likeness of God."[66] This dualism maligns the body but praises the spirit, one that is subjugated to carnal sin and the other as a transcended intellect.

Christ, the Eucharist, the "altar screen" – they are the material realization through the embodiment of something more than the thing. When viewers access the information projected to them at the live event, whether it be prerecorded images, laser designs, close-ups, or streaming statistics the "simulation" or mediatized event is enhanced and inevitably becomes an inherent part of the live experience. The live and the mediatized embody the entirety of the relationship to the live experience. If we return to Plato's puppets and shadows, we once more find that there is parallel truth – the shadows cast on the cave wall were indicative of the true nature of the real – that which is truth. This construct is often modified as a visual gag utilized in film or television, where we see a disguised person's true nature revealed by a mirror reflection or misshapen shadow cast behind them. Not only does this visually reveal to the viewer the true nature of the disguised, that which is not seen, but it is emblematic – the embodiment of their true selves. What was envisaged as an ancillary accouterment, then an accommodating technology for large crowds, becomes an inseparable component of the live event. The narrative on the altarpiece is much the same as the cast shadows and mirrored reflections. In the *Seilern Triptych*, the body of Christ descends from the altar imagery to the ciborium on the altar proceeding as the mediatized framework that simultaneously performs the perception of the penitent.[67] During the fifteenth century, this naturally perpetuated the popularity of the *corpus christi*, feeding the mass desire for proximity. The divine imagery *projected* on the surface of the altarpiece, then, was beyond mere reenactment.[68]

"Show's over folks?"

In many instances, when the mass is over, the image remains *in situ*. What does it mean, then, once a projection of the live becomes a replay? What was authentically live is called into question through the highly criticized phenomenon of lip-syncing during live performance. Citing concert culture, rock music recordings, and such controversial figures as Milli Vanilli, Auslander analyzes the changing meaning of the authentic. Rock music, like many other genres of music, is consumed in live performance as well as prerecorded media. Additionally, the ever-popular recorded album of a "live concert performance" further perpetuates the immediacy and intimacy of listening and experiencing the liveness at home. Audibly bearing witness to the happening that is the recorded live performance conjures Bogosian's romantic notions discussed earlier. These precepts, among others, call into question the ideology of authenticity. Auslander notes that these ideologies are largely determined by audience perception.

> Nostalgia assumes its full meaning when the real is no longer what it used to be. There is a proliferation of myths of origin and signs of reality; of second-hand truth, objectivity and authenticity. There is an escalation of the true, of the lived experience... And there is a panic-stricken reproduction of the real and the referential.[69]

The audience shares neither temporal form nor physical location with the performed imagery, yet experiences it out of time from its initial performance, whether that is the live event of transubstantiation or the historical Crucifixion itself.[70] Auslander explains the perception of the live through a recording: "live recordings allow the listener a sense of participating in a specific performance and vicarious relationship to the audience for that performance not accessible through studio productions." Here looking at the devotional image recorded on the altarpiece scarcely differs from the suspended sacramental gaze discussed earlier.[71] Therefore, our understanding of what is live – like live television or radio – has expanded far beyond its original meaning. Liveness is not determined by our willingness to interact nor its real-time interaction with the viewer, rather a thing is live because "we perceive a real-time response" and "our willingness to accept its claim."[72] As technology continues to change and morph into entirely new forms of immediate, mediated, and live interaction, our understandings and definitions of temporality and liveness will evolve along with them. For instance, pre-coded technologies, like computer programs, the internet, and an eReader, simulate a sense of liveness as the viewer inputs information, the computer synthesizes and

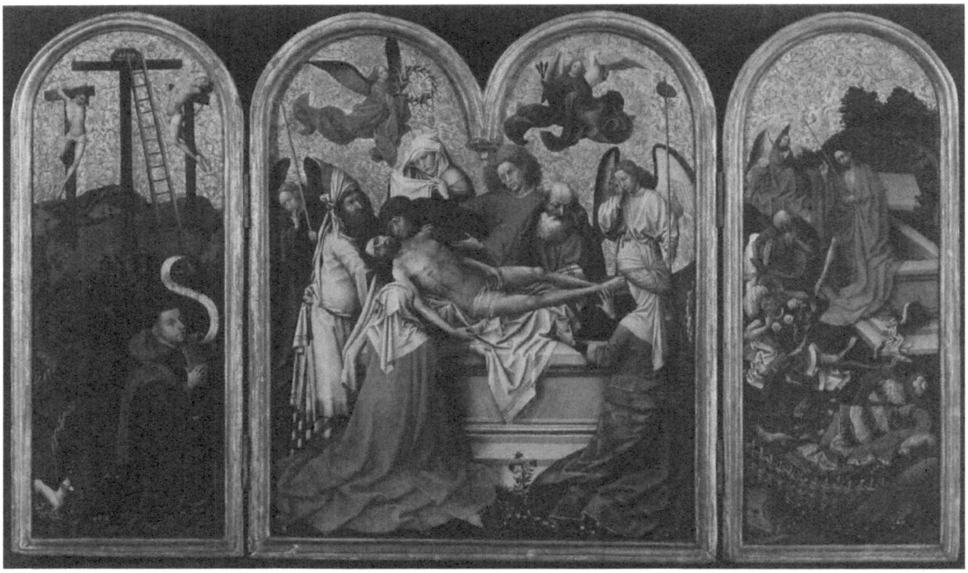

FIGURE 6.1 Robert Campin (1378/1379–444). *The Entombment, known as "The Seilern Triptych,"* ca. 1425. Oil on panel: The Courtauld, London.

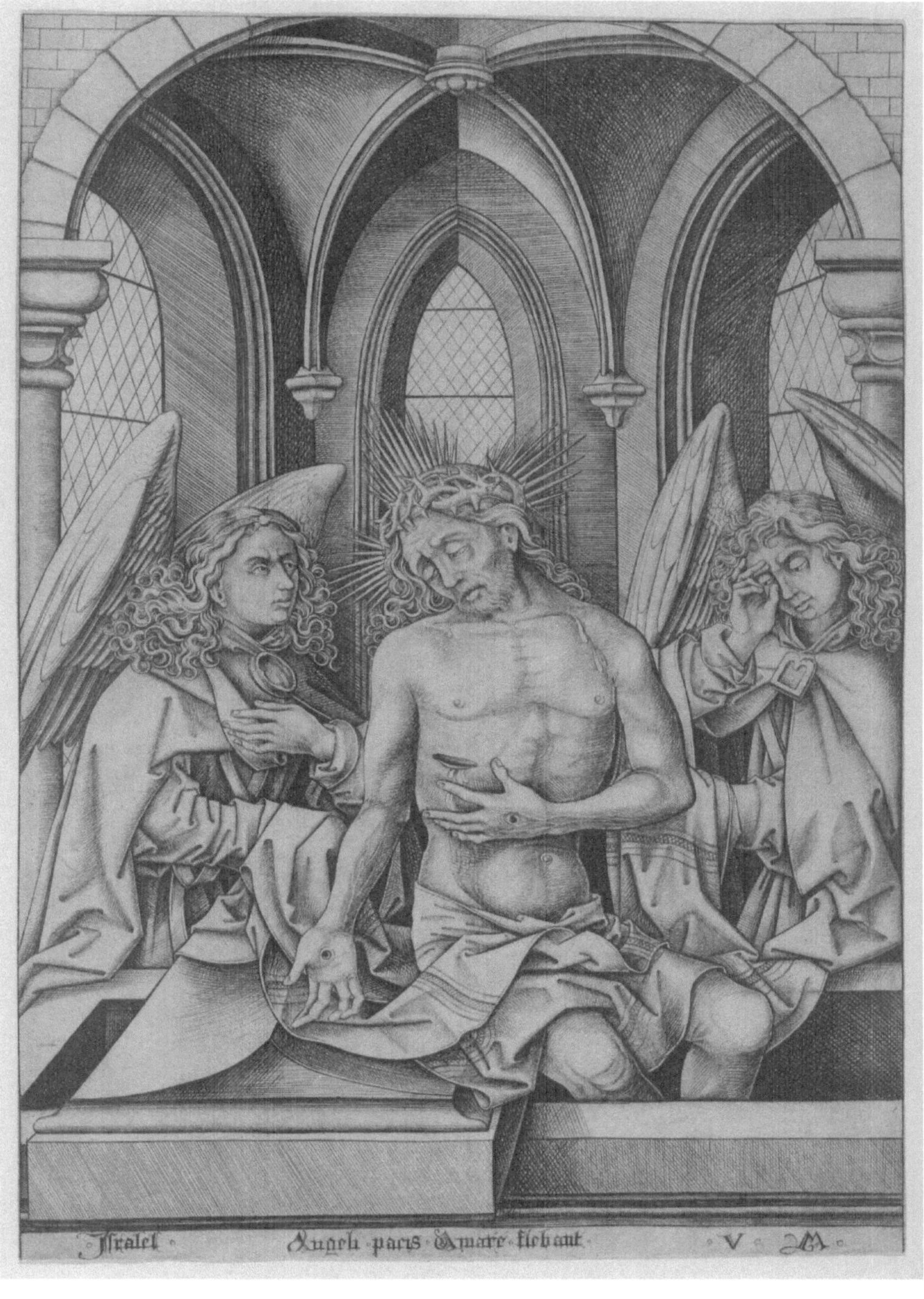

FIGURE 6.2 Israhel van Meckenem (German, Meckenem ca. 1440/1445–503 Bocholt). *Christ as the Man of Sorrows between Two Angels*, ca. 1500. Engraving, Sheet: 10 5/8 × 7 5/16 in. (27 × 18.5 cm).

displays action and meaning in real time. Though in the instance of a Kindle for example, the pages that appear on my screen are a simulation of a simulation, i.e. the remediation of an actual novel. Where in reading a leather-bound book, I would turn the paper page

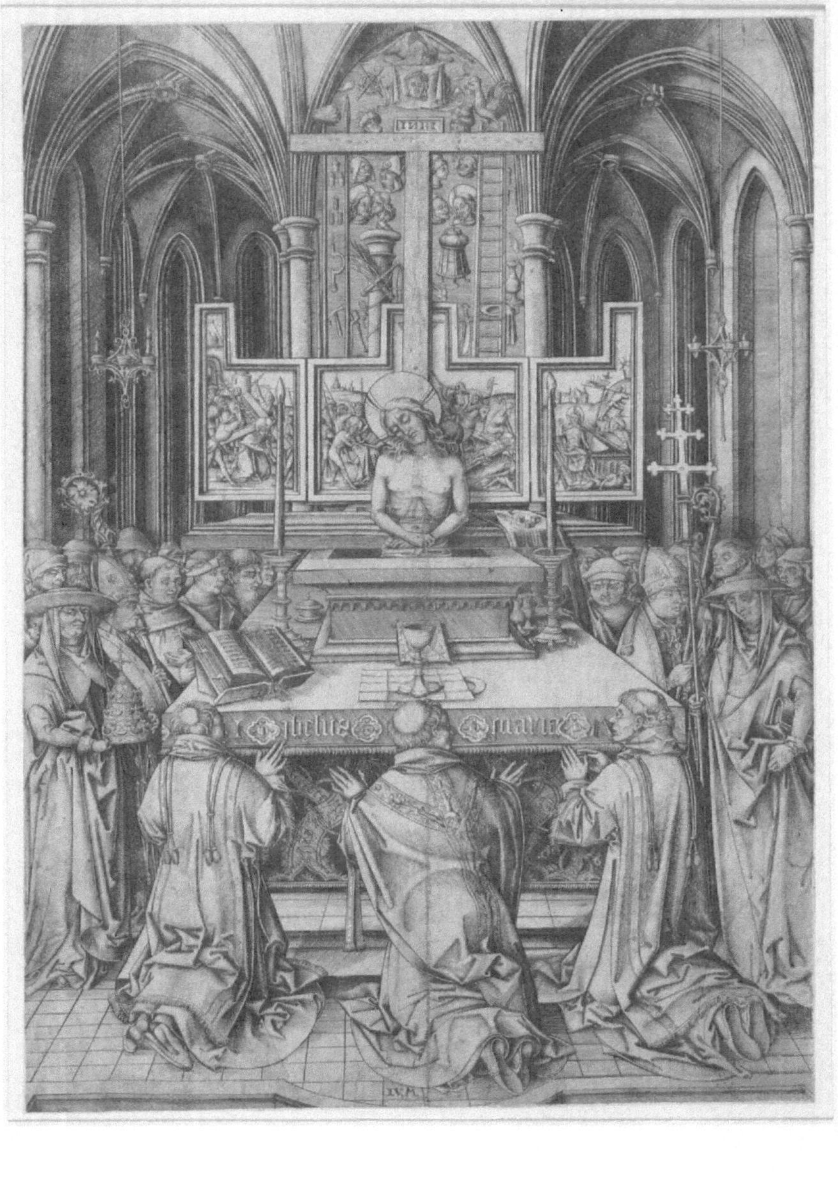

FIGURE 6.3 Israhel van Meckenem (German, Meckenem ca. 1440/1445–503 Bocholt). *Mass of Saint Gregory – With an Indulgence of 20,000 Years* (the largest of ten engravings) ca. 1490–50. Engraving 46.5 × 29.4 cm (18 5/16 × 11 9/16 in).

thereby advancing the story pressed onto the pages, with my digital book I merely swipe left to simulate the turned page. Are my digital words, constructed with binary code, any more or less real than the paper technology? Of course not; because I perceive it to be real. Therefore, in terms of reconciling the live and the mediated, I resolve that the live is dependent on viewer perception.

Notes

1 Philip Auslander explores the status of live performance where our philosophical views on media much align. See Philip Auslander, *Liveness: Performance in a Mediatized Culture* (New York: Routledge, 1999) and Auslander, *Liveness*, 13. He also discusses this concept in "Digital Liveness: A Historico-Philosophical Perspective," *A Journal of Performance and Art* 34, no. 3 (September 2012): 3–11.
2 Eric Bogosian, *Pounding Nails in the Floor with My Forehead* (New York: Theatre Communications Group, 1994), xii.
3 Eleanor Bloomfield, "Sacred Staging: Dramatic Magic in the Medieval Mass," *Platform* 12, no. 2 (Winter 2018): 34.
4 Thora Brylowe and Stephen Yeager, "Introduction: The Medieval/Media Concept," in *Old Media and the Medieval Concept*, eds. Thora Brylowe et al. (Montreal: Concordia University Press, 2021), 14.
5 Anne Winston Allen, *Stories of the Rose: The Making of the Rosary in the Middle Ages*, (University Park: Pennsylvania State University Press, 1997), 38. The sumptuous Middle Ages collections held in the Wallraf - Richartz Museum boasts some of the most beautiful examples of this type. https://www.wallraf.museum/en/collections/middle-ages/information/.
6 Christa Grössinger, *Northern European Panel Paintings: A Catalogue of Netherlandish & German Paintings before 1600 in English churches & Colleges* (New York: Oxford University Press, 1992), 10.
7 Petrus Christus, "The Lamentation, ca. 1450." *The Metropolitan Museum of Art*, https://www.metmuseum.org/art/collection/search/435898?sortBy=Date&when=A.D.+1400–1600&ft=lamentation&offset=0&rpp=40&pos=5.
8 Robert Meadows White and Robert Holt, *The Ormulum, with the Notes and Glossary, of R.M. White* (Oxford: Clarendon Press, 1878). Secundum Lucam VIII, 11. 3270–387.
9 Robert Meadows White and Robert Holt, *The Ormulum*, 121, 11. 3522–35.
10 Richard Kieckhefer, "Major Currents in Late Medieval Devotion," in *Christian Spirituality: High Middles Ages and Reformation*, Vol. 2, eds. Jill Raitt with Bernard McGinn and John Meyendorff (New York: Crossroad, 1987), 100 and Scribner, 94.
11 Israhel van Meckenem, "Christ as the Man of Sorrows between Two Angels, ca. 1500," *The Metropolitan Museum of Art*, https://www.metmuseum.org/art/collection/search/384416?sortBy=Date&when=A.D.+1400–1600&ft=Israhel+van+Meckenem&offset=40&rpp=40&pos=44.
12 Shirley Neilsen Blum, *Early Netherlandish Triptychs: A Study in Patronage* (Berkeley: California Studies in the History of Art, 1969), 9.
13 A. Nicholas Vardac, *Stage to Screen: Theatrical Method from Garrick to Griffith* (Cambridge: Harvard University Press: 1949), 237.
14 Steve J. Wurtzler, "She Sang Live, But the Microphone Was Turned Off: The Live the Recorded, and the *Subject* of Representation," in *Sound Theory Sound Practice*, 87–103, ed. Rick Altaman (New York: Routledge, 1992), 88.
15 Philip Auslander, *Liveness: Performance in a Mediatized Culture* (New York: Routledge, 1999), 3.
16 Auslander, "Live and Technologically Mediated Performance," in *The Cambridge Companion to Performance Studies*, 107–19, ed. Tracy C. Davis (Cambridge: Cambridge University Press, 2008), 109.
17 See Jane Feuer, "The Concept of Live Television: Ontology as Ideology," in *Regarding* Television, 12–22, ed. E. Ann Kaplan (Frederick, MD: University Publications of America, 1983).
18 Sean Street, *A Concise History of British Radio, 1922–2002* (Devon, UK: Kelly Publications, 2002), 65.
19 Auslander, *Liveness*, 14,.
20 Auslander, *Liveness*, 13. He also discusses this concept in "Digital Liveness: A Historico-Philosophical Perspective," *A Journal of Performance and Art* 34, no. 3 (September 2012), 6.
21 Auslander, *Liveness*, 13.

22 Ken Wlaschin, *Gian Carlo Menotti on Screen Opera, Dance, and Choral Works on Film, Television, and Video* (Jefferson, NC: McFarland, 1999), 127.
23 Lenox R. Lohr, *Television Broadcasting: Production, Economics, Technique* (New York: McGraw-Hill, 1940), 52.
24 See Jane Feuer, "The Concept of Live Television."
25 Nick Couldry, "Liveness, 'Reality,' and the Mediated Habitus from Television to the Mobile Phone," *The Communication Review* 7, (2004): 354–5.
26 Auslander discusses this in Chapter 2: "Live Performance in a Mediatized Culture," in *Liveness*, 1999.
27 Auslander, *Liveness*, 11–13.
28 Auslander, *Liveness*, 24.
29 Marshall McLuhan discusses extension and amputation theory in connection to media in his *Understanding Media: The Extensions of Man* (London: Routledge, 1964). He describes the concept that though media is an extension of the self, we lose something in that extension. An example is in the disembodiment of the extended voice through the telephone.
30 Christopher Borrelli, "Video Screens Sharpen Concert Debate," *Chicago Tribune*, last modified July 5, 2011, https://www.chicagotribune.com/entertainment/ct-xpm-2011–07-05-ct-ent-0705-focus-video-screens-20110705-story.html; Auslander, *Liveness*, 88–89.
31 J. David Bolter and Richard A. Grusin, "Remediation," *Configurations* 4, no. 3 (1996): 339.
32 Vardac, *Stage to Screen*, 143.
33 R.W. Scriber, *Religion and Culture in Germany (1400–1800)* (Boston, MA: Brill, 2001), 116.
34 Walter Benjamin, "The Work of Art in the Age of Mechanical Reproduction," trans. Harry Zohn, in *Video Culture: A Critical Investigation*, ed. John G. Hanhardt (Layton, UT: Peregrine Smith Books, 1986 [1936]): 31–2.
35 Kees Van der Ploeg, "How Liturgical Is a Medieval Altarpiece?," in *Italian Panel Painting of the Duecento and Trecento*, ed. Victor M. Schmidt (Washington, DC, New Haven, CT and London: National Gallery of Art and Yale University Press, 2002), 103. These were related to the 1215 Lateran Council. The elevation was introduced around 1200. Van der Ploeg notes that it is likely to have been a practiced much earlier than that. However, the Council did not make stipulations regarding the *elevatio*. For more discussion see Van der Ploeg, "How Liturgical," 103–5.
36 Van der Ploeg, "How Liturgical," 115–16; Julian Gardner, "Altars, Altarpieces, and Art History: Legislation and Usage," in *Italian Altarpieces 1250–1550: Function and Design*, eds. Eve Borsook and Fiorella Superbi Gioffredi (Oxford: Clarendon Press, 1994), 6.
37 David Rosand, "'Divinità di cosa dipinita': Pictorial Structure and the Legibility of the Altar-piece," in *The Altarpiece in the Renaissance*, eds. Peter Humfrey, et al. (Cambridge: Cambridge University Press, 1990), 147.
38 Scribner, *Religion and Culture*, 116.
39 John 19:5; Scriber, *Religion and Culture*, 116–17.
40 Lunn F. Jacobs, "Strategies in Intimacy: Memling's Triptych of Adriaan Reins," in *The Primacy of Image in Northern European Art 1400–1700*, eds. Debra Taylor Cashion, et al. (Boston, MA: Brill, 2017), 7.
41 Assaf Pinkus, "The Founder Figures at Vienna Cathedral: Between 'Imago' and 'Symulachrum,'" *Marburger Jahrbuch Für Kunstwissenschaft* 40 (2013): 63.
42 Assaf Pinkus, "The Founder Figures at Vienna Cathedral," 63.
43 Assaf Pinkus, "The Founder Figures at Vienna Cathedral," 79. What remained from the Platonic distinction between imago and simulacrum was the core of their essence: imago is everything which is permanent, stable, and a-temporal; simulacrum is that which is changeable and temporal. Even if at times he uses both terms interchangeably, William assigns to the imago a closer affinity to the eternal arche- type, while simulacrum is attributed to the signs of the temporal material world.
44 Assaf Pinkus, "The Founder Figures at Vienna Cathedral," 78.
45 Assaf Pinkus, "The Founder Figures at Vienna Cathedral," 78.
46 Plato, *Allegory of the Cave*, trans. Benjamin Jowett (Los Angeles, CA: Enhanced Media Publishing, 2017), 9.
47 Aristotle, *The Poetics of Aristotle*, trans. Stephen Halliwell (Chapel Hill: University of North Carolina Press, 1987), 34.
48 Assaf Pinkus, *Sculpting Simulacra in Medieval Germany, 1250–1380* (Burlington, VT: Ashgate Publishing Limited, 2014), 5.
49 William of Conches, Plato's *Glosae super Timeum*, trans. after Dronke (as note 50), 106, quoted in Assaf Pinkus, "The Founder Figures at Vienna Cathedral," 79.

50 Pinkus, "The Founder Figures at Vienna Cathedral," 79.
51 See Kathryn Blair Moore, *The Architecture of the Christian Holy Land: Reception from Late Antiquity Through the Renaissance* (Cambridge: Cambridge University Press, 2017), 9; and see for further reading: Jean Gailliard, *Recherches sur l'élise de Jérusalem à Bruges: suivies de données historiques sur la famille du fondateur* (Bruges: Gailliard, 1843).
52 Dunbar Ogden, "The Use of Architectural Space in Medieval Music-Drama," *Comparative Drama* 8, no. 1 (1974): 67–8. An entire discussion of these simulacra is found in this article.
53 Ogden, "The Use of Architectural Space in Medieval Music-Drama," 68.
54 Kathryn Blair Moore, *The Architecture of the Christian Holy Land*, 53.
55 Assaf Pinkus, *Sculpting Simulacra in Medieval Germany, 1250–1380* (2017), 179.
56 St Bonaventure of Bagnoregio, "Chapter II: On the Sight of God in His Vestiges in this Sensible World," in *The Journey of The Mind into God*, 295–316, trans. From the *Quarrachi Edition of the Opera Omnia S. Bonaventurae Vol. V (1891)*, 211. Digital transcript access January 1, 2022, http://www.franciscan-archive.org/index2.html.
57 Cyril Barrett, ed., *History of Aesthetics Vol. II Medieval Aesthetics* (Berlin: Mouton de Gruyter, 2015), 21.
58 Caroline Walker Bynum, *Wondrous Blood: Theology and Practice in Late Medieval Northern Germany and Beyond* (Philadelphia: University of Pennsylvania Publishing, 2007), 8.
59 Bonaventure, "Chapter II," 305.
60 See Jean Baudrillard's *Simulacra and Simulation* (Ann Arbor: The University of Michigan University Press, 1981).
61 Auslander, *Liveness*, 86.
62 Peter Dronke, *Fabula: Explorations into the Uses of Myth in Medieval Platonism* (Leiden: Brill, 1974), 34.
63 Thierry Lenain, *Art Forgery: The History of a Modern Obsession* (London: Reaktion Books Ltd., 2012), 374 --summary from Gilles Deleuze, "Simulacre et philosophie antique," in *Logique du sens*, 292–324 (Paris: Les. Éditions de Minuit, 1969).
64 I must thank my dear colleague Dr. Darren Hick who has, on more than one occasion, made this remark to me. It has always made me laugh.
65 Suzannah Biernhoff, *Sight and Embodiment in the Middle Ages* (New York: Palgrave McMillan, 2002), 17–19.
66 New Testament sources for Augustine's outer and inner man include col.3.9–10 and 2 Cor.4.16. St Augustine, *Eighty-three Different Questions*, trans. D.L. Mosher, in *Fathers of the Church*, Vol. 70 (Washington, DC: Catholic University of America Press, 1963), 355 (12.8); 315 (11.1); 342 (12.1).
67 Auslander discusses performance and perception in Chapter 2 of *Liveness*.
68 John F. Moffitt, *Painterly Perspective and Piety Religious Uses of the Vanishing Point, from the 15th to the 18th Century* (London: McFarland & Company, Inc. Publishers, 2014), 141, 209–10; Judith Sobre, *Behind the Altar Table* (Columbia: University of Missouri Press, 1989), footnote 50; Cynthia Robinson, *Imagining the Passion in a Multiconfessional Castile: The Virgin, Christ, Devotions, and Images in the Fourteenth and Fifteenth Centuries* (University Park: Pennsylvania State University Press, 2013), 236. Assaf Pinkus, "The Founder Figures at Vienna Cathedral: Between 'Imago' and 'Symulachrum.'" *Marburger Jahrbuch Für Kunstwissenschaft* 40 (2013): 63–92.
69 Jean Baudrillard, *Simulations*, trans. Paul Foss, Paul Patton, and Philip Beitchman (New York: Semiotext(e), 1983), 12–13.
70 Auslander posits that "a work of art from a past of which we have no direct experience becomes fully present to us when we grasp it as cotemporaneous. Auslander, "Digital Liveness," 8.
71 Scribner, 95.
72 Auslander, "Digital Liveness," 8–9.

Bibliography

Aristotle. *The Poetics of Aristotle*. Translated by Stephen Halliwell. Chapel Hill: Chapel Hill University of North Carolina Press, 1987.

Auslander, Philip. *Liveness: Performance in a Mediatized Culture*. New York: Routledge, 1999.

———. "Live and Technologically Mediated Performance." In *The Cambridge Companion to Performance Studies*, 107–19. Edited by Tracy C. Davis. Cambridge: Cambridge University Press, 2008.

———. "Digital Liveness: A Historico-Philosophical Perspective." *A Journal of Performance and Art* 34, no. 3 (September 2012): 3–11.

Barrett, Cyril, ed. *History of Aesthetics Vol. II Medieval Aesthetics*. Berlin: Mouton de Gruyter, 2015.

Baudrillard, Jean. *Simulacra and Simulation*. Ann Arbor: The University of Michigan University Press, 1981.

———. *Simulations*. Translated by Paul Foss, Paul Patton, and Philip Beitchman. New York: Semiotext(e), 1983.

Benjamin, Walter. "The Work of Art in the Age of Mechanical Reproduction." Translated by Harry Zohn. In *Video Culture: A Critical Investigation*, 27–52. Edited by John G. Hanhardt. Layton, UT: Peregrine Smith Books, 1986 [1936].

Biernhoff, Suzannah. *Sight and Embodiment in the Middle Ages*. New York: Palgrave McMillan, 2002.

Bloomfield, Eleanor. "Sacred Staging: Dramatic Magic in the Medieval Mass." *Platform* 12, no. 2 (Winter 2018): 34–48.

Blum, Shirley Neilsen. *Early Netherlandish Triptychs: A Study in Patronage*. Berkeley: California Studies in the History of Art, 1969.

Bogosian, Eric. *Pounding Nails in the Floor with My Forehead*. New York: Theatre Communications Group, 1994.

Bolter, Jay David and Richard A. Grusin. "Remediation." *Configurations* 4, no. 3 (1996): 311–58.

Borrelli, Christopher. "Video Screens Sharpen Concert Debate." *Chicago Tribune*. Last Modified July 5, 2011. https://www.chicagotribune.com/entertainment/ct-xpm-2011-07-05-ct-ent-0705-focus-video-screens-20110705-story.html.

Brylowe, Thora and Stephen Yeager, eds. *Old Media and the Medieval Concept*. Montreal: Concordia University Press, 2021.

Bynum, Caroline Walker. *Wondrous Blood: Theology and Practice in Late Medieval Northern Germany and Beyond*. Philadelphia: University of Pennsylvania Publishing, 2007.

Couldry, Nick. "Liveness, 'Reality,' and the Mediated Habitus from Television to the Mobile Phone." *Communication Review* 7, no. 4 (2007): 353–61.

Deleuze, Gilles. "Simulacre et philosophie antique." In *Logique du sens*, 292–324. Paris: Les. Éditions de Minuit, 1969.

Dronke, Peter. *Fabula: Explorations into the Uses of Myth in Medieval Platonism*. Leiden: Brill, 1974.

Feuer, Jane. "The Concept of Live Television: Ontology as Ideology." In *Regarding Television*, 12–22. Edited by E. Ann Kaplan. Frederick, MD: University Publications of America, 1983.

Gailliard, Jean. *Recherches sur l'élise de Jérusalem à Bruges: suivies de données historiques sur la famille du fondateur*. Bruges: Gailliard, 1843.

Gardner, Julian. "Altars, Altarpieces, and Art History: Legislation and Usage." In *Italian Altarpieces 1250–1550, Function and Design*, 5–39. Edited by Eve Borsook and Fiorella Superbi Gioffredi. Oxford: Clarendon Press, 1994.

Grössinger, Christa. *Northern European Panel Paintings: A Catalogue of Netherlandish & German Paintings Before 1600 in English Churches & Colleges*. New York: Oxford University Press, 1992.

Jacobs, Lunn F. "Strategies in Intimacy: Memling's Triptych of Adriaan Reins." In *The Primacy of Image in Northern European Art 1400–1700*, 3–17. Edited by Debra Taylor Cashion, Henry Luttikuizen, and Ashley D. West. Boston, MA: Brill, 2017.

Kieckhefer, Richard. "Major Currents in Late Medieval Devotion." In *Christian Spirituality: High Middles Ages and Reformation*, Vol. 2, 75–108. Edited by Jill Raitt with Bernard McGinn and John Meyendorff. New York: Crossroad, 1987.

Lenain, Thierry. *Art Forgery: The History of a Modern Obsession*. London: Reaktion Books Ltd., 2012.

Lohr, Lenox R. *Television Broadcasting: Production, Economics, Technique*. New York: McGraw-Hill, 1940.

Lupinacci, Ludmila. "'Absentmindedly Scrolling through Nothing': Liveness and Compulsory Continuous Connectedness in Social Media." *Media, Culture & Society* 43, no. 2 (March 2021): 273–90.

McLuhan, Marshall. *Understanding Media: The Extensions of Man*. London: Routledge, 1964.

Moffitt, John F. *Painterly Perspective and Piety Religious Uses of the Vanishing Point, from the 15th to the 18th Century*. London: McFarland & Company, Inc. Publishers, 2014.

Moore, Kathryn Blair. *The Architecture of the Christian Holy Land: Reception from Late Antiquity through the Renaissance*. Cambridge: Cambridge University Press, 2017.

Ogden, Dunbar. "The Use of Architectural Space in Medieval Music-Drama." *Comparative Drama* 8, no. 1 (1974): 67–68.

Pinkus, Assaf. "The Founder Figures at Vienna Cathedral: Between 'Imago' and 'Symulachrum.'" *Marburger Jahrbuch Für Kunstwissenschaft* 40 (2013): 63–92.

———. *Sculpting Simulacra in Medieval Germany, 1250–1380.* Burlington, VT: Ashgate Publishing Limited, 2014.

Plato. *Allegory of the Cave.* Translated by Benjamin Jowett. Los Angeles, CA: Enhanced Media Publishing, 2017.

Robinson, Cynthia. *Imagining the Passion in a Multiconfessional Castile: The Virgin, Christ, Devotions, and Images in the Fourteenth and Fifteenth Centuries.* University Park: Pennsylvania State University Press, 2013.

Rosand, David. "'Divinità di cosa dipinita': Pictorial Structure and the Legibility of the Altarpiece." In *The Altarpiece in the Renaissance*, 107–19. Edited by Peter Humfrey and Martin Kemp. Cambridge: Cambridge University Press, 1990.

Scriber, R.W. *Religion and Culture in Germany (1400–1800).* Boston, MA: Brill, 2001.

Sobre, Judith Berg. *Behind the Altar Table.* Columbia: University of Missouri Press, 1989.

St Augustine. *Eighty-three Different Questions.* Translated by D.L. Mosher. In *Fathers of the Church*, Vol. 70. Washington, DC: Catholic University of America Press, 1963.

St Bonaventure of Bagnoregio. "Chapter II: On the Sight of God in His Vestiges in this Sensible World." In *The Journey of The Mind into God*, 295–316. Translated from the *Quarrachi Edition of the Opera Omnia S. Bonaventurae Vol. V* (1891). Digital transcript accessed January 1, 2022. http://www.franciscan-archive.org/index2.html.

Street, Sean. *A Concise History of British Radio, 1922–2002.* Devon, UK: Kelly Publications, 2002.

Van der Ploeg, Kees. "How Liturgical Is a Medieval Altarpiece?" In *Italian Panel Painting of the Duecento and Trecento*, 147–59. Edited by Victor M. Schmidt. Washington, DC, New Haven, CT and London: National Gallery of Art and Yale University Press, 2002.

Vardac, A. Nicholas. *Stage to Screen: Theatrical Method from Garrick to Griffith.* Cambridge: Harvard University Press, 1949.

White, Robert Meadows and Robert Holt. *The Ormulum, with the Notes and Glossary, of R.M. White.* Oxford: Clarendon Press, 1878.

Winston Allen, Anne. *Stories of the Rose: The Making of the Rosary in the Middle Ages.* University Park: Pennsylvania State University Press, 1997.

Wlaschin, Ken. *Gian Carlo Menotti on Screen Opera, Dance, and Choral Works on Film, Television, and Video.* Jefferson, NC: McFarland, 1999.

Wurtzler, Steve J. "She Sang Live, But the Microphone Was Turned Off: The Live the Recorded, and the *Subject* of Representation." In *Sound Theory Sound Practice*, 87–103. Edited by Rick Altaman. New York: Routledge, 1992.

PART IV

Teaching "Tools" and Accessibility

7

SIMULATING THE SEVENTEENTH-CENTURY DUTCH ART MARKET IN THE TWENTY-FIRST-CENTURY CLASSROOM

Margaret Mansfield

Engaging and maintaining the interest of students in a Renaissance and Baroque art history survey course is a challenge. Even for the most charismatic lecturers, darkening the room for the optimum viewing of PowerPoint slides can result in students dozing off or not-so-stealthily scrolling on their phones or laptops. With the darkness of the room and distraction of technology aside, one hurdle is the nature of the lecture format itself as a vehicle for conveying information about specific objects and the complex circumstances surrounding their production and consumption. The objects discussed in class have been removed from their context of display and use, warped in size, and projected onto a screen. Also, the time and attention constraints of the class period mean a lecturer can only introduce a small number of objects on the slides. She often must present them unmoored from the circumstances of their production and consumption. The limitations of a lecture are particularly constricting when teaching the seventeenth-century Dutch art portion of a Western survey course, as it is such a departure from everything the students have encountered thus far in the course. This portion of the course is not merely art history with a bit of religious context thrown in: It also involves political, economic, and social history.

In the seventeenth century, the Dutch Republic established the Western world's "first modern economy."[1] Art historians and economic historians, including Maarten Prak, J. Michael Montias, Marten Jan Bok, Michael, North, Neil de Marchi, Hans Miegroet, Jan de Vries, and Ad van de Woude, agree that the "market forces" of the period "helped shape, if not caused the development of Dutch painting in the seventeenth century and its specific forms."[2] A far more socio-economically diverse swathe of the population owned artwork in their homes than ever before. In this proto-capitalist economy, the middle class, known as *burghers*, created broad demand for artistic products: ceramics, paintings, prints, maps, books, furniture, and textiles. The increased volume of demand necessitated a more "industrial" production of these items and new modes of purchase.[3] With such demand, the number of master artists working in the period increased by seven to eight times in the first half of the seventeenth century.[4] The variety of subject matter, range of monetary and cultural value of objects, shifts in artist-patron relations, and entirely new demographics of

DOI: 10.4324/9781003295082-12

consumers with the first truly open market are hallmarks of the seventeenth-century Dutch art. To this point in the survey course, the artwork was made by a small number of artists almost exclusively on commission in the context of feudal or gift economies. A lecture or two cannot convey the liveliness and diversity of the social, artistic, and economic networks and forces that shaped the art of the seventeenth-century Netherlands.

How do you approach ideas of seventeenth-century Dutch art including the boom in production in all genres, changes in personal and cultural taste, the various modes of buying and selling on the open market, and the regulatory body of the St. Luke's guild in a concise manner such that students can process and retain the information? To better convey the dynamism of the period and complexities that defined it, I developed an interactive role-playing exercise in which the entire class simulates the seventeenth-century Dutch art market. This enables students to creatively interface with each other while addressing far more objects than could fit into a traditional lecture. As they buy and sell, amassing collections, the students learn how these paintings and prints related to one another and to the networks of actors, and the circumstances of production. Rather than understanding objects as atomized, they understand them in relation to and informing/informed by one another. By performing social interactions that they are already familiar with, they teach themselves about the performativity of the market. This format not only helps students learn about the art produced in the Dutch Republic, but it also makes the introduction of the complexities of confessional differences, the emergence of the Dutch East and West India Companies, and the political challenges of an emergent Republic more easily digestible. This approach intrigued students, so much so that a Physics major arrived in class wearing a black rain jacket zipped to the top with tufts of Kleenex protruding from the circumference of his collar and sleeves, mimicking the lace ruff and cuffs fashionable in the era.

For one class session, twenty-five to fifty students actively engage with the buying, selling, and marketing of paintings and prints. Each student is assigned to play the role of a specific artist, dealer, or potential buyer. The roles are specific to seventeenth-century individuals who lived in the Netherlands and vary in socioeconomic status, confessional background, and gender. This approach provides students access to far more artists, paintings, and prints from the era than they would be able to consume in a normal lecture. They are challenged to consider how these objects played a role in seventeenth-century Dutch businesses, homes, and relationships. Rather than being distracted from a lecture by their laptops, tablets, and phones, they are encouraged to use their technology to their advantage in any way they like. The integration of technology continues to expand with each iteration, making the exercise more dynamic each time.

In real-time, students collectively establish trends that capriciously change with the whim of the market or opt to stick with an approach that better suits their strengths and comfort level. Students portraying artists can use their technological devices to emphasize the intricacies of the quality of their work or to flood the market with quantity asking for a smaller sum for each painting or print. As collectors, they can display their acquisitions and encourage their classmates to approach them for conversation and negotiation. Buyers, ranging the socio-economic ladder from Prince of Orange to fishwives, mingle with one another and haggle over the prices of paintings and prints to display in their homes and businesses. The exercise and subsequent debriefing helps students learn that the seventeenth-century art market involved the skills of networking, negotiation, budgeting, socio-economic structures, and the cultivation of personal and socially recognized taste.

This embodied and experiential approach to learning brings the experience of buying and selling of art, complete with its challenges, from centuries ago to life in our classroom.

Setting the Stage

The assigned readings for the week are excerpts from Eric Jan Sluijter's essay, "All Striving to Adorne Their Houses in Costly Peeces" and Jo Kirby's article "Studio Practice and the Training of Artists." Sluijter explains the boom in Dutch demand for paintings, noting that by 1640, approximately two-thirds of the Dutch population lived in homes decorated with paintings.[5] In the city of Delft, for example, the average household had eleven paintings.[6] Unlike the paintings studied in previous weeks, these were not financed and owned by titled wealthy individuals or the Church. A 1640 account by visiting Englishman, Peter Mundy, observed that it was the custom of the Dutch to decorate their homes, particularly the more public or street-facing rooms with paintings. This cultural phenomenon, he explained extended to average tradesmen: Butchers, bakers, and blacksmiths.[7] The Dutch hung paintings not only in the public and private rooms in their homes but also in their places of business as a signifier of cultural and intellectual capital. Kirby's article informs the students that artists, even those as famous as Rembrandt, collected the works of contemporaneous artists to be used both as learning tools for themselves and their students as well as markers of social status. Kirby's article also explains the process of an artist's education and apprenticeship, and the impact that association with one's master artist had on the perceived value of their work. She explains that a master's original began to be associated with a higher cost than a studio version, made by students under the master's instruction.

The lecture before the exercise builds on the content in the Sluijter and Kirby excerpts. I explain to students that Dutch artists of the seventeenth century created some objects on commission, as artists had previously elsewhere in Europe. The commissions in the predominantly Protestant Republic of the Netherlands came from a wider variety of social backgrounds and the subject matter tended to be more secular, albeit not exclusively so. An example of a secular commission is group portraits. Civic guards, guild governors, and regents of charitable organizations commissioned the best portrait artists to capture their legacy to display in their meeting places. The most famous examples of these being Rembrandt's *Night Watch* (1642) and his *Anatomy Lesson of Dr. Nicolaes Tulp* (1632). With these examples, they learn that group portraits involved multiple patrons, with each subject paying a portion reflective of their relative prominence of size and location in the painting. Although some who could afford it continued to commission artists to create custom works for them throughout the seventeenth century, far more paintings and prints were produced for the open market.

Dutch artists, I explain, did not have the job security of being court painters as there were no courts in the Netherlands. Rather, they sold their work directly from their own studios, through knowledgeable and socially connected dealers, at art auctions, or in lotteries hosted by the St. Luke's guild. It was not uncommon for individuals to buy and sell artwork second or third-hand either. Some of the determining factors of price were size, genre, originality of composition, number of figures, attribution of the artist, and the artist's reputation. Some artists were able to accrue enough income to sustain themselves completely through their artistic output. It was not uncommon, however, for artists to have a second job to sustain themselves and their families. For example, Adam Pynacker was a wine merchant and Jan

Steen was a brewer. The students also learn that social networking and connection played a major factor in the successful sale of artwork. Which studio an artist was educated or apprenticed with, whom they were related to, one's religious or confessional association, and any sort of clubs or group memberships could help or hinder successful sales.

Before the class is dismissed, each student receives a card with the identity that they will assume the following day. Each card has a character summary including the individual's name, lifespan, confessional affiliation, location(s) within the Netherlands, and bullet points that will be helpful in the exercise. These points include familial and professional relationships with others in the simulation, professional specialties, approximate annual budget, interests or dislikes, and other facts that will significantly impact their experience. The identity cards provide the premises on which the class will improvise. Some students are given specific objectives such as commissioning a particular painting, whereas others have more open-ended preferences included and are meant to buy and sell on the open market. Although identities could be dealt out at random, I try to carefully assign roles such that more gregarious students must depend upon quieter classmates for business and social relationships. I give students who have established a penchant for negotiating deadlines roles in which those skills shine. The assignments create a cohesive group while concomitantly representing the social and economic diversity of the seventeenth-century Dutch art market.

About one-third of the students are assigned to be artists who need to sell their own work, including Pieter de Grebber, Frans Hals, Judith Leyster, Jan van Goyen, Jan Steen, and Rachel Ruysch. They are given some cards with their own work on them. Some of these paintings are meant to be created on a specific commission, others through dealers, the remainder on the open market. The artists included a range in reputation, genre specialty, and output during the century. Some are related to one another, and others are established rivals. To reflect the historical reality, the identity cards include positive and negative personal and financial facts. Rembrandt's card states that his marriage to the niece of prominent Amsterdam art dealer Hendrick van Uylenburgh, Saskia, helped launch his career in the bustling capital city. His card also includes that Rembrandt's penchant for overspending meant that he had to declare bankruptcy in 1656. Emmanuel de Witte's card denotes his penchant for gambling and fighting with other artists and that he must indenture himself to his art dealer Joris de Wijs after his wife and adolescent daughter were arrested for theft. Both Rembrandt and De Witte's dealers are assigned identities, meaning the students in these roles must interact with one another. Judith Leyster's card notes that she is the first female artist appointed to the St. Luke's Guild of Haarlem, that she was married to fellow artist Jan Miense Molenaer, and that she had male students and apprentices of her own. Consistent with the background lecture, some artists, such as Jan van Goyen, are not able to support themselves and their families solely on their artistic output; these artists have indications of their supplementary professional endeavors on their identity cards. Jan van Goyen, painted over 1,000 landscapes using the quicker wet-on-wet technique and made additional income as an art dealer and seller of tulip futures and in real estate by renting a home to the painter Paulus Potter. With his own paintings, van Goyen's identity card notes that he aimed for the number of sales at lower prices rather than selling fewer quality paintings that would take far longer to create. To demonstrate the impact of the social network on the artists, Jan van Goyen's student and son-in-law Jan Steen also has indications of challenges with money on the identity card. Steen, the co-founder of Leiden's St. Luke's Guild and painter of humorously raucous paintings, is saddled with some of his extended family's financial woes and so has the supplemental occupation of owning and operating an unsuccessful brewery, called "The Snake."

A handful of students are assigned to be art dealers that act as intermediaries between the artists that they represent and potential buyers. For some, such as Joris de Wijs, the financial and legal arrangement between them and a specific artist is noted on their identity card. Other dealers, like Hendrick van Uylenburgh, who launched the career of Rembrandt and other artists in Amsterdam, only have indications of their professional connections and brief training as an artist but have more freedom in negotiation. The students in these roles get to negotiate the specific terms of their relationships with their associated artists. Depending on the number of students in the class, there may also be several anonymous dealers who are assigned a specific focus that helps stimulate the market.

The niche dealers have included individuals specializing in prints, the work of female artists, and Catholic works. Prints were generally less expensive than paintings, making many of them affordable to buyers of lesser means. Some painters, such as Rembrandt, turned to printmaking as an additional source of income. Rembrandt would change the plate just enough between runs to make different states or variations on the same composition. Keen collectors would aim to accrue one of each of the states in their collection. The Netherlands was a predominantly Protestant country. Laws changed several times over the course of the century, making the public practice of Catholicism illegal. Yet many Catholics still lived and worked in the Low Countries, including artists Jan Steen and Jan van Goyen as well as wealthy collector Hendrick Bugge van Ringe. Paintings with religious subject matter were made both for individuals for private use in their homes and for the decoration of clandestine, or hidden, Catholic churches. According to an article by Xander van Eck, the confessional differences did not preclude Protestant artists from creating work for Catholic buyers or vice versa.[8] In the context of this exercise, a dealer specializing in Catholic work can help students overcome inhibitions in the buying and selling of Catholic works in what they have learned is a Calvinist atmosphere.

The remainder of the class is potential buyers at all levels of Dutch society. Most of these individuals would never be covered in a traditional survey course as they are too far removed from the canon. Their inclusion demonstrates the diversity of the art market and a greater understanding of the historical reality of the Netherlands in the seventeenth century. Some students are tasked with securing specific commissions for themselves, their families, or groups with which they are affiliated. Dirck Dicx, the flag bearer in the St. George's Civic Guard of Haarlem, is tasked with commissioning his company's group portrait. Husband and wife, Fredrick Henrdrick, Prince of Orange, and Amalia von Solms are tasked with solidifying their individual and family legacy and political agendas through the commissioning of portraits, paintings for reception rooms in the palace, and objects reflecting their personal interests.

Other buyers' identity cards do not come with instructions to seek out specific commissions. Some buyers instead receive an indication of the parameters which would impact the purchases made on the open market: their socio-economic status, confessional concerns, professional interests, personal relationships, and budget. Atlas-maker for the Dutch East India Company, Willem Blaeu, whose maps were featured in paintings by Johannes Vermeer, is encouraged to purchase works that indicate his professional and intellectual pursuits. His identity card notes interests in mathematics and astronomy as well as a social connection to René Descartes. Hendrik Bugge van Ringe's card indicates that he is a wealthy

Catholic with a personal fondness for *fijnschilderij* (a technique that is richly detailed leaving almost no indication of brushstrokes). It also indicates that his fortune enables him to amass a personal collection boasting the works of over ninety-eight artists and to construct a hidden chapel, for his family and other Catholics to surreptitiously attend mass, in his attic (which also would require artwork). Petronella Dunois' card indicates that she is a wealthy art collector who not only wants paintings for her home but also to accompany the miniature Raphael's *Madonna* in her famous dollhouse. Individuals of more modest means, such as the brewster, Grietje Moyses, a cheesemonger, a fish wife, a spice merchant, and a tulip broker are also represented in the exercise. Each of these individuals is assigned their objectives in the market, their budget, and personal interests. The baker Arent Oostwaert's card notes that he earns 300 guilders per year and wants to purchase paintings to decorate both his home and his bakery. The variety of professional and social backgrounds of the buyers reveals to students how art fits into the existing economy.

With Greater Use of Technology Came More Potential for Learning

The first iteration of the in-class simulation was completely analog. Students enacted their assigned identities as they mingled with one another buying, selling, and dealing the limited number of paintings they had been provided printed onto notecards. All students had to keep track of their sales and purchases by hand, on a printed ledger. Students could use a desk to represent their home or place of work and to display the artwork they purchased. This exhibition of one's collection became the backdrop for future interactions and negotiations. As in the seventeenth century, what kind of art was in a collection and the exhibition acted as an extension of the collector's identity. The social performance of buying and selling art as well as using one's collection to prompt conversations underlines the importance of not only financial capital, but also social and intellectual capital. Rather than being overwhelmed by the number of objects they were seeing in the exercise and the variety of subject matter, students began to see how collections were established and the function that art played in a thriving society such as the seventeenth-century Netherlands.

Throughout the exercise, I also circulated through the class. I did not play the role of a specific historic individual. I ensured that the simulation ran smoothly by encouraging specific connections between timid students to be made. I interjected encouragement and reminders about the art market and artistic production that would aid further connections and sales. I also acted as the St. Luke's Guild, handling disputes among artists, dealers, and buyers. The simulation is not meant to occur within a specific year or years of the seventeenth century. The goal is for the students to understand the general principles of the way the market functions. Occasionally throughout the exercise, however, I would announce that it was a particular year or event of significance to individual students or combinations of them. Events, such as Rembrandt's bankruptcy would change the stakes or approach to the market, making the simulation simultaneously more interesting and more historically accurate. In the last few minutes, the class would reconvene and briefly discuss their impressions of the market. I ask students to share what surprised them, what challenged them, and what goals they had to leave unaccomplished. Students are then asked to write a single-page reflection of their experience in the market, citing images that they bought and sold and the rationale for their decisions in the simulation.

The limiting factor with this analog approach is that very few of the students were assigned artists or historical figures they had ever heard of, so they had little investment in the role they played. Once the "artists" had sold and possibly resold the handful of paintings they had been provided, the exercise began to stagnate. As most of the course up until this point had been focused on religious history paintings, even with an introduction to more genres such as still life, landscape, and genre painting, students heavily privileged history paintings particularly with religious themes. Students with assignments such as Rachel Ruysch, a still life painter specializing in flower paintings and seller of the most expensive individual painting of the seventeenth century, struggled to sell their works to their fellow students. As a collective, in the analog version, they struggled to move past the trends they learned with the Italian Renaissance earlier in the course and the name recognition of the few familiar Dutch artists such as Rembrandt and Vermeer. This myopic view of the artwork also expanded students' understanding of the economic realities of the emerging market.

Cultural and fiscal exchange being completely intertwined in a capitalist context is something students experience daily. Yet when simulating the seventeenth century, they hesitated to apply this knowledge. There was still so much more potential for learning that was untouched in the initial analog run. For it to have the pedagogical impact I wanted, students needed to be more invested in their identities and the premise of the art market. By providing the option to research their assigned identity in advance and encouraging engagement with technology during the activity, students were able to learn far more from the simulation. Rather than specifying what technology to use and how to use it, I opened the exercise up to the addition of technology and let them learn from one another. With the use of technology, the students feel more comfortable with the exercise and are better able to absorb information about the seventeenth-century Dutch art market. This enables a more organic reproduction of the unpredictability and inflexibilities of changing tastes within the constraints of a capitalist structure.

Having been provided their assigned identities the day before, students had time to research. Even with minimal online research, students were more invested in their identities, social relationships, and challenges. As a result, they were far more enthusiastically involved. Finding further information on Emmanuel de Witte, the student playing Joris de Wijs took the indenture of the artist more seriously, making sure they were present for sales and taking a percentage of any painting sales as part of the agreement. Students whose identities would not be covered within a canonical typical survey course such as travelogue publisher, Jacob van Meurs, and naval hero, Michiel de Ruyter, had been undesirable in the analog version. With basic web searches, the student playing van Meurs began to enjoy a healthy competition with their classmate playing Blaeu in the collection of images celebrating the Dutch increasingly global presence through the East and West India Companies. The student assuming the role of De Ruyter enjoyed the celebrated position in society and felt more comfortable shopping for personal tastes rather than conforming to what they thought they should want.

Some students discovered new social connections and others discovered the breadth of the artist's *oeuvre*. Once in class, they would not only buy and sell the works printed onto notecards but additional objects that they looked up using their phones or tablets. Further, opportunities for learning emerged from the infusion of the market with digital objects. In one version of the exercise a student approached me with the following complaint: "I am Frans Hals, and I was looking for the perfect buyer for my portrait of René Descartes," she explained as she gestured to the notecard with the painting. "I was talking to Willem Blaeu and realized that they are friends, but that one of the dealers had already sold the portrait from their phone." I responded,

> You have some options here as the artist of this work, with the original in your hand. You could negotiate to sell it for more as it is your original work, and originals are worth more than copies. Or you could appeal to the St. Luke's Guild to file a complaint about fraud paintings in circulation.

Overhearing this conversation, other students decided to bring their issues to me as the representative of the St. Luke's Guild. This prompted conversations about how important authenticity was, the relative prices of a master's version versus a student's copy, and the specific role the dealer played as the intercessor between artist and buyer.

I encouraged students to use their devices however they were pleased to enliven the simulation. Beyond research, students used their devices for marketing and advertisement. In the analog version, one resourceful student who was assigned the role of Fredrick Hendrick took out his notebook and wrote "I am King of the Netherlands! I've got money to burn!" Although the sign inaccurately conflated the stadholder's position with that of the monarch, he was right in assuming the power of his position and the depth of his coffers. His sign lured artists and dealers to him as he sat still. In the more technologically supplemented iterations, students took similar approaches with their devices. One student, playing the role of Paulus Potter, opened an app on his tablet and wrote in hot pink letters: "Paulus Potter: The Best Cow Painter There Is!" He then inserted a.jpeg of one of his cow paintings and scribbled grass across the bottom of the screen. He left his tablet on a desk with a notepad so that his classmates could leave notes next to his advertisement if they were interested in his work. He would alternate between mingling with others to sell his work and checking in with his digital billboard and notebook to optimize his sales.

Students assigned to artists whose work was considered less desirable in the analog version also used technology to their advantage. The student playing Clara Peeters, a still life painter, attracted buyers by showing her paintings on her phone, zooming in to show the intricate hidden details. What was dismissed or undersold before as a basic still life with cheese was now being sold at a much higher price. She achieved this by zooming in on high-resolution images to let potential buyers marvel at the hidden signature etched into the knife that extends precariously off the edge of the table into the viewer's space. To elevate the price further, she zoomed in on her hidden self-portraits in the reflection on both glass and metal objects, demonstrating her understanding of optics in the ways that each material impacted the reflection. This particularly enterprising student understood that her work could appeal to the cheesemonger as a mode of advertising and to more elite female collectors such as Petronella Dunois and Amalia von Solms. Seeing the power of the zoom tool, other students used this approach to their advantage too. Artists whose work was very labor intensive given the level of detail were able to negotiate higher prices for their work. Other students used technology to look up the dimensions of the works. They did this to demand higher prices for larger works.

Students who did not accrue much income from the sale of paintings or prints began to wonder how they could make an additional income to further participate in the active market. In one iteration of the activity, the student assigned to be Jan Steen approached me with a complaint. "The only painting I have been able to sell is, *The Baker Oostwaert and his Wife*. My card says that I own a brewery, and my paintings just aren't selling well, what can I do?" My answer was simple, "Brewers sell beer and the Dutch love beer. Go for it!" A few minutes later, she returned to me gleefully reporting that she had struck a deal with Dirck Dicx, the civic guardsman. Not only did she sell several theoretical barrels of beer for a civic guard celebration, but in doing so she struck a deal for *The Rhetoricians* (1665). He liked that there was a flagbearer like him in it. Word quickly spread through the class that they could sell other pretend wares related to their identity. Cheese, shoes, tulips, and beer all entered the market prompting business negotiations and solidifying social relationships between the students' characters.

In one particularly enterprising class, a brewer, cheesemonger, and tulip broker teamed up to form a party-planning committee to make more money and boost their social positions. They then could bring artists and dealers together with buyers who might have overlooked their work when each student was operating independently. Although students understood that they were simulating a cash economy, they began to understand that their wares had value both intrinsic and negotiable. The value of paintings was commensurate with other objects, but also could be inflated or minimized depending on their social value and the potential cultural value the object posed to the buyer. In that same class, the student playing Judith Leyster was having trouble selling her work for as much as other male artists, so she asked if she could take on students. As Leyster had taken on several students, I let her do so and she negotiated a significant price. Those students who "studied" under her then began negotiating higher prices for their work as "Students of Judith Leyster – first woman appointed to the St. Luke's Guild of Haarlem – student of Frans Hals." Seeing students do this demonstrated to me their understanding of the power of social and business connections.

The Future of the Simulation

The integration of technology into this seventeenth-century art market has enabled students to learn far more from one another and from the activity than they were able to before. Ideally, this exercise will further integrate technology in increasingly helpful ways in the future. Perhaps, at some point, students can have an assignment in which they have to build a profile page of their assigned identity in which they can flesh out who they are, and market their works as a seller or advertise their interests as a buyer. If students had to create these pages a week in advance, the whole class could have access to them, and students could pre-plan some of the connections that they would want to make. Students would be using tools similar to the social media that many of them already use on a daily basis but from the perspective of their seventeenth-century identity.

It would also help facilitate the market simulation if I could develop a platform for the students to make the financial exchanges in real time. I envision this to be in a digital format that tracks all the individual and collective transactions. It would include a ledger to track their purchases and sales, rather than the paper version they presently use. Such a program would help students regulate prices amongst themselves and keep track of their budgets. With this type of shared interface, it would be easier to introduce historical events that had major impacts on the art market. Throughout the exercise events such as the establishment of the Dutch East India Company (1602), the burst of the Tulip Futures Bubble (1637), and the Disaster Year (1672) could be announced, and students would have to react accordingly given the assigned personas. The specific impact on each student could be distributed digitally. Ideally, I would like to see the introduction of objects that do not fall within the definition of fine art being bought and sold in this simulation. For example, Willem Blaeu could sell his atlases and Jacob van Meurs his travelogues. I would also love to see the students handle the influx of imported items such as Chinese porcelain, Japanese lacquerware, and Indonesian spices that were a major aspect of the seventeenth-century Dutch reality.

It is important for the simulation to remain a hybrid approach of in-person mingling and the use of technology. Technology has certainly enabled students to absorb far more of the nuances of the seventeenth-century Dutch art market than they did when the exercise was fully analog. They are able to get a better understanding of the actual size and level of detail of the objects they are buying and selling and are more engaged with their identities. With further innovations, they will be better able to advertise and track their sales and purchases. Meanwhile, the in-person interactions (which they rarely have with all their classmates in such a dynamic way) provide an opportunity for students of a wide variety of learning styles and disciplinary backgrounds to shine and learn from one another. The social connections of their assigned roles prompt interactions between individual students who normally would never speak to one another.

The break from the lecture format introduces students to far more paintings and prints than they would be able to absorb in the traditional setting. Not only are they learning about more images and more artists in this way, but they are teaching themselves about the first modern economy from which this artwork emerged and through which it was sold. Students also are learning how the consumption of art was occurring in various strata of Dutch society. The in-person, interactive approach to this exercise reinforces the impact of relationships and networks on negotiations. They learn that much like their twenty-first-century reality, both men and women occupy a variety of professions and amass collections of art. Ideally, the students will come away with a richer understanding of the Dutch art market of the seventeenth century. By forgoing the lecture format for one day, the class as a collective can work through the complexities of the interconnectedness of the economy, politics, social change, art production, and consumption in the Netherlands during the seventeenth century. This role-playing simulation, particularly when supplemented by technological engagement, makes even the most jaded students excited to learn about the Dutch art of the seventeenth century.

Notes

1 Jan de Vries and Ad van der Woude, *The First Modern Economy: Success, Failure, and Perseverance of the Dutch Economy, 1500–1815* (Cambridge, UK: Cambridge University Press, 1997), iii.
2 Maarten Prak, "Guilds and the Development of the Art Market of the Dutch Golden Age," *Simiolus: Netherlands Quarterly for the History of Art* 30, no. 3/4 (2003): 237.
3 Jan de Vries and Ad van der Woude, *The First Modern Economy: Success, Failure, and Perseverance of the Dutch Economy, 1500–1815* (Cambridge, UK: Cambridge University Press, 1997), 342.
4 Ibid., 343.
5 Jo Kirby, "Studio Practice and the Training of Artists," in *National Gallery Technical Bulletin: Rembrandt*, ed. David Bomford (London: National Gallery, 2006), 14–19.
6 Eric Jan Sluijter, "All Striving to Adorne Their Houses in Costly Peeces," in *Art and Home: Dutch Interiors in the Age of Rembrandt*, ed. Mariet Westermann (Denver: Denver Art Museum, 2001), 103–27.

7 Peter Mundy, *The Travels of Peter Mundy in Europe and Asia, 1608–1667, vol. 4, Travels in Europe, 1639–47*, ed. R. Carnac Temple (Cambridge: Hakluyt Society, 1925), 70.
8 Xander van Eck, "The Artist's Religion: Paintings Commissioned for Clandestine Catholic Churches in the Northern Netherlands, 1600–1800," *Simiolus: Netherlands Quarterly for the History of Art* 27, no. 1/2 (1999).

Bibliography

Baer, Ronni, Henk van Nierop, et al. *Class Distinctions: Dutch Painting in the Age of Rembrandt and Vermeer*. Boston: Museum of Fine Arts Publications, 2015.

Bok, Marten Jan, and Tom van der Molen. "Productivity Levels of Rembrandt and His Main Competitors in the Amsterdam Art Market." *Jahrbuch Der Berliner Museen* 51, no. 4 & 5 (November 2009): 61–8.

De Marchi, Neil. "The Role of Dutch Auctions and Lotteries in Sharping the Art Market(s) of 17th Century Holland." *Cultural Economics: The Arts, the Heritage, and the Media Industries* 28, no. 2 (January 1995): 203–21.

De Marchi, Neil, and Hans Joris van Miegroet. "Art, Value, and Market Practices in the Netherlands in the Seventeenth Century." *Art Bulletin* 76, no. 3 (June 1994): 451–64.

———. "Rules versus Play in Early Modern Art Markets." *Recherches Économiques de Louvain/Louvain Economic Review* 66, no. 2 (2000): 145–65.

de Vries, Jan, and Ad van der Woude. *The First Modern Economy: Success, Failure, and Perseverance of the Dutch Economy, 1500–1815*. Cambridge: Cambridge University Press, 1997.

Kirby, Jo. "Studio Practice and the Training of Artists." In *National Gallery Technical Bulletin: Rembrandt*, edited by David Bomford, 14–19. London: National Gallery Press, 2006.

Montias, John Michael. *Artists and Artisans in Delft: A Socio-economic Study of the Seventeenth Century*. Princeton: Princeton University Press, 1982.

Mundy, Peter. *The Travels of Peter Mundy in Europe and Asia, 1608–1667, vol. 4: Travels in Europe, 1639–47*. Cambridge: Hakluyt Society, 1925.

North, Michael. *Art and Commerce in the Dutch Golden Age*. New Haven: Yale University Press, 1997.

Prak, Maarten. "Guilds and the Development of the Art Market of the Dutch Golden Age." *Simiolus: Netherlands Quarterly for the History of Art* 30, no. ¾ (2003): 236–51.

Rasterhoff, Claartje. *Painting and Publishing as Cultural Industries: The Fabric of Creativity in the Dutch Republic, 1580–1800*. Amsterdam: Amsterdam University Press, 2017.

Sluijter, Eric Jan. "All Striving to Adorne Their Houses in Costly Peeces." In *Art & Home: Dutch Interiors in the Age of Rembrandt*, edited by Mariet Westermann, 103–232. Denver: Denver Art Museum, 2001.

Tummers, Anna, and Koenraad Jonckheere. *Art Market and Connoisseurship a Closer Look at Paintings by Rembrandt, Rubens and Their Contemporaries*. Amsterdam: Amsterdam University Press, 2008.

van Eck, Xander. "The Artist's Religion: Paintings Commissioned for Clandestine Catholic Churches in the Northern Netherlands, 1600–1800." *Simiolus: Netherlands Quarterly for the History of Art* 27, no. 1/2 (1999): 70–94.

Westermann, Mariët. "Playing the Market: The Artist as Agent in the Dutch Golden Age." In *Artwork through the Market*. Bratislava: Nadácia - Centrum Súčasného Umenia, edited by Ján Bakoš, 93–105, 2004.

8

THE VIRTUAL RENAISSANCE

Adopting Virtual Reality to Transform How Art History is Taught

Eric R. Hupe and Caitlyn Carr

Introduction

The two-dimensional photographs we project on the screens of our darkened classrooms continue to be an indispensable component of any art history course, and in many respects, the academic discipline remains tethered to the technologies that reproduce the works we study. As any instructor knows, these images fail to convey the essence of a three-dimensional work of art or architectural space. Art history students, especially those who lack easy access to museums or cultural sites, are expected to grasp a work's significance through the mediated images projected in class or reproduced in the textbooks they skim half-heartedly. As an American art historian who studies and teaches the Italian Renaissance, I struggle to convey to my students the experience of art – whether that be the divine rationality of Brunelleschi's *Pazzi Chapel* or the unsettling grandeur of Michelangelo's *Laurentian Library*. As the field of art history embraced contextual studies, the need to experience a work of art *in situ* became increasingly relevant. We want students to understand the function of space and the art that adorns it but lack the tools to provide rich situated experiences that strengthen their connection with the material they study. We may convey to our students the necessity of travel, urging them to see the monuments in person, but that will never provide access for every student. Given the discipline's reliance on image technology, as that technology advances, so too must the methods we use for teaching and conducting our research.[1]

Emergent technologies and art history – not to mention Italian Renaissance art history – may appear at first as incompatible areas. This chapter, however, outlines and reflects on the recent work done by Professor Eric Hupe who, in collaboration with several undergraduate students at Lafayette College including Caitlyn Carr, is adopting immersive technology to transform the way we teach and understand art history. The digital initiative, Zeuxis VR: Immersive Art History, reconstructs three-dimensional models of Italian Renaissance monuments to allow students to explore them in virtual reality (VR) independently or as a class.[2] We see several benefits and potential outcomes to our work. First, VR provides an opportunity to fuse the conventional study of art history with state-of-the-art technologies.[3]

DOI: 10.4324/9781003295082-13

Second, the implementation of VR in the classroom creates an entirely new method for teaching and learning about art history that empowers students to have more meaningful encounters with works of art. Finally, and most importantly, VR provides greater access to cultural heritage sites. Student travel for genuine immersion remains fraught with obstacles such as limited financial resources, physical disabilities, safety, and time constraints. We consider VR a solution to these barriers by allowing students to step into the spaces relevant to their coursework and traverse hundreds of years and thousands of miles effortlessly.

In addition to enhancing the classroom experience, this project promotes a more collaborative version of art history. Like many other humanities disciplines, the field struggles to involve students in the active production of knowledge. We see this chapter as a testimony to how immersive technology can help incorporate students directly into faculty research. By engaging with technology, students and faculty are compelled to navigate this unfamiliar terrain as peers with a common goal of changing established educational practices, and relearning how we learn, together. What follows is our reflection on that process. We begin by surveying the project, its methods, and practices, and then discussing the impact this technology has on student learning. Eric Hupe will speak to the benefits and challenges as an educator while Caitlyn Carr, the current student project leader, will speak to the student perspective.

Project Overview

Zeuxis VR is a faculty and student-led digital project that creates VR environments of cultural sites to enhance student engagement in object-focused research. Our work currently focuses on Italian Renaissance monuments, but we intend to expand our portfolio to include sites representing the entire history of art. The project delivers innovative approaches for teaching art history that harness the full potential of immersive technology and learning. Immersive learning transports a student to a sensory-rich environment that increases their sense of presence and connects them to the content they study.[4] Rather than relying on two-dimensional images to recreate the experience of an architectural space, students will now be able to encounter these sites with their instructors. This mediated form of learning can allow students to feel that they are genuinely visiting new physical environments, creating memorable learning experiences.

We train students involved in the project in photogrammetry, 3D modeling, WebXR, and game engine platforms to generate the VR environments used in classes. The immersive scenes provide students with a social, interactive, and situated experience that encourages intensive contextual learning. The adoption of VR allows students to engage with works of architecture, painting, and sculpture in a way that encourages them to consider the context and function of art in the Early Modern period. The project adopts new documentation and representational methodologies that enrich traditional art historical analysis. It does so by recreating the event of teaching and learning art *in situ* using social VR platforms and multiplayer gaming technology, thus creating an immersive and lasting encounter with historical art. The central mission of Zeuxis is to expand access to art historical sites by providing an Open Educational Resource (OER) that instructors can use.

One of the challenges we face with emergent technology remains that the barrier of entry is high. Instructors are expected to have familiarity with gaming systems in which they possess no training, and adding any advanced technology to the classroom can be daunting. This has limited the success and deployment of VR technology. The cost of equipment also remains an issue. VR headsets, until recently, were prohibitively expensive and often needed a dedicated gaming PC to run the VR models. These tethered systems required students to take turns viewing the VR environment. The result was an impressive but isolating experience that prevented active discussion and shared learning. As a team, we are exploring these problems and producing solutions that will ensure even the most technophobic instructor succeeds in deploying our models in their classrooms. To accomplish this aim, we currently rely on the VR social platform Mozilla Hubs, which allows an instructor to easily import our models into a "chat room" space where a class of twenty-five individuals can discuss, annotate, and explore together.[5]

Methods and Practices

Our methods and practices are continually evolving. With every milestone reached, we find new techniques and resources that improve efficiency and deliver more impressive results. As we continue to work and revise our workflow, we have developed a generalized plan involving photogrammetry, 3D modeling, and VR scene-building.

Photogrammetry allows us to build accurate and photorealistic models of cultural sites. The process relies on a software program that analyzes photographic images to reconstruct a 3D model of the space. Though there are alternative methods such as Lidar scanning, we have chosen photogrammetry because of its convenience, flexibility, and affordability. Lidar scanning provides a high degree of accuracy but the equipment remains prohibitively expensive. Furthermore, Lidar scanning produces colossal data sets that exceed our needs and still require photographs to create photorealistic textures. Photogrammetry alone can yield results that are equal in accuracy and quality to Lidar scanning and have proven best suited to our project.

Once we have chosen a site to recreate, we begin the photography stage, capturing the site from varying heights and angles to create our dataset. This provides students the opportunity to encounter cultural sites in a new way by gaining privileged, unimpeded access to the space. These photographing sessions are a rare chance to engage with the cultural site without the presence of tourists. Students can explore the monument for a longer period of time than they would if they were casually visiting. Since these sessions require capturing thousands of photos and usually take place over a series of days to accurately record every detail of the room, the students have ample time to familiarize themselves with the space and study it. Besides acquiring the necessary photos to proceed to the next step of the process, students also improve their skills of visual analysis as they meticulously analyze the space and its details.

We then refine the data set based on the quality of each photo. This stage promotes increased visual acuity because every image requires close scrutiny to confirm there is no blur, grain, or equipment in the frame that would weaken the data set. After sorting these photos, we edit the approved images in Adobe Lightroom to extract the most information from each. By experimenting with settings like exposure, contrast, highlights, and shadows, we can optimize each image to improve its clarity and accuracy. After achieving a clean data set with high-quality images, we progress to the next step: inputting the images into the photogrammetry software. We are currently experimenting with both Reality Capture and Agisoft Metashape.[6] Both have similar functionalities, so we use the two in tandem to accomplish the best models. The programs help lead us through a series of steps. We first align the photos to clarify the subjects that will be recreated in 3D, and then we create a dense point cloud that provides a series of coordinates in a 3D plane to give the first glimpse of how the model will look (Figure 8.1). The program then builds a mesh model, which is a solid rendering of the dense point cloud and will show the proper dimensions and architecture of the site (Figure 8.2). A miscommunication in the data or a faulty picture can lead to physical gaps or inaccurate bumps in the mesh model, so this step allows us to review our data and correct the program if it has misplaced any features of the original architecture. We can fix some of the holes with control points, manually match the feature points within images, and run the model again. At this stage, the model remains whitewashed and bare of any color or pattern, so we must then texture it. We optimize by reducing the geometry and then applying the textures, which wrap the model in our original photographs to achieve a photorealistic quality. The result is a faithful 3D model of the physical space (Figure 8.2).

We run multiple models for each room, experimenting with different settings and comparing different results, to ensure we are producing the best model possible. Once we are satisfied, we can export the model to another program where users can explore it in a digital environment (Figure 8.3). We are currently using Mozilla Hubs because it is user-friendly and allows us to easily input our model, but it was also designed as a social chatroom for people to interact in private rooms accessed with a unique code. Because downloading the models and uploading them to different programs might prove too complex for some educators, we see Mozilla Hubs as a great alternative to programs like Unity, which might be better suited for those with more experience. We plan to use Unity to create 3D environments in higher detail that are not limited by online constraints, but we will continue to use Mozilla Hubs for its convenience and the possibility of hosting our models on their website to further simplify the downloading process for educators. By offering different levels of our models, we hope to meet educators and students where they are comfortable and provide the resources for them to try advanced methods that require more experience.

Reimagining the Early Modern Classroom Teaching the Virtual Renaissance, Eric Hupe

Like so many travelers to Rome, I still remember my first visit to the Sistine Chapel. I was a junior in college studying abroad finally seeing first-hand the places and works of art I had studied in class. While it sounds cliché, the event was transformative and inspired me to devote my life to the study and teaching of art history. Years later, as a graduate student, I returned to Rome to co-teach my first study abroad trip. On a chilly January day, I had the privilege and slightly hellish experience of leading two groups through the maze of the Vatican Museum. At the end of the tour, I prepared my students for entering the Chapel by advising them to proceed to the entrance wall before looking up: "Then you will see the ceiling as Michelangelo intended it," I remarked. For me, it was about taming what can otherwise be a frustrating viewing experience and creating for my students an encounter where the art was front and center. More than half of the group followed me into the chapel, heads bowed to their feet. They held onto each other as they snaked through the crowd until they reached the small porphyry disc by the entrance door. In unison, we turned and craned our necks heavenward. Their reaction was priceless and the bewilderment on their faces transported me to my first visit a decade earlier. This is something they too would remember for decades to come.

As a professor of Early Modern art, I struggle to convey to my students the experience of a work of art. When not teaching in Italy, I find myself longing for a way to engage my students in meaningful ways to recreate what is so often lost in the translation of photography to PowerPoint. I cannot replicate the anticipation that builds when marching through the Gallery of Maps or tapestry corridors, nor can I imitate the Sistine Chapel's perfume of incense mixed with damp stone and time.

I want students to understand the function and ritual of space along with the art that adorns it through embodied experiences that strengthen their connection with the material they study. With limited resources, I began thinking of ways to replicate the situated learning experiences students have on-site.[7] Several years ago, I began experimenting with various forms of immersive technology. At first, I employed 360° stereoscopic photos and Google Cardboards (inexpensive VR viewers for smartphones) to transport students to the various sites we visited.[8] While the bar was low regarding the cost and technology, the images were of uneven quality and static, limiting one's ability to explore and navigate a space on their own. The technology isolated the students and prevented them from interacting with each other or the professor during the lessons. The Cardboards enriched classroom learning, but it remained a watered-down version of the immersive experience I envisioned. Students were able to increase their sense of presence when viewing the art, but the tours were prescriptive and prevented free exploration. In some ways, the technology – or at least my handling of it – reinforced the sage-on-the-stage pedagogy and prevented students from asking questions as they arose.

To counter these challenges and create moments of rich situated learning, I began Zeuxis VR. Photogrammetry provides an inexpensive, easy, and accurate method for generating 3D models of architectural spaces that I foresee revolutionizing the traditional art history classroom. The VR environments we create are not meant to replace the actual encounter with a work of art, but rather to enhance an ever-growing toolbox of techniques instructors can use to engage students. The impact this technology has on students' learning is notable. We have run several test studies to solicit feedback from students and gauge the interest and success of the technology. Across the board, students described the experience as "engaging" and "immersive." While important, I want to ensure that the VR space is not an art history Disneyland but a place where real substantive learning can happen. One student noted:

> This was an extremely interesting and different experience than anything I have had in any art history class. It is really different looking at art on a screen in comparison to being inside of it, able to walk around and interact with it. It gives you a different perspective, especially about size. It was really cool to be able to walk around and get up close to the artwork. One of my favorite things about classes is being able to go and actually see some of the work in person. Obviously, this is not possible in all scenarios, so the Oculus is really a great resource to be able to experience art and even have class in a completely different yet fascinating way.

Another student commented:

> Specifically with art history, it is difficult to see all of the artwork that we cover in a class in person because these pieces are housed all over the world. VR gives students

> the opportunity to gain a new perspective by being able to walk around a space and actually feel like you are seeing the work in person. This is the closest and most representative experience to actually traveling around the world and visiting these places in person.

The benefits, however, are not limited to the classroom. Students who are involved in the project and collaborate to build the VR environments are involved at every step of the process – from photographing the sites to the final export. In the process, we train these students in digital art history and the digital humanities while developing specific skills in photogrammetry, 3D modeling, and game engine development. These outcomes lie outside the conventional curriculum in art history (either undergraduate or graduate). In this way, we are preparing our students to think about how emergent technologies can intersect with the humanities and providing them with the skills necessary to stand at the forefront of those developments.

Inside and outside the classroom we are granting students access to technology – albeit in an unconventional setting – that will benefit them in the future. Over the past two years, newspapers and periodicals have been abuzz with talk of the Metaverse and the future of VR/XR technology. The social network company formerly known as Facebook was rebranded, changing its name to Meta, indicating that the future of the internet was the Metaverse. While some may dismiss this recent craze as a passing fad, I advocate a different approach. I am confident that as VR technology improves and costs come down, VR's popularity will only grow. This is true of Meta's success with the Quest 2 headset that we use in our classes.[9] Advertised for recreational use, the device remains the top-selling VR headset in the world and was one of the most sought-after holiday gifts in 2021.[10] The Metaverse is here to stay. Educators have an opportunity to harness the potential of this technology, helping to educate and train the next generation who will inevitably shape its future. This work complements the recent push in higher education to sharpen information and digital literacies.

The process of creating and adopting VR has also transformed the way I teach, causing me to reexamine my pedagogy. The situated learning experiences provided by this technology have taught me to prioritize depth over breadth. I must admit, I am not overly concerned with whether my students remember a lengthy slide list of objects – committing to memory their dates of production, medium, and significance. I have always found the rote memorization that art history courses often require to be highly artificial, not long-lasting, and a detractor for students. I still remember preparing for art history exams as an undergraduate, creating stacks of index cards with an image of the work on one side and key facts on the reverse. In the process of studying the art remained an estranged, abstract entity mediated by a 3 × 5 photograph. As a professor, I am now concerned with what students will remember in five, ten, or twenty years after taking my class. I want them to be empowered to appreciate, analyze, and associate with art. The specific works do not matter, it is about the tools with which we provide them. I tell my Renaissance Art students that it is not about remembering every David or Madonna and Child but what you can say about them. I often give the hypothetical example of them traveling to Italy and visiting a small regional museum. When they encounter the art – often by non-canonical artists – what will they be able to say about the works and how will they begin to process and understand it? In the end, VR may help our students transfer the knowledge gained in the classroom to the real world beyond.

Creating and Learning in the Virtual Renaissance, Caitlyn Carr

I have walked countless laps around the *New Sacristy* in San Lorenzo, Florence, and I know the tiled floors, faces of each statue, and enormity of the dome like the back of my hand. Yet, I have never set foot in Italy. These may sound like the opening lines to a confusing riddle, but it is much less perplexing when I explain the remarkable way in which I have been able to accomplish this seemingly impossible task: VR.

My first interaction with the intersection of art history and VR began with my Italian Renaissance course taught by Professor Hupe in Fall 2020. COVID-19 was at its most isolating moment, so I was quite eager to put on my Google Cardboard and get lost in the Palazzo Medici. It was a unique experience, but the interface was a bit clunky and the technical difficulties I encountered took me out of the environment, reminding me I was sitting in my basement in sweatpants and had not gotten fresh air in more than a few days. Still, I was fascinated by the possibilities of the technology and continued to explore spaces with the Google Cardboard. When asked if I would like to explore an old English hall using the Oculus VR headset, I jumped at the opportunity and was amazed by what I saw. I knew that I was still standing in the art building on my campus, but my vision was fully enveloped with an unbelievable rendering of a room that felt so real that it was easy to believe I was digitally transported to this new location.

VR has the ability to create memorable experiences with art that make learning more powerful and enjoyable for students. It provides an opportunity to engage with a work of art, which approximates the physical encounter that occurs in a museum or on-site. VR proves much easier to implement in the classroom than physical travel to sites, which can be overly expensive, limited by time constraints, and require extensive planning to accommodate large groups of students. Meanwhile, an educator can use VR within an hour lecture on a college campus to allow students to explore sites in-depth and then proceed to their next class.

The sense of being there will appeal to many students studying art history. Professors frequently comment on the scale of objects from tiny individual rosary beads to colossal cathedrals, usually followed by the sentiment that we must visit the works to truly understand the overwhelming emotions of awe, fear, and wonder associated with them. What better way to comprehend the enormity of a Gothic church than to stand in the nave and look up at the ceiling? VR can convey that same sensation of jaw-dropping surprise, translating pictures from textbooks and outlines into digital experiences that look and feel real and therefore become real memories and encounters with the art.

Working on this project has provided great benefits to me as a student who both develops and uses the content. Creating the models has definitely enhanced my education. I had never even heard of photogrammetry when we began working, but I am now very familiar with different workflows and techniques to produce results from our data in programs like Metashape, RealityCapture, and Lightroom. Besides increasing my technical skills, I have also acquired a keener eye for analyzing art. Processing photos to determine their quality meant hours of scrutinizing images of the same room. I had to become much more critical and observant to see the differences between photos of the same subject. Constructing the model and seeing it improve with each stage has given me a deeper appreciation for the work itself and led to more introspective thoughts about the effort required to build it. Just as Michelangelo used marble to create the sculptures *Day* and *Night*, we are following in his footsteps to recreate them in illusionary marble by way of digital code and programming. In this way, we become digital successors of great Renaissance artists because they have created the original art but we must then undertake an entirely new workflow to build the same creation in a virtual format. It is both gratifying and humbling: successfully rendering a believable model that emulates a space like the New Sacristy is exciting, but I am thoroughly reminded of Michelangelo's genius and ability when the program malfunctions and we have to start again from scratch. Though my painting and sculpting skills are lacking in comparison to Michelangelo, I remain amazed at just how close our digital models come to the originals.

Testing our project with other art history students illuminated the possibilities of this project and where it can go from here. As we worked on the project, we remained focused on the student experience and how we could best accommodate their needs, so it was fulfilling to see a group of students finally test it out together. The experiment was set up in the large lobby of Lafayette College's Williams Center for the Arts, and we spread out the students within their own sizable boundaries. My first impression was that of watching newborn animals try to walk for the first time – timid, uncertain, and honestly comical. Though we had created large areas where students could walk comfortably, they planted themselves in the center and swiveled their heads around like owls. I tried to encourage them to take a few steps forward and reassure them that there were no possible obstacles in their path. Seeing new students tackling the VR learning curve reminded me of my first attempt in which I tried to walk up virtual steps while still standing on a flat floor.

Even so, the students conquered unfamiliar technology quickly and easily. My peers are quite tech-savvy, and I think this trait of my generation makes these students the perfect candidates to introduce to VR learning. Most students have been exposed to computers from a young age and they can navigate interactive features found on devices like smartphones or in video games effortlessly. Professor Hupe gave a short lecture in the virtual New Sacristy environment using Mozilla Hubs and was able to move around and physically point to areas of interest while teaching. This program has features like a pen or pointer that the digital avatars can then pick up and use to highlight or draw on surfaces. It was quite funny when a student, ambitious to master the controls, discovered the virtual pen and accidentally graffitied the walls of the New Sacristy. I cannot imagine that going over well in Florence, but the undo button conveniently erased the scribble and opened the door to using the tool to annotate particular aspects of the space.

We solicited feedback from the students in the form of a survey. Taking these responses into consideration, we have continued to optimize our models, build our website, and find ways to meet students and educators at their levels of comfort. This has required a great deal of effort from the team, but it has truly been worth the many hours staring at computer progress bars that seem to be moving backward or reading articles filled with techno-jargon. This initiative will motivate and aid students in their pursuit of art history by providing them with a valuable educational resource that can virtually take them across the globe in a matter of minutes. I am confident that Zeuxis VR will kindle the passion and inspiration necessary to study art history in students. As a student who has seen the models more times than I can count, I am always awestruck each time I encounter them in VR.

Benefits and Considerations

Our initial feedback from students who have explored and learned with the prototype environments reveals significant benefits. VR increased student engagement, both exciting them to study and creating memorable moments that will remain for years to come. One of the reasons we chose to focus on multiplayer and social VR was to recreate the experience of learning in a traditional classroom setting. For example, Mozilla Hubs features spatial audio, meaning the further away you are from someone the fainter their voice. This allows students to discuss in teams without a cacophony of voices. As a result, conversations can occur more naturally, as they would in a physical classroom. Social VR allows students and teachers to experience the space and explore together.

In our testing, we have found that full immersion in the VR space for the duration of a 50–75-minute class would be challenging. For one, motion sickness and eye fatigue are common issues with using VR. There are ways to mitigate these side effects (chewing gum or sucking on candy can help alleviate motion sickness – and who doesn't love an excuse to eat candy?) and frequent breaks alleviate eye strain. One student noted in a feedback survey that they "missed having their notes available" in the VR space. Allowing students to transition between VR and real space allows them to reflect on what they experienced and provides an opportunity for them to write down any necessary information and observations. For this flexibility to move between real and VR space, students and professors must be well versed in the technology. Because participants must have ample time to learn the technology, the technology used must have a low bar of entry. We suggest dedicating an entire class to familiarizing students with the headsets and VR platform. Have students gather in a generic Mozilla Hubs room so they can practice locomotion and using the various tools like camera, pen, and laser pointer. The user experience must not be cumbersome, and students must be able to easily access the VR environments to mitigate lost class time.

Mozilla Hubs also allows professors to upload slide presentations (saved as PDFs) into the VR space. Slides can provide additional contextual information, comparative images, or high-resolution details of the site they are visiting. One of our students found the inclusion of slides "help bridge the gap between the conventional structure and the new structure that comes to fruition with VR." There are issues with Mozilla Hubs, such as limitations by file size, meaning the models we make available for use in Hubs require less complex geometry and lower-quality textures. The result is an environment that lacks some detail. We are currently working to address these issues. One solution may be to use 3D Tiles that parse the environment into different levels of detail. As you move through the space or closer to an object, tiles with higher levels of resolution are activated.[11] Despite these challenges Mozilla Hubs and other WebXR platforms provide the greatest level of accessibility. WebXR allows VR headsets to interact with virtual and augmented reality content through the internet browser. As a result, our environments can be viewed across a range of devices including VR headsets, computers, and smartphones. In other words, one is not limited in experiencing these cultural sites based on their access to a VR headset though the level of immersion will vary depending on the device. Since accessibility is our primary goal, WebXR promises to reach the widest audience.

The Future of Art History?

The last ten years have been filled with intellectual debate on how to define digital art history.[12] In her influential article, Joanna Drucker set out to define the difference between *digitized* and *digital* art history.[13] While both rely on technology, digitized art history makes information accessible for study, while digital art history produces innovative approaches to analysis and interpretation. Undeniably, technology has allowed for more efficient ways to find and organize images to aid traditional methods of art historical study. Digital art history moves a step further, harnessing the potential of emergent technology to transform the way we think about objects and spaces. Detractors of digital art history fret that the humanity of art history becomes obscured by elaborate computational methods, but digital art history is more than mere reproduction by automated programs.[14] In fact, digital art history uses technology to emphasize the humanity of art, reshaping the way we analyze and engage with temporal, spatial, and visual relationships within the history of the work. We can better appreciate the artists involved in the creation, the society in which the work was executed, and the effects the work has on the modern audience studying it. Paul Jaskot, while discussing the intersection of digital methods in social art history, remarked that this work is not performed for amusement – the sheer complexity and scale of evidence provided by digital methods is the most meticulous and thorough we can achieve.[15] Zeuxis VR engages with digital art history by heightening users' individual and collective experience and altering the way we understand the cultural site and our relationship with it.

VR provides an opportunity to enhance our understanding of built space. We now have the potential to not only recreate architectural environments as they exist today, but also reconstruct what they looked like in the past, visualizing the evolution of art through time. Similarly, paintings and sculptures that are today preserved in museums can be returned to their original context adorning the walls of a Renaissance home, or the altar of a church. Moving beyond the visual, audio can be introduced to these environments in an attempt to recreate historical soundscapes and invite new phenomenological insights into these spaces. From a pedagogical perspective, VR fundamentally changes how students learn and encourages new lines of inquiry about the art, its historical creators, and viewers. Projects like Zeuxis VR allow students to explore environments together to better understand how the site functioned and who might have participated in its creation and use. The ability for students to make these connections is predicated on VRs ability to increase the student's sense of presence within the space.

Presence allows a user to feel as though they are standing in a particular setting, even if the user is physically located somewhere else.[16] To be fully present, users must also be involved in a series of actions that keep them stimulated and focused on remaining in the environment and immersed in this space by allowing themselves to believe they are actively existing in the setting. By wearing a VR headset that fills one's field of vision and dominates their hearing, users can easily be involved, immersed, and present in the digital environments that we have created. We have recorded testimonies of the students who participated in the VR test and they shared these positive sentiments of VR in their surveys after the trial. We anticipate collaborating with the Psychology Department to secure an Institutional Review Board approval so that we may acquire results that quantitatively demonstrate the benefits of VR.

One of the greatest benefits of working in digital art history is the necessity of partnership and Zeuxis VR is beginning to team up with several other institutions to strengthen the project. We believe that the future of higher education and humanities scholarship is collaborative, open access, and public facing. These invitations to work together span not only colleges and universities but act as a call to unity between different academic disciplines. Art history has always been interdisciplinary, but digital art history provides an opportunity to actively integrate the social sciences and STEM fields into art history and open these fields to the richness of art historical study. Most importantly, digital art history possesses the potential to break down the silos between faculty and students by challenging them to look to each other as peers with the same goal of better understanding, spurring them to ask new questions and find the answers together.

This technology and concept of digital art history are recent and ever-changing, so there is still much that we are learning. We hope that Zeuxis VR will play a vital role in this digital evolution and will flourish as a pedagogical tool for the study of art history. This process has been eye-opening to how we perceive works of art and how we can strengthen our relationships with art through immersion in both the developmental and experiential perspectives. Immersive learning through VR has the potential to transform education by allowing students to familiarize themselves with the art without overly complicated and often difficult planning and travel. With VR accelerating in popularity and capability, we

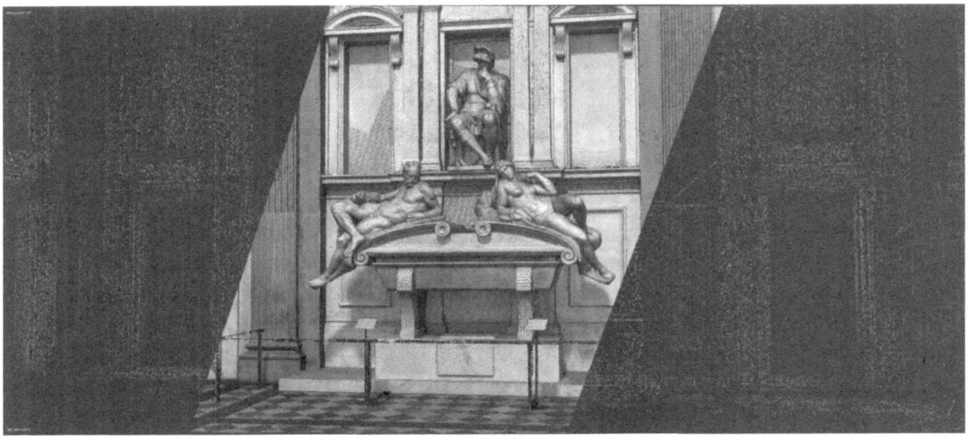

FIGURE 8.1 Detail of sparse and dense cloud from 3D model of Michelangelo's *New Sacristy*, Florence. Rendered using Agisoft Metashape.

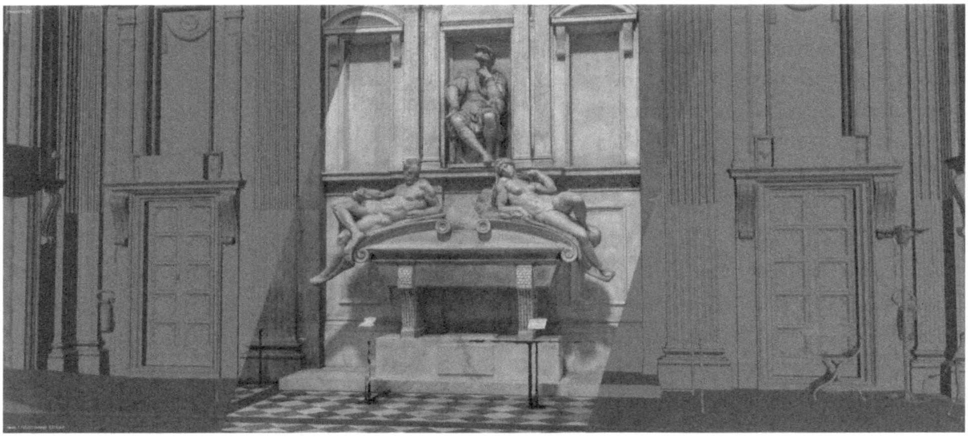

FIGURE 8.2 Detail of solid and textured mesh from 3D model of Michelangelo's *New Sacristy*, Florence. Rendered using Agisoft Metashape.

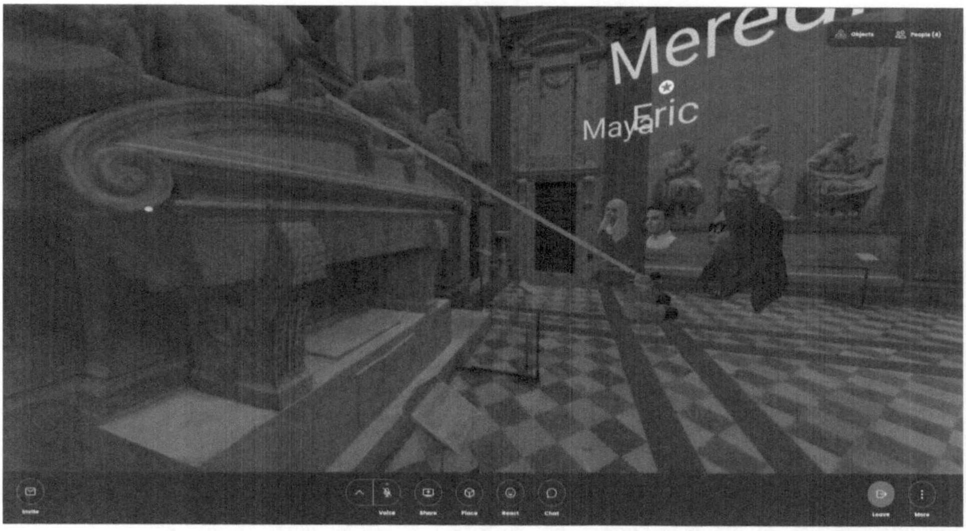

FIGURE 8.3 Students learning in the virtual environment of Michelangelo's *New Sacristy* using Mozilla Hubs.

cannot say for certain where this technology will lead. The burgeoning determination and enthusiasm for collaboration by our growing team, however, along with students' eagerness for more VR experiences, indicate promising developments for art historical pedagogy. One thing is certain: The future of art history is bright, especially when viewed through VR goggles.

Notes

1 Similar questions about digital technology's impact on art history were raised by Robert S. Nelson, "The Slide Lecture, or the Work of Art 'History' in the Age of Mechanical Reproduction," *Critical Inquiry* 26, no. 3 (2000): 414–34.

2 For more information on the project and our workflow please refer to our website: www.zeuxisvr.com.

3 Virtual reality and digital art games have been experimented with since the 1980s. For an overview of some of these projects read, Erik Champion and Anna Foka, "Art History, Heritage Games, and Virtual Reality," in *The Routledge Companion to Digital Humanities and Art History*, ed. Kathryn Brown, 238–52 (New York: Routledge, 2020); Hubert Cecotti, et al., "Virtual Reality for Immersive Learning in Art History," *2020 Proceedings of the 6th International Conference of the Immersive Learning Research Network*, ed. Daphne Economou (Piscataway: IEEE, 2020): 16–23; Matthew Brennan and Leif Christiansen, "Virtual Materiality: A Virtual Reality Framework for the Analysis and Visualization of Cultural Heritage 3D Models," *Digital Heritage* (2018).

4 For background on immersive learning, refer to Samson Tan, "The Rise of Immersive Learning," *Journal of Applied Learning & Teaching* 2, no. 2 (2019): 91–4; Andreas Dengel and Jutta Mägdefrau, "Presence Is the Key to Understanding Immersive Learning," in *Communications in Computer and Information Science Immersive Learning Research Network. iLRN 2019*, ed. D. Beck, et al. (New York: Springer, 2019): 185–98; Andreas Dengel and Jutta Mägdefrau, "Immersive Learning Explored: Subjective and Objective Factors Influencing Learning Outcomes in Immersive Educational Virtual Environments," in *Proceedings of 2018 IEEE International Conference on Teaching, Assessment, and Learning for Engineering*, ed. Mark J. W. Lee (Piscataway: IEEE, 2018), 608–15.

5 "Hubs by Mozilla," Hubs, accessed January 28, 2022, https://hubs.mozilla.com/.

6 "Photogrammetry with Metashape," Agisoft Metashape, accessed January 28, 2022, https://www.agisoft.com/; "RealityCapture," RealityCapture: Mapping and 3D Modeling Photogrammetry Software - CapturingReality.com, accessed January 28, 2022, https://www.capturingreality.com/.
7 For a discussion of situated learning consider Lisa Dawley and Chris Dede, "Situated Learning in Virtual Worlds and Immersive Simulations," in *Handbook of Research for Educational Communications and Technology*, 4th ed., eds. J. M. Spector et al. (New York: Springer, 2013), 723–34.
8 "Google Cardboard," Google Cardboard – Google VR, Google, accessed January 28, 2022. https://arvr.google.com/cardboard/.
9 "Oculus Quest 2," Oculus, accessed January 28, 2022, https://www.oculus.com/quest-2/.
10 Jonathan Ammerman, "Oculus Quest 2 is the Best-Selling Oculus Headset by a Significant Margin," *Game Rant*, March 31, 2021, https://gamerant.com/oculus-quest-2-best-selling-oculus-headset-significant-margin/; Mike Boland, "5 Signs of Quest 2's Holiday Surge," *AR Insider*, January 3, 2022, https://arinsider.co/2022/01/03/5-signs-of-quest-2s-holiday-surge/.
11 The New York Times Research and Development team recently launched an open access 3D tile loader we hope to use. "A-Frame Scenes Using Our 3D Tiles Loader Component:" A-Frame 3D Tiles Component, accessed January 29, 2022, https://nytimes.github.io/aframe-loader-3dtiles-component/.
12 For an overview of the history of digital art history and its development see Alexander Brey, "Digital Art History in 2021," *History Compass* 19, no. 8 (2021).
13 Johanna Drucker, "Is There a 'Digital' Art History?," *Visual Resources: An International Journal of Documentation* 29, no. 1–2 (2013): 5–7.
14 For counter perspective on digital art history, see Claire Bishop, "Against Digital Art History," *International Journal for Digital Art History*, no. 3 (2018): 1–14.
15 Paul B. Jaskot, "Digital Art History as the Social History of Art: Towards the Disciplinary Relevance of Digital Methods," *Visual Resources* 35, no. 1–2 (2019): 21–33.
16 Bob G. Witmer and Michael J. Singer, "Measuring Presence in Virtual Environments: A Presence Questionnaire," *Presence: Teleoperators and Virtual Environments* 7, no. 3 (1998): 225.

Bibliography

"A-Frame 3D Tiles Component." Research and Development. *The New York Times*. Accessed January 18, 2022. https://nytimes.github.io/aframe-loader-3dtiles-component/.

Ammerman, Jonathan. "Oculus Quest 2 Is the Best-Selling Oculus Headset by a Significant Margin." *Game Rant*, March 31, 2021. https://gamerant.com/oculus-quest-2-best-selling-oculus-headset-significant-margin/.

Bishop, Claire. "Against Digital Art History." *International Journal for Digital Art History*, no. 3 (2018): 123–31.

Boland, Mike. "5 Signs of Quest 2's Holiday Surge." *AR Insider*, January 3, 2022. https://arinsider.co/2022/01/03/5-signs-of-quest-2s-holiday-surge/.

Brennan, Matthew, and Leif Christiansen. "Virtual Materiality: A Virtual Reality Framework for the Analysis and Visualization of Cultural Heritage 3D Models." *Digital Heritage* (2018).

Brey, Alexander. "Digital Art History in 2021." *History Compass* 19, no. 8 (2021): 1–14.

Cecotti, Hubert et al. "Virtual Reality for Immersive Learning in Art History." In *Proceedings of the 6th International Conference of the Immersive Learning Research Network*. Edited by Daphne Economou, 16–23. Piscataway: IEEE, 2020.

Champion, Erik, and Anna Foka. "Art History, Heritage Games, and Virtual Reality." In *The Routledge Companion to Digital Humanities and Art History*, edited by Kathryn Brown, 238–52. New York: Routledge, 2020.

Dawley, Lisa, and Chris Dede. "Situated Learning in Virtual Worlds and Immersive Simulations." In *Handbook of Research for Educational Communications and Technology*, 4th ed., edited by Jonathan M. Spector, Marriner D. Merreill, Jan Elen. MJ Bishop, and J. M. Spector, M. D. Merrill, J. Elen, and M. J. Bishop, 723–34. New York: Springer, 2013.toec

Dengel, Andreas, and Jutta Mägdefrau. "Immersive Learning Explored: Subjective and Objective Factors Influencing Learning Outcomes in Immersive Educational Virtual Environments." In *Proceedings of 2018 IEEE International Conference on Teaching, Assessment, and Learning for Engineering.* Edited by Mark J. W. Lee, 608–15. Piscataway: IEEE, 2018.

Dengel, Andreas, and Jutta Mägdefrau. "Presence Is the Key to Understanding Immersive Learning." In *Communications in Computer and Information Science Immersive Learning Research Network. iLRN 2019.* Edited by D. Beck et al., 185–98. New York: Springer, 2019.

Drucker, Johanna. "Is There a 'Digital' Art History?" *Visual Resources* 29, no. 1–2 (2013): 5–13.

"Google Cardboard." Google Cardboard – Google VR. Google. Accessed January 28, 2022. https://arvr.google.com/cardboard/.

"Hubs by Mozilla." Hubs. Accessed January 28, 2022. https://hubs.mozilla.com/.

Jaskot, Paul B. "Digital Art History as the Social History of Art: Towards the Disciplinary Relevance of Digital Methods." *Visual Resources* 35, no. 1–2 (2019): 21–33.

Nelson, Robert S. "The Slide Lecture, or the Work of Art 'History' in the Age of Mechanical Reproduction." *Critical Inquiry* 26, no. 3 (2000): 414–34.

"Oculus Quest 2." Oculus. Accessed January 28, 2022. https://www.oculus.com/quest-2/.

"Photogrammetry with Metashape." Agisoft Metashape. Accessed January 28, 2022. https://www.agisoft.com/.

"RealityCapture." RealityCapture: Mapping and 3D Modeling Photogrammetry Software - CapturingReality.com. Accessed January 28, 2022. https://www.capturingreality.com/.

Tan, Samson. "The Rise of Immersive Learning." *Journal of Applied Learning & Teaching* 2, no. 2 (2019): 91–4.

Witmer, Bob G., and Michael J. Singer. "Measuring Presence in Virtual Environments: A Presence Questionnaire." *Presence: Teleoperators and Virtual Environments* 7, no. 3 (1998): 225–40.

PART V

Digital Viewing and Reflections

9

REFLECTIONS

Relating Medieval Modes to Modern Multimodal Literacies in the Digital Humanities

Lane J. Sobehrad and Susan J. Sobehrad

This chapter is, in some ways, a postscript to the preceding chapters. Readers have learned about how medieval people engaged with their media using the technology around them, and how twenty-first-century investigators use twenty-first-century media and technology to access and interpret extant medieval evidence in new and exciting ways. But the rubber has yet to meet the road, so to speak, and this volume needs to explicitly address the "so what?" that has been implicit in its structure. Each author has developed a new perspective that has allowed them to generate meaning for themselves influenced by the composition of their resources, both material and immaterial.[1] At the same time, the chapters resulting from their use of resources both articulate the authors' generated meaning and are, in and of themselves, resources intended to generate further meaning for its readers. Some understanding is explicitly directed to the audience, such as a thesis statement or concluding sections that indicate what the audience will learn or should have learned based on what the author wanted the audience to learn. However, additional understanding is generated unintentionally, which results in most narrative research projects having statements indicating the audience will likely have their own meaning developed in parallel to the meaning prescribed by the author:

> For historians they do not provide documentary evidence, but rather illuminate the way that premodern people understood the world around them.
>
> *(Forniotis, p. 73)*

> Indeed, this intersection between accounting and penance testifies to the creative ways in which medieval subjects used the technologies and strategies from that expanding marketplace to teach each other the various responsibilities they owe to their fellow humans.
>
> *(Jiang, p. 25)*

DOI: 10.4324/9781003295082-15

> As technology continues to change and morph into entirely new forms of immediate, mediated, and live interaction, our understandings and definitions of temporality and liveness will evolve along with them.
>
> *(Scherff, p. 106)*

It is standard practice in academic scholarship both to note the limitations of a given research project and to explicitly leave space for future contributions and, thus, additional generated understanding. But the space for generated understanding is neither restricted to academic research nor is it limited to a narrative format.

In educational research, a teaching resource that intentionally shapes the way people generate meaning for themselves or others is called a *mode*. Anyone who has written a lecture, built a lesson plan, or developed a recipe has created a modality through which others receive information and create products based on the learning engaged in, whether it be class notes, a group project, or a cake. Modes, as suggested by their inclusion here, are not restricted to pedagogy, as the contributors to this volume have articulated physical, visual, literary, and spiritual modalities medieval people used as well as the modalities medieval scholars have recommended for modern audiences to generate meaning from the Middle Ages.

Users must develop various *literacies* in order to generate meaning scaffolded by their modality. As seen above, these literacies extend far beyond traditional reading and writing, both for medieval people and medieval scholars. Medieval people, as Michael Clanchy long ago suggested, were more literate than historians have traditionally given them credit for, whether through the communication of cultural meaning in chorograhies, literary meaning accessed through learned techniques and tools like the *ars combinatoria*, or spiritual meaning acquired through a visual contemplation of altarpieces. It is critical to note these medieval literacies had to be learned, as they should consequently inform how we develop our own twenty-first literacies and the ways in which we communicate the Middle Ages to our peers, students, and the general public.[2] This chapter situates itself between medieval and modern modes of meaning through a discussion of the literacies needed to both navigate medieval resources and resources about the medieval. By understanding this skillset, it is our aim that readers be able to more effectively communicate the importance and applicability of historical phenomena to a twenty-first-century audience, particularly in a learning environment.

Multimodal Literacy

First and foremost, the definition of "literacy" has changed over time and has, at no point in those changes, had a singular definition. Indeed, education researchers have long noted that "Definitions of literacy shape our perceptions of individuals who fall on either side of the standard (what a "literate" or "nonliterate" is like) and thus in a deep way affect both the substance and style of educational programs."[3] Michael Clanchy spends a great deal of his introduction toiling over the assumptions that the association of literacy and formal education has had a negative effect on how modern scholars and the general public perceive medieval literacy.[4] His conclusions are much the same as UNESCO's global literacy initiatives. Their definition does restrict itself to using printed and written materials, "to identify, understand, interpret, create, communicate and compute," but critically extends beyond the formal educational environment in, "a continuum of learning...enabling individuals to achieve their goals, to develop their knowledge and potential, and to participate fully in their community and wider society."[5] That is, literacy is certainly about people learning to read and write, but it is also just as much about learning to explore the world around them and use that acquired knowledge, learning to navigate society to make their lives better, and developing the ability to navigate new technologies to adapt to a rapidly changing world.[6]

Arguably, the most significant change to how we perceive literacy is demonstrated in McLuhan's periodization of the electronic age (See intro, p. 3). Modes of communication have multiplied in number and complexity beyond direct, in-person orality and physically created texts and images. Websites, for example, offer a choose-your-own learning pathway where learners can click on links of their choice, read bits and pieces, look at images from across the globe, and listen to a text in its original language. Videos, podcasts, interactive simulations, instant graphing, and data analysis have all introduced a much more complex environment for meaning making. Added to the vast changes in the materiality of modes, individuals now must also navigate a global virtual space that impacts the immateriality of the modes – geography, social interaction, culture, and community, and even space and time, impact meaning made in the digital world. Practical literacy has evolved into a multimodal process that requires its own specific literacy in order to access digitally located information. In the pre-electronic age, no special technical skills were required to operate a book, assuming one understood reading conventions and had learned the ability to read the language of the text. This is not the case with computer-based texts. One must know how to turn a computer on, use a mouse and keyboard, navigate an operating system to locate and open a file folder or website, and operate the text's viewing platform – and then also understand reading conventions and have the ability to read. That is, digital literacy can be a barrier to traditional reading and writing literacy. The World Economic Forum has noted that in low-income countries, only 32% of people had basic digital skills, and even high-income countries plateaued at 62%.[7] In a learning environment today, the ability to navigate modes and interact with their complex material and immaterial attributes is essential in order to learn, communicate, and make sense of the world. This transformation of meaning making from traditional two-dimensional textual literacy to multidimensional, multimodal literacies requires adaptation by both instructors and students.

As Sister Albert Marie Surmanski suggested in her discussion of the tongue, competency in reading literacy helps one make sense of the world by offering well-structured interpretive frameworks to help a reader pull meaning from text. By contrast, multimodal literacies draw-out meaning by making connections between modes and all the material and immaterial attributes that go with them. Beatrice Bottomley and Arianna Dalla Costa show us this with the *ars combinatoria*. Reading literacy is not enough to draw out hidden meanings contained within texts. One must also become literate in using the cipher disks to be used in conjunction with the text. As with computers, these additional literacies create a barrier to meaning making. Though many examples could be articulated, and the parameters of multimodal literacy are vast, in an effort toward clarity and brevity, it will be useful to describe some general categories of multimodal literacy. While not an exhaustive list, Sean Cordes outlines some specific literacies necessary to effectively navigate digital spaces as presented to *The International Federation of Library Association and Institutions*:

1 **Information literacy**: the ability to use the latest technology to find, analyze, and use information from different sources.

2 **Visual literacy**: the ability to use visual images to create online products and develop critical thinking skills.
3 **Multicultural literacy**: the ability to perceive, compare and contrast, and empathize with people who hold different beliefs and values in a virtual, global context.
4 **Media literacy**: the ability to process and evaluate information from a wide variety of digital sources in a range of genres and different media formats.
5 **Aural and spoken literacy**: the ability to listen, comprehend, and participate in academic conversations and presentations using digital tools.[8]

Analysis of historical artifacts through this kind of multimodal lens can shed light on social, political, cultural, economic, and environmental conditions that existed at the time the artifact was created. For example, Surmanski shares how Thomas Aquinas used multimodal attributes of the tongue to mediate meaning between the self and others, and even between the self and God. In this way, the tongue may be considered to be a mode that influences what people think and believe. According to Surmanski, the Psalms were about real battles, with concomitant moral teachings about warfare. However, Aqiuinas' *Commentary* was presented to young theologians who were training to "wield language" not weapons in battle. Therefore, Aquinas interpreted sword and arrow references in the Psalms as "violent speech" in order to reveal the lessons related to the dangers of having a "sharp" tongue. These moral teachings were investigated, learned, and expanded upon using medieval media and technologies like the codex, libraries, and textual communities (information literacy).[9] The time and effort it took to assemble such resources were considerable in the Middle Ages and required a great deal of patience, both in the time it took to acquire new information and in the acceptance of limited materials. The opposite is true in twenty-first-century literacies. New information is nearly instantaneous with the right keywords.

Metaphorical usage of the tongue often resulted in visual imagery making its way onto the parchment of medieval authors, visually enhancing the text while offering a distinct interpretive lens (visual literacy).[10] It bears mentioning that in a space restricted, image restricted as often come part-and-parcel with publication, digital spaces allow additional content with a few easy taps on a keyboard and mouse. We have no space for images, despite some fantastic tongue images as seen in a thirteenth-century Bible Showing David sticking out his tongue in a conversation with God, a Dominican who holds the personification of Slander in a headlock while a nun prepares to cut off his tongue in *Roman de la Rose*, or a cow sprouting an arm holding a sword from its mouth in Jean de Feshal's treatise on livestock bits. But you can click or copy the URL in the footnote below and see all three in less than sixty seconds if you have the necessary media literacy skills.[11]

Aural and spoken literacy are somewhat obvious for the Psalms Surmanski references, but it is important to recognize the environments in which people may have engaged with them. Monastic hours reciting the Psalms suggest both a different cultural context and different meaning than the itinerant friar reading his Psalter or the priest reading to his flock. Likewise, the difference in interpretations by a lay audience hearing Psalms in Latin or their vernacular offers a considerably altered lived experience in the sacred space further impacted by the visual imagery contained in a church, as Katharine Scherff suggests. The "mediating" tongue, in this perspective, is less about establishing vice and virtue, and more about establishing access to information.

Literacy training provides the skills necessary to extract information from various modalities, allowing the user to generate meaning and understanding of the subject. In a modern context, one primary function of the medievalist is not just to communicate information about the past, but to provide access to the tools that allow others to acquire this information, too. On this, Aquinas agrees, noting that teaching something is impossible if,

> they are signs of things that he does not know, he can learn nothing therefrom: for instance, if one were to speak Greek to a man who only knows Latin, he would learn nothing thereby. Therefore in no way can a man cause knowledge in another by teaching him.[12]

Modalities in the Learning Environment

Though not all literacies are needed for a given inquiry or project, the chapters in this book do reveal the importance of modal affordance in the context of literacy. That is, the idea that different modes are especially suited to specific kinds of meaning-making. Modal affordances are tied to both mode and the way that the mode has changed over time, and specifically to why one mode is chosen over another. According to Jewitt et al., modal affordances can be broken down into two categories – (1) transduction, the shift in meaning that occurs when the mode is reconfigured (for example, a set of steps is changed into a diagram); and (2) transformation, which occurs when there are internal changes in a single mode that alters meaning making.[13] Brittany Forniotis does this in her treatment of chorographies. She describes various theoretical interpretation of maps, wherein mapmakers, "make theoretical knowledge about the three-dimensional world physical again in a two-dimensional form," while a map user, "engages intellectually with the map through the act of viewing, each time creating new knowledge for themself" (Forniotis, p. 64). But still, maps can provide accurate guidance from one physical location to another, while chorographies cannot. This is transduction. The cartographic modality that encompasses maps and map-related forms has overarching interpretive frameworks, but by changing the spatial representations, it changes the ways in which audiences interact with the media. Chorography is a form of visual literacy that uses images, icons, and symbols to help viewers understand the culture of a specific place at a certain time, separate and distinct from the geometric and mathematical representations of a landscape on a two-dimensional surface seen in maps. Transformation occurs within the chorography itself, as seen in the digital presentation of the chorographies included in this volume and the references to archival websites. It is still offering meaning through the original artifact, but accessing its meaning now requires the additional burden of digital literacy, inherently changing the meaning generated through interacting with the artifact.

Elsewhere, the Vernon Table described by Nancy Jiang is a medieval mode or resource used for making meaning. Its materiality consisted of a physically large codex inscribed with a pattern that allowed users to tally vices and virtues by moving roundels to designate types and numbers of these actions. Its immateriality lay in its ability to influence a "collective penitential vigilance against spiritual debts," whereby the individual interpreted and modified their own behaviors according to what they observed on the Vernon Table. The meaning the individuals took away from this was personalized and specific and depended on their own prior actions. When this spiritual tool was used in conjunction with accounting technologies like tally sticks and accounting ledgers, fiscal policy and statistical principles morph into moral guidance, and spiritual accountability for whole communities. In order for appropriate meaning to be generated in the context of later medieval England, readers must have both a competent understanding of their religious penitential system as well as an understanding of accounting principles. In all cases, the acquisition of particular literacies was necessary for medieval people to navigate their respective modalities in order to both obtain and generate meaning. The same is true today.

In education research learning typically happens in formal and informal environments. Formal environments typically include settings like classrooms, lecture halls, workshops, and conferences where the learning is systematic and structured. Informal environments include settings like museums, zoos, and the home where learning is *not* systematic or structured. Anne Betty Weinshenker asks readers to engage in informal learning to engage in a more robust evaluation of eighteenth-century art. Importantly, she notes, "The initiation and rapid expansion of electronic communications have been serving to remove the geographic restrictions that limited access," to her previous research on Owen McSwiny's work (Weinshencker, p. 59). Furthermore, digital investigation offers a different modality through which to engage with the art, observing fine details that might otherwise be overlooked but are of some significance to the viewer. As noted above (Intro, p. 5), this type of work has been ongoing since the 1990s, but has had a significant impact on the ways in which both researchers and teachers engage themselves and others in investigations of the past. What has been less common is the inclusion of informal learning in digital spaces into formal scholarly settings such as an edited volume Weinschencker notes, in particular, that the "utilization of digital techniques greatly facilitates conducting research that requires comparison of the variant forms and details of a single image" (Weinshencker, p. 57). While the reduction in travel and legwork required to compare images is certainly a practical benefit to digitized images, it only scratches the surface of what imaging software is capable of today. Project Mirador, for example, not only allows viewers to multiple images for comparisons, but also provides tools to annotate, organize, and mark uploaded images. That is, users control the media, they are not subject to static viewership. This creates art that is not only a useful tool to add to Weinshencker's toolbox for her next project, but it is also an invaluable teaching tool that allows endless opportunities to engage students in high-quality images that they are able to view, annotate, and manipulate themselves that would otherwise be impossible either due to geographic or archival constraints.

Medieval and modern modes converge in the chapters addressing teaching strategies. Margaret Mansfield describes a project-based simulation of a seventeenth-century Dutch art market, while Eric Hupe and Caitlyn Carr describe the use of virtual reality to examine the visual arts of the Italian Renaissance. In the first instance, students posed as artists, dealers, or potential buyers, charged with buying, selling, and marketing paintings and prints. Each student was assigned a role to play, and given basic information about their characters in advance. The paintings and prints in play were printed on cards to use as artifacts in the market. Students kept their records by hand on ledgers. The simulation was designed as a non-digital activity to demonstrate to students the general principles of the way the market functioned, along with insights about how historical events impacted the process. Most students were assigned artists or historical figures they had never heard of, so there was little connection to the roles they played, and once the "artists" had sold the paintings they had been given, students lost interest. To inject more enthusiasm into the simulation, technology was introduced as a factor in the simulation. Mansfield claims, "It enable[d] a more organic reproduction of the unpredictability and inflexibilities of changing tastes within the constraints of a capitalist structure" (Mansfield, p. 123). Students used their phones and computers to research online, keep track of their purchases, seek out different interpersonal connections, and even different products that the artists were historically known to sell. Students even used marketing and sales tactics on their devices that encouraged participation and generated excitement.

This simulation has been transduced, both materially and immaterially. The addition of completely new modes changed the materials students used to make meaning and altered their interactions with one another. And while smartphones and computers were not technologies available to the purveyors of art of seventeenth-century Dutch art in the seventeenth century, Mansfield scaffolded access points that allowed students to engage in the content and simulate the intensity, competition, and excitement that was surely present in an early modern art market. This type of authentic engagement is critical in a learning environment and has long been recognized as such. Seneca, for example, describes that the current state of teaching left students, "starving vomiters who keep the body at the feeding trough while the mind grows feeble for lack of nourishment."[14] Multimodality is at the heart of good teaching and learning that "sticks."[15] Mansfield's technology-infused simulation was a multimodal experience for students that no doubt left an impression on students, both for its engaging activities and the content retained by students. Information literacy was encountered as they learned about the artists, the art, and the economics of the market, visual literacy as they learned to recognize painting styles and unique attributes of an artist's work, multicultural as they assumed different points of view, and media and aural literacy as they used both written, visual, spoken, and digital artifacts to make their sales. Digital tools were used to enhance the authenticity of the experience by providing students tools for which they already had the necessary literacies.

For Hupe and Carr, students work together with their instructors to create three-dimensional models of Italian Renaissance monuments. Once created, students are able to explore the monuments in a virtual reality setting. In this way, students can get a sense of proportionality and orientation, and walk up to and around the monuments, immersing themselves in the scene and experiencing the art in a setting that closely resembles the real thing. Like a digitized chorograph, virtual reality transforms the piece into a virtual representation while maintaining the original purpose of the work, which allows students to engage in "object-focused research" (Hupe and Carr, p. 129). Unique to the modality of virtual reality, virtual immersion makes it possible to interact with art and monuments in a way that mimics reality. Students are able to walk around statues, talk to other patrons, and take notes on what they see. Other aspects of the experience are unlike what one might experience in a real-world setting, such as being able to digitally draw on the art. In this way, the medieval is *reproduced* by the modern, but does not detract from its original purpose. Hupe and Carr describe how virtual reality can reproduce not only the art, but the original setting that housed the art, providing additional insight into their provenance that was not previously possible. These virtual reality experiences make it possible for students to access artifacts in parts of the world they might never be able to reach in person, thereby expanding their worldview and revealing potential contextual connections between historical figures, societies, and ideas. Digital tools share artifacts with audiences not limited by space, time, or money and preserve them in a way that ensures their historical significance will not be lost or forgotten.

Engaging students via multimodality requires capitalizing on their digital fluency, while at the same time altering their perception of authenticity and real worldness. In her investigation, Katharine Scherff asserts that altarpieces are mediating images (altar screens) that enhance the "liveness" of sacred performance in the medieval church by using visual imagery to inspire piety. Scherff went on to explain that because people in the Middle Ages usually only received Communion once a year, the *elevatio* of the Eucharist, which allowed people to see the consecrated host, became a substitute for Communion. In both cases, visual imagery was used to remind the congregation of the underpinnings of their faith, and induce a reverent piety. Similarly, jumbotrons and large viewing screens found at stadiums affect the viewing experience for their audiences by using larger-than-life visual imagery to ensure that every member of the audience is able to witness the events occurring on the field, inspiring a reverent awe for the athleticism of the players with replays of perfect pitches and impossible catches. In each instance, the meaning of the live experience is enhanced by the incorporation of visual images designed to elicit specific responses from the crowd.

Scherff also relates arguments that propose that simulations and imitations (as opposed to live, in person experiences) of real things "defraud" the viewer; however, she goes on to share research that contends that the practice of imitation can show what is hard to express in words, and help lead the mind to "intellectual understanding." It is this thought that has application in the classroom. A triptych or painting, a wall of graffiti, a live-stream video, or a medieval monument in a virtual reality setting are all representations, or imitations of real life, past or present. And, upon study, they are inherently multimodal. The choice of subject and medium, the intended message, and the socio-political environment in which they were made were all influential in their creation and therefore helped shape the resultant meaning. Multimodal literacies allow researchers to offer new insight over the previously trodden ground. They also allow instructors a more dynamic pathway to engage their learners in an investigation of the past using interfaces that are familiar to them. In the various presentations of media, technology, and their interactions in the medieval and modern periods presented in this volume, readers should reflect on the ways in which medieval and modern people engage with *their* literacies to generate meaning in their respective contexts.

Notes

1 Carey Jewitt, Jeff Bezemer, and Kay O'Halloran, *Introducing Multimodality* (New York: Routledge, 2016), 71–2.
2 Michael Clanchy, *From Memory to Written Record: England, 1066–1307*, 3rd edition (Malden: Wiley-Blackwell, 2012).
3 Sylvia Scribner, "Literacy in Three Metaphors," *American Journal of Education*, 93 #1 (1984): 6.
4 Clanchy, *From Memory to Written Record*, 7–15.
5 http://uis.unesco.org/en/glossary-term/literacy.
6 Brian Street, "Understanding and Defining Literacy," *Literacy for Life*, Education for All Global Monitoring Report 2006 (UNESCO, 2005), 21–5.
7 World Economic Forum, *Accelerating Digital Inclusion in the New Normal* (Geneva: World Economic Forum, 2020), 6.
8 Sean Cordes, "Broad Horizons: The Role of Multimodal Literacy in 21st Century Library Instruction," *Paper presented at the World Library and Information Congress: 75th IFLA General Conference and Assembly "Libraries Create Futures: Building on Cultural Heritage,"* (Milan, August 2009), 1–18, as paraphrased in Lane Sobehrad and Susan Sobehrad, *Medieval History in the Modern Classroom: Using Project-Based Learning to Engage Today's Learning* (Leeds: Arc Humanities Press, 2022), 155–6.

9 Brian Stock, *The Implications of Literacy: Written Language and Models of Interpretation in the Eleventh and Twelfth Centuries* (Princeton: Princeton University Press, 1983).

10 Jesse M. Gellrich, "The Art of the Tongue: Illuminating Speech and Writing in Later Medieval Manuscripts," in Colum Hourihane (ed.) *Virtue & Vice: The Personifications in the Index of Christian Art*, 93–119 (Princeton: Princeton University Press, 2000).

11 Morgan Library, Bible, MS. M.295, fol. 284v, http://ica.themorgan.org/manuscript/page/27/77409, accessed May 31, 2022; Morgan Library, Roman de la Rose, MS M.48 fol. 83r, http://ica.themorgan.org/manuscript/page/22/76878, accessed May 31, 2022; Jean de Feschal, *Traité d'hippiatrie, Traité d'embouchure* (Paris: Bibliotheque Nationale NAF 28881, https://gallica.bnf.fr/ark:/12148/btv1b10071549r/f9.item, accessed November 28, 2022.

12 Thomas Aquinas, *Summa Theologica* Prima Pars, Q.117.A.1, https://www.newadvent.org/summa/1117.htm, accessed May 31, 2022.

13 Carey Jewitt, Jeff Bezemer, and Kay O'Halloran. *Introducing Multimodality* (New York: Routledge, 2016), 71–2.

14 Seneca, *Letters on Ethics: To Lucilius*, trans. Margaret Graver (Chicago: University of Chicago Press, 2015), 88.19, 312–13.

15 Brigid Barron and Linda Darling-Hammond, "Teaching for Meaningful Learning: A Review of Research on Inquiry-Based and Cooperative Learning," from *Powerful Learning: What We Know About Teaching for Understanding*, ed. Linda Darling-Hammond (San Francisco: Jossey-Bass, 2008), 11–70.

INDEX